Zones of Twilight

Zones of Twilight

Wartime Presidential Powers and Federal Court Decision Making

Amanda DiPaolo

LEXINGTON BOOKS

A division of

ROWMAN & LITTLEFIELD PUBLISHERS, INC.
Lanham • Boulder • New York • Toronto • Plymouth, UK

Published by Lexington Books
A division of Rowman & Littlefield Publishers, Inc.
A wholly owned subsidiary of The Rowman & Littlefield Publishing Group, Inc.
4501 Forbes Boulevard, Suite 200, Lanham, Maryland 20706
http://www.lexingtonbooks.com

Estover Road
Plymouth PL6 7PY
United Kingdom

British Library Cataloguing in Publication Information Available

Library of Congress Cataloging-in-Publication Data

DiPaolo, Amanda, 1979–
Zones of twilight : wartime presidential powers and federal court decision making/ Amanda DiPaolo.
p. cm.
Includes bibliographical references and index.
ISBN 978-0-7391-3833-5 (cloth : alk. paper) — ISBN 978-0-7391-3834-2 (pbk. : alk. paper) — ISBN 978-0-7391-3835-9 (electronic)
1. War and emergency powers—United States. 2. Courts—United States. 3. Judicial process—United States. 4. Executive power—United States. 5. Legislative power—United States. 6. Separation of powers—United States. 7. National security—Law and legislation—United States. I. Title.
KF5060.D57 2010
342.73'062—dc22 2009032225

Printed in the United States of America

∞™ The paper used in this publication meets the minimum requirements of American National Standard for Information Sciences—Permanence of Paper for Printed Library Materials, ANSI/NISO Z39.48-1992.

To my parents,
Judy and Jim DiPaolo

Contents

Preface

What I believed to be the defining shift in American foreign policy in my lifetime was the fall of the Soviet Union and the lack of direction that resulted from it. Many believed Huntington's predicted clash of civilizations to be likely, while others subscribed to Fukuyama's thought that liberal democracy had won out, resulting in the eventual spread of freedom around the world. However, all this changed with the terrorist attacks in New York and Washington in 2001. After eight years of the Bush administration, there are no signs that the Obama administration has any intention of shifting course away from fighting international terrorism. In the years to come, the Supreme Court is likely to remain involved in disputes over individual liberties being limited by the Executive.

My interest in constitutional law began in my first year of the PhD program at Syracuse University, when my teaching assistant duties were reassigned from Western Traditional of Political Philosophy to Constitutional Law, a topic I knew nothing about. For the next two years, I cultivated a fondness for the federalism cases and developed a keen interest in how the Court would decide the limits of power held by each branch of government, including its own. My interest in war powers emerged as the Bush administration took actions to fight its war on terrorism without getting explicit congressional approval, with critics charging the administration was not only acting unilaterally, but also unconstitutionally. With the limited knowledge I gained about presidential action in times of war, I knew Bush was not the first to expand presidential authority, though from the sound of the administration's critics, you would have thought so. I started to wonder how the Court historically decided such cases where the Executive limited individual liberties at home. As the Supreme Court made its initial rulings in this new area of American foreign policy in 2004 and again in 2006, there appeared to be some deference, not to the Executive, but rather to Congress. If the Court perceived the president to have the authorization of Congress, then the Court would be more lenient. With Justice Jackson's concurrence in *Youngstown* in mind, I began to wonder if Jackson had been right all along. Does the Court defer to the political branches when they work together, even if it means our protected rights will be limited?

As I worked to answer the questions in which I had become interested, along the way I received an enormous amount of support from mentors and colleagues for which I am grateful. Many members of Syracuse University's faculty were instrumental in my finishing this book. Jeffrey Stonecash, with one phone call, ensured that I would finish what I started—even if he didn't know it. Keith Bybee, Ralph Ketcham, William Banks, Thomas Keck, Margaret Thompson, and Stonecash, members of my dissertation committee, from which this book is based, were invaluable in their comments and suggestions. I am most grateful to Keith Bybee and Ralph Ketcham, both supportive of my work and influential since my first day entering graduate school in 2002, who continue to be so today. Not only have they influenced my research agenda, but also have shaped my teaching style in the classroom.

St. Thomas University in Fredericton, New Brunswick, Canada, provided me with a fellowship that afforded me the opportunity to finish the first draft of what would eventually become this book. I am thankful to Dr. Michael McGowan and Senator Noel Kinsella for that opportunity. Richard Meyers, Thomas Bateman, Joe Masciulli, Shaun Narine, and Mikhail Molchanov, members of the political science department, read drafts of these chapters and provided me with insight and advice. I am also most grateful to Patrick Malcolmson who has been my mentor since 1997 and who has and continues to have the biggest influence on my academic career.

At Middle Tennessee State University, I am thankful for the institutional support I have received to cover some financial costs that had become associated with the manuscript. I am also grateful to John Vile for reading earlier chapters and providing valuable insights as well as to John Maynor for his advice on what to do with the manuscript once completed.

I would also like to thank an anonymous reviewer for Lexington Books who provided me with excellent feedback, ultimately resulting in a much stronger product. I would also like to thank Alia Morgan for her support as my research assistant.

Finally, I owe much to my family. To my brother Jeff, and my sister Jaime, her husband Leigh, and their two beautiful daughters, Rebecca and Sarah, for their continued love and support. They have each helped me in a number of ways, from coffee breaks to sleepovers. Lastly, to my parents, Judy and Jim DiPaolo, for providing me with years of unwavering support in all my endeavors. They have followed my interest in constitutional law both as loving parents and as interested readers, having each carefully read the entire manuscript and providing comments along the way. I dedicate this book to them.

Chapter 1

Introduction

When Justice Samuel Alito was questioned before the Senate Judiciary Committee hearing, he was asked how he would evaluate the Executive's war powers under Article II of the Constitution. Specifically, Alito was asked how he would judge the president's authority to engage in electronic surveillance in regard to the warrant requirement of the *Foreign Intelligence Surveillance Act* (1978). Alito answered that he "might" look to Justice Robert Jackson's framework presented in *Youngstown Sheet & Tube v. Sawyer,* 343 U.S. 579; 1952. Alito explained that Jackson divided war powers into three categories: "where the President acts with explicit or implicit congressional approval, where the President acts and Congress has not expressed its view on the matter one way or the other, and the final category, where the President exercises executive power . . . in the face of explicit or implicit congressional opposition to it."[1] What is interesting about Justice Alito's answer is that he did not mention the Bill of Rights, or, more specifically, the Fourth Amendment's protections against unreasonable search and seizure.

The extent and scope of the executive's authority during war is of renewed concern since the terrorist attacks on American soil in 2001. During the course of 8 years in office, the Bush administration held American citizens as enemy combatants, denied the writ of habeas corpus to foreign citizens, examined phone records of American citizens that major telecommunications companies handed over to government officials, and conducted electronic surveillance without a warrant on individuals phoning people with known links to terrorist organizations outside the country. Each of these situations resulted in Supreme Court cases with decisions of great importance in shaping how individual rights will be protected (or not) during war in the future.

Americans have come to expect federal courts to declare actions by the government which are contrary to the Bill of Rights as unconstitutional. However, it is often argued that "[w]hen national emergencies strike, the executive acts, Congress acquiesces, and courts defer" (Posner & Vermeule, 2007: 3). My findings show that when liberties are limited during national emergencies, the Judiciary, more often than not, will defer to the political branches of government when they are working together. This means that the Court has been less influenced by rights provisions and more concerned with the separation of powers, or congressional approval, of executive actions. In other words, the Judiciary is more than willing to examine cases concerning the limitation of individual rights during times of war through a separation of powers framework rather than through the lens of the Bill of Rights and other constitutional limitations. Courts routinely decide cases in accordance with whether or not the individual justices on the bench are adequately convinced that Congress has authorized[3] the Executive's actions. As such, cases concerning the war powers become questions of procedure (which branch of government has authority to act), rather than a question of substance (can the government do that without infringing upon individual rights). As a result, the federal courts often decide war-powers cases based on statutory claims by looking at authority, or lack of, delegated to the president by Congress. Incidentally, when this emphasis on the separation of powers occurs, this means that the rights-based claims concerning issues such as the right to be free from unreasonable searches and seizures and the right not to be detained arbitrarily take a backseat to questions such as Congress has written into statute the authority for the Executive to detain individuals without laying charges, and so forth.

When individual liberties cases reach the federal courts, observers expect the justices to use rights-based language in formulating their decisions. Phrases like "equal protection" and "due process" have become staples in contemporary constitutional dialogue concerning rights-based issues. Litigants look to the Bill of Rights as protection against usurpation of power by government agents. It is reasonable to expect that the government cannot infringe individual rights even if the particular limitation is believed to be in the best interest of society at large (Dworkin, 1991; 91–93). Despite such a claim, no right is absolute and when the nation is in a perceived state of emergency, there is always a possibility that individual liberties will be limited as a national security precaution. In fact some aspects of the Bill of Rights specifically are listed as not applicable in a time of war. The Third Amendment prohibits the quartering of soldiers in a time of peace but does not forbid it during war, so long as a law is passed to prescribe it. The Fifth Amendment guarantees a civil trial, except in cases that arise from the land or naval forces during times of war. These notable exceptions to the Bill of Rights would suggest that the other clauses are indifferent to wartime or peacetime situations and thus equally applicable in both. It should therefore be the case that "the Bill of Rights limits governmental authority in the conduct of foreign relations as in other federal activity" (Henkin, 1996; 285). If this realistically is the case, what rationale is behind Justice Alito's search for congressional authorization of executive activities that limit individual liberties during war rather than the restrictions placed on the Executive by the Bill of Rights?

Limiting individual liberties during armed hostilities is different than when the Executive infringes rights in times of perceived peace because when "new threats appear, the balance shifts; government should and will reduce civil liberties in order to enhance security in those domains where the two must be traded off" (Posner & Vermeule, 2007; 5). The potential destruction of the State is given as a reason why freedom gives way to the security needs of the nation. Cicero's oft-quoted statement is that *inter arma silent leges*: in war, the law is silent. Yet it is expected that our rights will be protected whether the nation is at war or not. A hierarchy of judicial standards exists when the federal courts are asked to weigh the interests of the government against the constitutionally protected rights of the people. There are no special levels of review for wartime cases. When a fundamental right, guaranteed in the Bill of Rights, is limited by the government, courts typically apply the highest level of scrutiny. Detailed in footnote 4 to *United States v. Carolene Products, 304 U.S. 144; 1938,* the Court set up the idea of levels of scrutiny, a higher level being required for cases when fundamental rights are infringed. For a law to pass this highest form of judicial strict scrutiny, three prongs must be satisfied. First, the government must be advancing a compelling state interest. Second, the government must use narrowly tailored means to achieve its interest. Third, the government must use the least restrictive means in limiting the people's rights. During World War II (WWII), the Court, for the first time, indicated that it would apply a strict review of race-based legislation. In *Korematsu v. United States,* 323 U.S. 214; 1944,[4] the Court applied strict scrutiny, but announced that the evacuation order of Japanese Americans satisfied the three prongs outlined above because the Court deferred to the military's judgment that the threat of sabotage to the West Coast was a large enough concern to warrant the removal of Japanese Americans from their homes in sensitive areas. The Court opted to defer to the military and Executive expertise in foreign affairs, but it did at least apply the test, albeit poorly. It is more common to see the federal courts not apply a heightened level of review because they are unwilling to address the Constitutional issues and are content with decided war powers cases when rights are limited using separation of powers and statutory arguments.

This book seeks to answer a number of questions by carefully examining the decisions of the federal courts in four issue areas where the government has infringed individual liberties during war: military detentions, warrantless electronic surveillance, emergency economic legislation, and restrictions to free speech. I will demonstrate that the Court often decides cases arising during wars that limited individual rights using a separation of powers framework rather than by examining of the Bill of Rights with the exception of the free speech cases.

With cases about the Executive limiting individual liberties due to national security concerns being decided based on the institutional separation of powers, a principled approach to war-powers adjudication is achieved. In fact, in answering why the courts are preoccupied with a separation of powers framework, I find this principled approach is a way for the courts to maintain their institutional legitimacy and even protect the Constitution itself during war. What results is a layer of protection for individual liberties during times of war that is unexpected.

The courts will defer to the Executive when the two elected branches of government are in agreement on the need to limit individual liberties, but limit executive authority when these actions are without authorization either explicitly through statute or implicitly through tacit consent by continued inaction on the part of Congress. This does not mean each and every time a federal court invalidates some action by the Executive that the cause of individual freedoms is advanced. In fact, a separation of powers approach to wartime judicial decision-making offers less protection to individuals than looking at the case through rights-based language and by answering the constitutional questions presented before the courts. However, the separation of powers offers a level of protection that is more than flat out deference to the Executive. Furthermore, the separation of powers ensure that overzealous judicial officers do not grant overbroad authority to the president using constitutional language that may do permanent damage to our liberties in times of peace. Does this mean, however, that the Bill of Rights is only respected during times of war when Congress places explicit limits on the powers of the Executive? In other words, does the Bill of Rights now depend on the will of Congress, the very will that encouraged many of the nation's framers of the need for a Bill of Rights to protect the people in the first place? If so, what are the results?

On the one hand, it is comforting to note that the Executive does not have the blank check that it is so often accused of receiving from the federal courts during times of national crisis. But on the other hand, the nation must come face to face with the realization that the blank check does exist and it is placed in the hands of Congress by the federal courts. If it comes as a surprise that rights-based claims are often decided using a separation of powers rationale rather than rights-based discourse found in the Bill of Rights, it will also come as a surprise that this emphasis on the separation of powers does not necessarily need to be a constant cause for alarm. In fact, James Madison believed that the Constitution protected individual liberty through the separation of powers between the federal and state governments as well as the two branches of the federal government. In a letter to Thomas Jefferson, Madison explained that individual liberties would be protected "by the manner in which the federal powers are granted." In the oft-quoted *Federalist #51,* Madison explains that "ambition must be made to counteract ambition . . . you must first enable the government to control the governed and in the next place oblige it to control itself." The aim of structuring the government in a way giving each office its own power, but also overlapping powers, made the branches of government dependent upon each other. At the same time, no branch of government would "possess, directly or indirectly, an overruling influence over the others in the administration of their respective powers" (Madison, *Federalist #48*).

THE CONSTITUTION, THE PROTECTION OF LIBERTY, AND THE WAR POWER

The interconnected nature of the three branches of government ensured that no concentration of power would occur in any one institution. Congress passes legislation which the Executive signs into law or will veto. Upon becoming law, the Executive becomes responsible for the law's implementation. The Executive also heads the Armed Forces, but cannot command troops without the Legislature appropriating funds. The Judiciary passes judgment on the laws of Congress and the actions of the Executive. This vision of government, with its appropriate checks and balances, created "a government which is to be administered by men over men," that "demands attention to fostering effective governance as well as to protecting liberty" (Madison, *Federalist #51*).

Madison further argued that "experience proves the inefficacy of a bill of rights on those occasions when its controul is most needed. Repeated violations of these parchment barriers have been committed by overbearing majorities in every State" (Madison to Jefferson, Oct. 17, 1788). Alexander Hamilton, in *Federalist #84,* argues the idea of a bill of rights is better in theory but did not work in practice. Furthermore, for Hamilton, the idea was actually a "dangerous" one because it presented "exceptions to powers not granted" to the federal government in the first place. This would undermine the view that government was limited with enumerated powers. Listing rights that could not be infringed implied that without the provision in place, Congress could in fact infringe the rights listed. The argument follows that the Bill of Rights adopted by the first Congress changed the Constitution from forming a government of limited power to a government with unlimited powers, minus the restrictions placed in the Bill of Rights as well as the various restrictions placed under the rubric of the separation of powers.

Despite Madison's claim that the powers of government were divided in a way to protect individual liberty, Thomas Jefferson was critical of the separation of powers argument. In a dialogue with Madison, Jefferson wrote that he did "not like . . . the omission of a bill of rights providing clearly . . . for freedom of religion, freedom of the press, protection against standing armies, restriction against monopolies, the eternal and unremitting force of the habeas corpus laws, and trials by jury in all matters of fact triable by the laws of the land and not by the law of nations" (Jefferson to Madison, 1787). Towards the end of the Constitutional Convention, George Mason did propose the inclusion of a bill of rights and one was drafted by Elbridge Gerry. The proposal was unanimously rejected as unnecessary by the framers.[5] The anti-federalists, fearing a strong national government, criticized the newly drafted Constitution for its lack of a bill of rights. Jefferson's vision regarding the importance of such safeguards to individual liberty won out over Madison's arguments and despite his initial lack of faith, it would be Madison who drafted and introduced the Bill of Rights for political reasons to the First Congress. Still, it would be the Constitution's structure of government that would go on to protect individual liberties when the Bill of Rights would not, when the nation was at war. The division of the war powers and their subsequent use over the last two centuries shows how Madison's vision of protecting individual liberties proves important today, more than two centuries later.

The main debate at the Constitutional Convention concerned the distribution of power between the national government and the states rather than the distribution of power between the two branches of the national government. In other words, "federalism considerations . . . trumped separation of powers" (Rakove, 2007; 87). That said, one goal of creating a new Constitution was, in fact, to "remedy what the convention believed were deep, structural flaws in the ability of government under the Articles of Confederation to defend the United States" (Kohn, 1991; 63). In fact, when deliberations opened at the Convention, a discussion ensued concerning the defects in the Articles of Confederation. The initial complaint was that the Articles "produced no security agai[nst] foreign invasion; congress not being permitted to prevent war nor to support it by th[eir] own authority" (Banks & Raven-Hansen, 1994; 27).

Madison was not ignorant to the defects of the Articles concerning the defense of the nation. In a letter to George Washington two months before the Convention convened, Madison suggested it was necessary for the federal government to have the financial capacity to raise an army (Madison to Washington, April 16, 1787).[6] Furthermore, in his *Vices of the Political System of the United States,* Madison suggested that international laws and treaties were broken under the Articles of Confederation due to the numerous legislatures all acting on their own interests with a lack of coherency among state actions (Madison, 1787).[7] At the Convention, the governor of Virginia, Edmund Randolph acknowledged the Articles deficiencies as Congress' inability to prevent wars between states or its inability to protect the nation from foreign attack (Farrand, Vol. 1; 25). This sentiment was echoed by the first secretary of foreign affairs, John Jay. Complaining about the post he held, created under the Articles by Congress, Jay, in a letter to Thomas Jefferson, expressed his sentiments that Congress was ill-suited to manage such affairs because of the "unseasonable delays and successive obstacles in obtaining the decision and sentiments of the Legislature" (Letter from Jay to Jefferson, Aug. 18, 1786, 1970, 3; 210). Jay also expressed the inability of Congress to act with secrecy since the "executive business of sovereignty, depend[ed] on so many wills" (Letter from Jay to Washington, Jan 7, 1787, 3; 227).

Despite Jay's warnings that the executive power should not rest in the hands of Congress, the framers' vision of the war powers differed from British practice, where such power lay exclusively in the hands of the Monarch.[8] Like many of the other debates in Philadelphia, there was no initial agreement on the separation of the war powers between Congress and the Executive. Before the delegates talked about congressional powers, the role the Executive would play in foreign affairs was already being debated (Irons, 2005; 19). Of course, when the Constitutional Convention first convened, it was not entirely certain there would even be an independent executive. It was not until Randolph presented the Virginia Plan on May 29, 1787, that there was a call for a national Executive.

The seventh paragraph of the Virginia Plan first officially called for a national executive to be instituted. The plan suggested the Executive "ought to enjoy the Executive rights vested in Congress by the Confederation" (Farrand, 1911; Vol. I, 236). These executive powers included the ability to declare war and peace, of sending and receiving ambassadors, making rules for the determination of which prize captures are legal, as well as granting letters of marque and reprisal during times of peace. When the proposal to give the National Executive the executive powers possessed by the Congress under the Articles of Confederation was debated on June 1, 1787, Charles Pinckney, from South Carolina, thought that an Executive that could declare war and peace would institute a monarchy "of the worst kind, to wit an elective one" (Farrand, Vol. 1; 65). In fact, Pinckney proposed that the Senate be vested with the power to make war as it was already knowledgeable in foreign affairs (Farrand, Vol 2; 318), having a part to play in regard to the treaty power as well as appointments made by the Executive which included ambassadors.

Federalists James Wilson from Pennsylvania and James Madison ensured the skeptics of a powerful national government that the powers of war and peace belonged to the Legislature, not the Executive. Wilson moved that the Executive be a single person because it would give the office the most authority and would at the same time allow for its powers to be restrained because its duties would not consist of those found under the British prerogative model of government, but would rather be to execute the laws the Legislature has passed (Farrand Vol. 1, 66).

Roger Sherman, in echoing Wilson's sentiments, considered the "Executive magistracy as nothing more than an institution for carrying the will of the legislature into effect." Sherman went so far as to propose that the Executive be appointed by the legislative branch (Farrand, Vol. 1, 65). However, Wilson placed emphasis on the importance of a democratically elected Executive by the people and was one of the main creators of the electoral college, rather than the Executive being chosen by the Legislature. This was yet another safeguard against the unlimited power of the Executive. The president would need to heed the will of the people or risk getting voted out of office. These sentiments again were proclaimed in Wilson's lectures on law which he gave at the University of Pennsylvania between 1790 and 1792. Wilson noted that "the restraints on the executive power are external. These restraints are applied with greatest certainty, and with greatest efficacy, when the object of restraint is clearly ascertained. This is best done, when one object only, distinguished and responsible, is conspicuously held up to the view and examination of the publick."[9] If, by chance, the people elected someone who exceeds the powers of the office in a way the citizens believe warrant not being reelected, "the person, who has once shamefully abused their generous and unsuspecting confidence, shall not have it in his power to insult and injure them a second time, by the repetition of such an ungrateful return" (Wilson, 1790; Vol.1, 278).

Madison picks up Wilson's argument from the Constitutional Convention and in *Federalist Paper* #48. Madison explains that the Executive's functions are limited "both in extent and duration of its power . . . it is against the enterprising ambition of this department (the legislature) that the people ought to indulge all their jealousy and exhaust their precaution." Madison's caution in regard to the Executive would suggest that it is the Executive that is checked by the Constitution's Article II, as Congress is the branch empowered with the Supremacy Clause as well as the ability to pass all laws that are necessary and proper to fulfill its enumerated powers and obligations. As such, Madison's president would only possess the executive powers that were specifically enumerated in the Constitution and those delegated to the president by Congress, in a familiar echoing of Justice Jackson's *Youngstown* framework. Under Jackson's framework this grant of authority to Congress is also recognition of the importance of a delegation of authority from Congress to the Executive through the passage of laws and incidentally falls within the first prong of the *Youngstown* framework where the Executive is at its most powerful. What is most important to note here is that it is appropriate for Congress to grant a broad scope of authority to the Executive to guard the nation's security. The hands of Congress are not tied in that it does not necessarily have to perform its own powers, thus allowing for the grant of power to the Executive from Congress possible in the first place.

Further evidence of the intention to achieve a balance of power where interbranch cooperation was meant to be the norm is found in the carefully chosen words the framers used in drafting the war powers. The original wording of the war powers was that the legislature could "make" war, thus excluding the Executive altogether from the process. Changing the wording to Congress having the power to declare war left open a role for the Executive to command the army in the field once the hostilities were initiated (Irons, 2005; 20). The president being the commander-in-chief was necessary, as Hamilton explains in *Federalist # 74* because war "most peculiarly demands those qualities which distinguish the exercise of power by a single head." In this vein, South Carolina's Pierce Butler put forth a motion to give all such power to the Executive. This was not well received. George Mason, for example, was "ag[ain]st giving power of war to the Executive, [as well as against giving the power to the Senate] because not safely to be trusted with it; . . . He was for clogging rather than facilitating war," and promoted "facilitating peace" (Farrand, Vol. 2, 319). While the convention certainly had proponents of executive authority over congressional and vice versa, cooler heads prevailed. On August 17, Madison and Gerry proposed a motion to change the wording from "make" to "declare" war, ensuring a role for the Executive to execute the war once declared. The states voted 9-1 in favor of this set up of the war power.

As passed, the Congress would decide in which military situations the United States would involve itself and the president, as commander-in-chief, would command the tactical side of the armed conflict as well as "repel sudden attacks" if need be (Ely, 1993; 5). This power to repel sudden attacks was supposed to be an emergency measure to protect the homeland or troops abroad. It should be noted that the phrase to "repel sudden attacks" is nowhere in the text of the Constitution, though it is implied in Article IV with the federal government being responsible to guarantee to each state protection against invasion. How far the president could take the power to repel sudden attacks and the defensive executive power in general is not well defined by the framers. However, Congress delegated such authority to the Executive in February 1795 and again in March 1807, passing acts which authorized the president to call up the militia and use the armed forces of the United States in cases of invasion by foreign nations as well as to suppress insurrections against the government of a state or the United States as a whole.[10]

According to Louis Fisher, "[p]residential use of force during the first few decades after the Philadelphia Convention conformed closely to the expectations of the framers. The decision to go to war or to mount offensive actions was reserved to Congress, for all wars: declared or undeclared" (Fisher, 1995; 13). And yet by 1815, the United States engaged in battle against Indian Tribes, which at the time the government considered to be foreign enemies, as well as involved in hostilities against the British, the French, and the Barbary States (Reverley, 1983; 2117). This came as no surprise to those in government. The framers were aware that armed hostilities were likely to occur. Justice Brandeis noted in his dissent in *Myers v. United States, 272 U.S. 52; 1926,* that "the doctrine of separation of powers was adopted by the Convention of 1787, not to promote efficiency but to preclude the exercise of arbitrary power. The purpose was, not to avoid friction, but, by means of the inevitable friction incident to the distribution of the governmental powers among three departments, to save the people from autocracy" (Brandeis' *Myers* dissent).

How the federal courts decide cases pertaining to the initiation of hostilities plays an important role in maintaining the framers vision of how the Executive and Congress have worked together to come to the defense of the State. The federal courts often continue to use the same separation of powers discourse in deciding war time individual liberties cases as used in those cases pertaining to the initiation of hostilities. It makes sense and is in fact necessarily the case that war-powers cases concerning which branch of government can initiate hostilities must be decided using a separation of powers framework. It is less clear why the courts would not adopt a judicial discourse using rights-based language to decide cases dealing with limits to individual liberties. This question seems relevant and timely as the United States partook in what the Bush administration called a war on terrorism, and the threat of terrorism by non-state actors on American targets continues to remain a top concern for the Obama administration.

As Justice Alito points out, the suggestion that the federal courts rely on the interconnected nature of the elected branches of government in deciding war-powers cases was articulated in 1952 by Justice Robert Jackson. Jackson's framework suggests how the courts not only do, but should, in fact decide cases during armed hostilities. My emphasis on Jackson's framework is important because I show its historical accuracy in regard to how the federal courts decide cases where the president limits individual liberties. Because Jackson's vision is founded on his belief in the original philosophy of the nation, I suggest the framework can be used to reshape conventional wisdom not only on how the courts often will decide war powers cases when individual liberties are at stake, but also in regard to the original allocation of the war powers between the branches of government.

JACKSON'S CONCURRENCE IN YOUNGSTOWN SHEET & TUBE V. SAWYER

The *Youngstown* decision resulted from President Truman seizing most of the nation's steel mills during the Korean War to prevent a labor strike in 1952. Justice Hugo Black wrote the Court's opinion, refusing to accept the government's position that the president had inherent power to seize the steel mills as part of the Executive's role to protect the nation from threats to its security. Black reasoned that if the president had authority to seize the mills, it would come from either congressional statute or directly from the text of the Constitution. No statutory authorization to seize the mills existed. Black's opinion emphasized that the Constitution's division of powers ensured that Congress alone could authorize seizing the steel mills to prevent a stoppage in production due to the labor dispute. Congress legislated on the issue, offering ways of settling labor disputes for the Executive to follow that did not include outright seizure of property. Black further held that "in the framework of our Constitution, the President's power to see that the laws are faithfully executed refutes the idea that he is to be a lawmaker" (Black's *Youngstown* opinion). When the president seized the steel mills, he effectively made a law calling for the nationalization of the industry. Such an action was not in the Executive's enumerated powers granted to the office in the Constitution and in fact infringed on those of Congress.

The *Youngstown* opinion was accompanied by five concurring and one dissenting opinion;[11] however, it is Jackson who recognizes an inherent role in regard to the war powers for the president to play, but only in congruence with Congress. Jackson's concurrence is cited in federal court opinions today as a framework to be used in deciding cases dealing with which branch of government has authority to use the war powers (Marcus, 2003; 731, Sharman, 1989; 578). In fact, the Supreme Court itself has cited Jackson's concurrence as having eclipsed Black's majority opinion "in terms of influencing the governing paradigm" (Stokes Paulsen, 2001; 224).[12]

Just as Justice Alito explained during his confirmation hearings in front of the Senate, Jackson divided executive authority into three categories. First, the president has the most authority when his actions can be linked as having explicit or implicit authorization from Congress. In these circumstances, the president's actions should be viewed with "the widest latitude" by the federal courts. If executive actions are held unconstitutional under this category, Jackson suggests, it would only be as a result of the federal government as a whole lacking the power to act. The second category of executive authority is when the president acts in the absence of congressional authorization, but when Congress has not denied authority either. In this situation, both the Executive and Congress may have overlapping and concurring powers or it may be uncertain which branch has the proper authority to act. Under such circumstances, Jackson argues the war powers constitute a "zone of twilight." The final category of authority finds the Executive at its "lowest ebb" and is where the federal courts must "scrutinize with caution" presidential actions. Here the president must act with specific constitutional authority and does so in direct or implicit contradiction to the wishes of Congress. If the federal courts allow the president's actions to stand, they do so only by denying Congress the ability to act on the issue. Jackson argued that Truman found himself in this third category because Congress passed other statutes that offered ways to deal with labor disputes, none of which allowed for the unilateral seizure of private property by the Executive.

Jackson's concurrence is an effort to determine the legitimate use of executive authority during armed hostilities, stating that "while the Constitution diffuses power the better to secure liberty, it also contemplates that practice will integrate the dispersed powers into a workable government. It enjoins upon its branches separateness but interdependence, autonomy but reciprocity" (Jackson's *Youngstown* concurrence). Jackson himself noted that both security and liberty could no longer be taken for granted and that "freedom is achieved only by a complex but just structure of rules of law, impersonally and dispassionately enforced against both ruled and the governed" (Jackson, 1951; 104). The importance of the separation of powers in protecting individual liberty becomes apparent when Jackson looks at other regimes and notes that those that provide for the safety and the liberty of their citizens require joint action by both political branches of government (Jackson, 1951; 108). As reiterated in *Youngstown,* the Constitution has no provision giving the Executive extra power in times of a national security crisis. That said,

Jackson went on to conclude that it was not for the Court to amend the Constitution to allow for such extraordinary powers. While Jackson contends that the power to delegate more authority in times of an emergency to the Executive belongs only in the hands of Congress, he does note that it is Congress alone that can assure, as an institution, it does not lose its own power.

The *Youngstown* decision concerns the "legitimate and proper effect on the judiciary of the constitutional interpretations of the political branches" just as much as it is about whether or not Truman was authorized to seize the nation's steel mills (Stokes Paulsen, 2001; 215). In fact, Jackson's framework represents best how the structure of government itself, one of "limited sovereignty—and the relation between human rights and government power" can best be used to "refute the notion that the 'laws' to be faithfully tended convey, but do not restrict, presidential authority" (Bobbitt, 2002; 11).

Despite Jackson's framework, when cases dealing with individual liberties are adjudicated, it is expected that cases be decided whether or not the federal government can limit individual liberties protected in the Constitution using language concerning those constitutionally protected rights. That the separation of powers does not necessarily and always collapse requires some explaining. The federal courts' willingness to, in many cases and areas of decision-making, focus on the separation of powers over the Bill of Rights in deciding these cases is an attempt at creating the balance of making hard decisions that respect the Judiciary's own institutional limitations. Rosen points out that "judicial unilateralism in wartime [which challenges executive authority to curtail liberty] may lead to political backlashes that hurt judicial power and civil liberties at the time . . ." with such actions being seen "in the face of constitutional uncertainty [as] counterproductive" (Rosen, 2006; 171–72).[13] In the very least, however, during armed hostilities, when pressure exists for the federal courts to rally around the flag and defer to the Executive, relying on the institutional division of powers to decide many of these war-powers cases provides some level of protection not only for individual liberties but also for the Judiciary.

In the chapters that follow, I look at federal court cases involving war powers controversies. In an attempt to say something relevant about the present and the future of judicial decision making concerning the adjudication of war powers cases when individual rights are at stake, it is important to look to the past for patterns of judicial activity. In particular, this book promotes that the separation of powers has a role to play in protecting individual liberties as James Madison envisioned so long ago.

The analysis to follow shows that Justice Jackson's framework presented in his concurring opinion in *Youngstown Sheet & Tube v. Sawyer* is a useful tool to guide the Judiciary in its war-powers adjudication. If the federal courts continue to decide war-powers cases concerning individual liberties by determining the proper scope of institutional balance based on the separation of powers, then it may be possible to better understand the rationale used when courts decide war-powers cases where individual liberties are at stake. While it is not always the case, as will be shown, that a separation of powers framework is used over the Bill of Rights in deciding these cases where individual liberties are limited, it is still true that the proper scope of authority between all three branches of government finds its way into the rationale of these decisions of the federal courts.

ENDNOTES

1. U.S. Senate Judiciary Committee Hearing on the nomination to the Supreme Court of Judge Samuel Alito. January 10, 2006.

2. Cases based on a separation of powers framework initially concerned the police powers of the state versus the commerce power of Congress. It was a question of which level of government, state or federal, had authority to act. The separation of powers framework used to adjudicate war-powers cases refers to the separation of the federal government's powers between the two elected branches of the federal government.

3. This is contingent, of course, on what each individual court accepts as congressional authorization. I am cognizant of this fact. Congressional authorization has come in the form of explicit authority in statute or resolution, the inability of Congress to act on an issue that is repeatedly conducted by the Executive, as well as the federal courts' interpretation of congressional acts to read into them implicit authorization, using legislative histories as a means to justify their decisions. While such ways of determining congressional authorization are vague and really up to the individual courts to decide, absent explicit congressional authorization in statute form, the language used by the courts stating authorization exists should be enough to note that the courts' rationale rests on their being able to find that Congress conferred power or delegated it to the Executive. Regardless of how strong the authorization may be, if the courts say it exists and bases its decision on its presence, then the case was decided predominantly using the separation of powers as a guide to its decision-making.

4. Justice Black states that "all legal restrictions which curtail the civil rights of a single racial group are immediately suspect. That is not to say that all such restrictions are unconstitutional. It is to say that courts must subject them to the most rigid scrutiny. Pressing public necessity may sometimes justify the existence of such restrictions; racial antagonism never can." Black's opinion fails to make any further analysis based on strict scrutiny and upholds the conviction because Congress authorized the exclusion order. This case will be looked at in greater detail in Chapter 3.

5. I often make reference to the thought or intention of the framers of the Constitution or of the founding generation. I acknowledge that there is no one intention of the framers or of the founding generation. The Constitution that resulted from the

Convention was one that had adopted many compromises that incorporated a variety of points of view. That said, however, the end result, I believe, can be looked at as encompassing an intent or vision of the framers that takes into account the variety of points of view represented in the final version of the Constitution. It is this comprehensive vision of the framers intentions that I refer to when I suggest that the intent of the framers is one that requires the elected branches of government to cooperate in formulating policies in foreign affairs.

6. http://www.constitution.org (May 9, 2007).

7. http:// www.teachingamericanhistory.org (May 9, 2007).

8. It should be noted that the royal prerogative had been successfully checked and limited by parliamentary struggles against the Crown. Charles I failed to obtain the funds in 1626 to wage a war. This victory for Parliament led to the Petition of Right in 1628, denying the sovereign's power to tax without Parliament's consent. In 1665, Parliament began dictating how taxes would be spent and began voting on military appropriations, giving Parliament more control over the standing army. Parliament substantially gained the power of the purse in 1688 with the passage of the British Bill of Rights. By the 18th Century, Parliament largely oversaw military actions. In 1702, the King lost control of the army to Captain General Lord Marlborough. After 1714, the Cabinet Council became the source of authority for the Captain General. This information is outlined in Keynes' 1982 work (24) and is used to suggest that by time Blackstone wrote his *Commentaries on the law of England* in 1765, the prerogative power he speaks of for the Monarch is not as all encompassing as it seems (for greater detail, see also Coolidge, 1970: 5–18. For a more recent account of the legislative restrictions on the prerogative powers of the British Crown, see also Rakove, 2007; 89). However, these reforms were not enough to convince even the strongest proponents of a powerful Executive that its powers should be unlimited in foreign affairs. The framers rejected notions of federative and prerogative power during armed hostilities, relying instead on the separation of powers. The framers decided to divide the powers between the Legislative and Executive branches of government, thus making it difficult to declare war (Keynes, 1982; 20). By separating the power of spending from the power of commanding the military, the framers sought to ensure a lack of military enthusiasm and tyranny at the domestic level (Huzar, 1950; 18-23).

9. James Wilson's papers http://www.constitution.org/jwilson (May 9, 2007).

10. Not everyone at the Constitutional Convention favored maintaining a standing army outside of participation in armed hostilities. Gerry opposed a standing army and suggested that its size be limited to two or three thousand soldiers in times of peace. On August 18, 1787, Gerry argued that the proposed Constitution offered no checks and balances against a standing army. This concerning him, Gerry stated that "he could never consent to a power to keep an indefinite number" of troops (Farrand, Vol. 2; 329). Two days later, on August 20th, Pinckney proposed that "[n]o troops shall be kept up in times of peace, but by consent of the Legislature' and that… 'no grant of money shall be made by the Legislature for supporting military land forces, for more than a year at a time" (Farrand, Vol. 2; 341). The final recommendation was that the appropriations for the army be limited to two years.

Appropriations for the military being in the hands of Congress provided a further check on the use of the military by the Executive as the House and Senate would have to agree to its funding. Despite such precautions, delegates Gerry, Luther Martin, and James McHenry of Maryland remained staunchly opposed to the possibility of a standing army in times of peace under any conditions. These delegates considered a standing army to be dangerous to the liberty of the people. Gerry even stated he would not sign the Constitution if a standing army was provided for (Farrand, Vol. 2; 509), and he kept his word. Martin argued his objections to the standing army in the Maryland legislature, stating that:

> Congress have also the power given them to raise and support armies, without any limitation as to numbers, and without any restriction in time of peace. Thus, Sir, this plan of government, instead of guarding against a standing army, that engine of arbitrary power, which has so often and so successfully been used for the subversion of freedom, has in its formation given it an express and constitutional sanction (Farrand, Vol. 3; 207).

Hamilton addressed these issues in *The Federalist Papers* trying to convince skeptics that allowing Congress the possibility to provide for the common defense as well as the ability to raise and support armies was necessary for the nation's protection.

In *Federalist #25*, Hamilton explained that without the power to provide for the nation's security, the United States, as a whole, would have to rely on the individual state's militias for security. This posed the problem of a couple of state militias being bigger than the others thus threatening and raising alarm in the rest of the states. In-fighting could start and the risk would be run of the state militias quarreling with each other. Other potential problems included states being unwilling or financially unable to maintain a militia, as well as unable or unwilling to offer said militia in the service of the federal government as a whole when it was called upon as necessary. The national government, Hamilton argued, must have the power to determine future threats to the State as well as the necessary amount of troops needed to deal with such threats. Hamilton goes on to suggest in *Federalist #25* that if the Constitution would not allow for a standing army, it would create "a nation incapacitated by its Constitution to prepare for defense before it was actually invaded." Hamilton also soothed concerns of the Executive creating a military dictatorship as for that to happen there would need to be "not merely a temporary combination between executive and legislature, but a continued conspiracy for a series of time." Finally, Hamilton reassured his anti-federalist colleagues, in *Federalist #24* that the "whole power of raising armies was lodged in the Legislature, not the Executive; that this legislature was to be a popular body, consisting of the representatives of the people periodically elected."

11. The *Youngstown Sheet & Tube v. Sawyer* decision and accompanying concurrences and dissent are more fully explored in Chapter 2.

12. In *Dames & Moore v. Regan*, 453 U.S. 654; 1981, citing the *Youngstown* framework, then Justice Rehnquist stated that "[b]ecause the President's action in nullifying the attachments and ordering the transfer of assets was taken pursuant

to specific congressional authorization, it is 'supported by the strongest presumptions and the widest latitude of judicial interpretation, and the burden of persuasion would rest heavily upon any who might attack it.'" More currently, in *Hamdan v. Rumsfeld*, 548 U.S. 507, 2006, Stevens states that "[w]hether or not the President has independent power, absent congressional authorization, to convene military commissions, he may not disregard limitations that Congress has, in proper exercise of its own war powers, placed on his powers" (Stevens' *Hamdan* opinion, footnote #23). *Youngstown* was Stevens reference for this argument.

13. This cautious vision of the federal courts is the vision that I believe shows to be the dominant position of the federal courts throughout American history during armed hostilities. This judicial restraint in regard to the use of a separation of powers framework rather than looking to the Bill of Rights in adjudicating rights-based litigation will be further examined in chapter 2.

Chapter 2

Guiding War Powers Judicial Decision-Making

During times of war, it is often the case that the federal courts look for the presence, or absence, of congressional approval of executive actions when individual liberties are limited. Instead of strict, intermediate or rational basis review, Justice Jackson presents a framework in his concurring opinion to *Youngstown Sheet & Tube v. Sawyer,* 343 U.S. 579; 1952, where the federal courts are offered three levels of analysis to decide rights-based legislation based on the institutional design of government powers. The federal courts decide cases based on a heightened level of analysis when the Executive acts without, or in contrast to, congressional authorization. Similarly, cases are adjudicated with a low-level of scrutiny, reminiscent of rational basis review, when the two elected branches of government are working together. When authorization sanctioned by Congress is not found, but the president is not acting contrary to the wishes of Congress either, adjudication is based on an intermediate level of scrutiny.[1]

This chapter highlights the relevance of Jackson's *Youngstown* concurrence and offers a rationale why the courts might choose to decide war powers cases concerning individual liberties using a separation of powers framework rather than the limitations presented in the Bill of Rights. First, I introduce the historical circumstances leading to the *Youngstown* case. After highlighting each of the case's opinions, I explain why Jackson's framework is a useful guide for the adjudication of war-powers cases. The concurring opinion's emphasis on the interconnected nature of the president and Congress in regard to the war powers as well as the flexibility required by all branches of government to provide for the continued safety of the nation is telling. The second part of this chapter presents an institutional argument. Jackson himself notes the federal courts' emphasis on the separation of powers in deciding war-powers cases is a way to ensure the federal courts protect the Constitution as well as the legitimacy of the Judiciary from granting too much authority to the Executive, thus potentially damaging rights enumerated in the Constitution beyond repair after the end of hostilities. The framework also protects the courts from limiting the Executive so much as to endanger national security, leaving political decision makers to ignore court rulings, weakening not only the institution of the Judiciary but the Constitution itself. The language of the Bill of Rights does not guarantee that the federal courts will find a violation of rights just because cases come up arguing that a violation has occurred. By leaving the language of the Bill of Rights alone, the courts protect rights that already existed before hostilities began.

THE YOUNGSTOWN FRAMEWORK

In an effort to contain the spread of communism, President Harry Truman committed American troops to fight in Korea on June 25, 1950. Truman made the decision because he thought neighboring states would be in jeopardy of falling to communism if the North Korean Army that invaded South Korea, was victorious. Truman relied on authority from the U.N. rather than from a congressional declaration of war. Truman did, however, ask Congress for funds to fight the war on July 10. In December of the same year, China entered the conflict on the side of North Korea. In response, Truman declared a national emergency, something he chose not to do beforehand. The proclamation automatically enacted over sixty "war" acts of Congress, giving the president extra powers. A couple of years after the initiation of the conflict, Truman would nationalize the steel mills, believing the looming labor strike would result in a shortage of war supplies being produced.

In the words of the late Chief Justice William H. Rehnquist, "what started as a labor dispute between the steelworkers' union and the major steel producers suddenly blossomed into a major constitutional crisis" (Rehnquist, 1987; 155). The United Steelworkers notified company owners of their intention to strike in December 1951; their contract with the steel companies expired at the end of the month. Federal mediation agencies attempted, but failed, to resolve the dispute. The president stepped in by asking the union members not to strike. The first strike notice was called off at the president's request but once settlement efforts again failed, the steelworkers set a nationwide strike for 12:01 a.m., April 9, 1952.

To prevent the strike, Truman issued Executive Order 10340 ordering Secretary of Commerce Charles Sawyer to nationalize the steel mills. The next day, Truman informed Congress that the steel mills were seized. He argued that his authority to seize the mills came both from the Constitution and the laws of the land. Despite the call to the laws of the United States as one source of his authority, Truman cited no congressional statutes. Truman wrote to Congress saying he would respect whatever it decided to do about the situation,[2] but Congress did not act. Twelve days after Truman first wrote to Congress, he sent another letter, this time specifically asking for authorization. Congress did not respond to the letter.

In the meantime, the steel companies asked for an injunction in federal court, which the District Court for the District of Columbia granted. Assistant Attorney General Holmes Baldridge claimed the authority for the president's actions came from his inherent powers as Executive. However, Judge David A. Pine held there was nothing in the Constitution that supported Truman's claims of an inherent power given to his office. Judge Pine stated that a strike "would be less injurious to the public than the injury which would flow from a timorous judicial recognition that there is some basis for this claim to unlimited and unrestrained Executive power, which would be implicit in a failure to grant the injunction" (Fisher, 1999; 102).[3]

That same day, the Truman administration asked for a stay by the Court of Appeals for the District of Columbia and also invoked a rule to bypass the court of appeals so the issue would go from the district court to the Supreme Court (Rehnquist, 2002; 163). The court of appeals voted 5-4 in favor of the government's request for the bypass. The case reached the Supreme Court nine weeks after the steel mills were seized.

Because Democratic presidents, Roosevelt and Truman, appointed all the justices on the bench at the time, some observers believed that the opinion was destined to favor Truman's seizure (Rehnquist, 2002; 171). However, the Supreme Court upheld Pine's decision by a 6-3 vote, and Truman directed the secretary of commerce to return the steel mills to their owners. Justice Hugo Black wrote a short and straightforward opinion for the Court majority. He addressed two questions. First, did the judiciary have the jurisdiction to hear the case and decide on the constitutional validity of the Executive Order and the motion for the injunction? Second, if the Court was within its jurisdiction to decide the case, did the president have the constitutional authority to seize the steel mills?

After determining the Court had jurisdiction to hear the case, Justice Black held that the president's authority to seize the steel mills must come from the Constitution itself or from an act of Congress. Black found no act of Congress that gave the president proper authorization to seize the mills, so Truman had to rely on his own power found in the text of the Constitution. Black found no explicit grant of authority in the text of Article II of the Constitution, outlining the powers of the president. Because Congress had flat out rejected an amendment to the *Taft-Hartley Act* that would have given the president the authorization to seize private property and instead passed an act that did not allow for seizure of property, Justice Black further concluded that it had neither given explicit or implicit authorization to the president to make such seizures. Black observes that there were two statutes, the *Labor-Management Relations Act* of 1947 (the *Taft-Hartley Act*) and the *Selective Service Act* of 1948, authorizing the president to "take both personal and real property under certain conditions. However, the Government admits that these conditions were not met and that the President's order was not rooted in either of the statutes" (Black's *Youngstown* opinion). Black was concerned that the president did not utilize the *Taft-Hartley Act.* Its provisions allowed for "maintaining the status quo for a period during which a labor dispute might be settled and whereby, in the case it threatened a dangerous stoppage of production, the Congress might be informed and proceed to authorize seizure, if it saw fit, in a lawful manner" (Richberg, 1952; 724).

The government's argument for seizing the steel mills was that the language of the Constitution implied discretionary powers to the Executive in Article II under the following provisions: "[t]he executive Power shall be vested in a President of the United States of America" as well as "[t]he President shall be Commander-in-Chief of the Army and Navy of the United States," and finally, that "he shall take Care that the Laws be faithfully executed." Black rejected the argument that these provisions either singly or together created inherent authority to seize the mills. He argued that the Constitution did not grant legislative authority to the president and that only the legislature had power to seize private property:

> in the framework of our Constitution, the President's power to see that the laws are faithfully executed refutes the idea that he is to be a lawmaker. The Constitution limits his functions in the lawmaking process to the recommending of laws he thinks wise and the vetoing of laws he thinks bad. And the Constitution is neither silent nor equivocal about who shall make laws which the President is to execute. The first section of the first article says that 'All legislative Powers herein granted shall be vested in a Congress in its place.'

Black acknowledges Truman's argument that the seizure was necessary to avert a "national catastrophe," and that "the indispensability of steel as a component of substantially all weapons and other war materials led the president to believe that the proposed work stoppage would immediately jeopardize our national defense and that governmental seizure of the steel mills was necessary in order to assure the continued availability of steel." However, while acknowledging the importance of world events in the Executive's decision to seize the mills, Black focuses on domestic policy for dealing with labor strikes. These domestic implications led Black to conclude that seizing the steel mills was not a legitimate exercise of the president's military power as commander-in-chief of the Armed Forces. Black continued, "[e]ven though 'theatre of war' [is] an expanding concept, we cannot with faithfulness to our constitutional system hold that the Commander in Chief of the Armed Forces has the ultimate power as such to take possession of private property in order to keep labor disputes from stopping production."

The controversy resulted in a total of seven opinions. Each member who signed the Court's opinion wrote a concurrence, and three justices signed a single dissent. Justice William Douglas' concurring opinion emphasized, like Black, that the Constitution placed the legislative authority in the hands of Congress. Douglas acknowledges that the president has more leeway in times of national crisis than in times of peace. However, he adds that checks and balances are in place to determine the allocation of such powers. The president could not legislate to seize the mills and execute the same order. Black and Douglas do not take into account "hypothetical situations, exceptions, limitations, contingencies, doubtful cases, or broad categories" (Stokes Paulsen, 2002; 218). The other concurrences reject the "rigid interpretation of separation of powers elucidated" by the majority opinion and the Douglas concurrence (Bigel, 1986; 139).

Justice Felix Frankfurter notes that according to the founding generation, the separation of powers was not just a theory but rather a "felt necessity." While there may be occasion for the Court to intervene "in determining where authority lies as between the democratic forces in our scheme of government," Frankfurter believes the Court must do so in a way that is "wary and humble. Such is the teaching of this Court's role in the history of the country" (Frankfurter's *Youngstown* concurrence). Focusing on the specifics of the case, Frankfurter rests his concurrence on the grounds that Congress had rejected a proposal to grant powers of seizure to the president leaving "no room for doubt . . . as a result of that legislation, the only recourse for preventing a shutdown in any basic industry, after failure of mediation, was Congress." Moreover, Congress had the prerogative to "disallow such power from the President" and in this case it "could not be more decisive if it had been written into . . . the *Labor Management Act.*"

Justice Harold Burton wrote a short concurrence. Addressing current acts of Congress that presented ways for settling labor disputes, he observed that none allowed for the seizure of private property as Truman had done. Burton, like Frankfurter, held that "Congress, within its constitutional delegated power, has prescribed for the President specific procedures, exclusive of seizure, for his use in meeting the present type of emergency." While recognizing that the United States was engaged in an armed conflict, Burton stated that "the present situation is not comparable to that of an imminent invasion or threatened attack" or "catastrophic situations." Burton also rejected that the current seizure "is in the nature of a military command addressed by the President, as Commander-in-Chief, to a mobilized nation waging, or imminently threatened with, total war."

Justice Tom Clark did not concur in the opinion of the Court, but only the judgment. Clark wanted to leave room for the possibility of inherent presidential powers and suggested that the gravity of the situation and the circumstances in question could lead to a different decision. Clark quoted Lincoln in suggesting the Constitution gives the president extra emergency powers, and, that for the sake of the Constitution's survival, such powers are necessary. Lincoln asked, "[I]s it possible to lose the nation yet preserve the Constitution?" Clark continues, "[I]n describing this authority, I care not whether one calls it 'residual,' 'inherent,' 'moral,' 'implied,' 'aggregate,' 'emergency,' or otherwise. I am of the conviction that those who have had the gratifying experience of being the President's lawyer have used one or more of these adjectives only with the utmost of sincerity and the highest purpose" (Clark's *Youngstown* concurrence). Yet Clark, like his colleagues, points out that Congress had specific procedures in place for the type of crisis confronting the president. As such, Truman was required to "follow those procedures in meeting the crisis" at hand.

Three justices dissented, including Chief Justice Fred Vinson. Joined by Justices Stanley Reed and Sherman Minton, Vinson argued that Truman's actions were extraordinary, but were tied to extraordinary times: "A world not yet recovered from the devastation of World War II has been forced to face the threat of another and more terrifying global conflict." The war efforts in Korea required "continued production of steel and stabilized prices for steel."

Vinson argued that Congress indirectly approved Truman's actions through previous efforts to "protect the free world from aggression." Congress initiated or approved through financial support the Administration's role in a number of military endeavors, including the Marshall Plan, the Truman Plan, and the *Mutual Security Act* of 1951, as well as American participation in the North Atlantic Treaty and presidential initiatives like the Korean War. As a result, the president's duty included executing those legislative programs. One such action included seizing the steel mills to avoid the labor strike. For Vinson, these legislative acts and treaty obligations "represent not merely legal obligations, but show congressional recognition that mutual security for the free world is the best security against the threat of aggression on a global scale" (Vinson's *Youngstown* dissent).

Vinson further suggests that Congress's failure to respond to the president's call for legislative action on his seizure of the steel mills strengthened his authority. Emphasizing the national emergency that existed, Vinson argues that "if the President has any power under the Constitution to meet a critical situation in the absence of express statutory authorization, there is no basis whatever for criticizing the exercise of such power in this case" (Vinson's *Youngstown* dissent).

JACKSON'S YOUNGSTOWN CONCURRENCE

In contrast to the other decisions that portray either the role of Congress or the role of the president as being dominant in foreign affairs, Justice Jackson's concurring opinion emphasizes a vision of shared powers. The president may have inherent power, but he wields it only with an endorsement from Congress, either by a positive act of legislation meant to endorse the action in question or through repeated inaction that accepts the role the Executive has taken.

There were calls for Jackson to recuse himself from the steel seizure case because of his previously stated positions on executive authority as Attorney General. On May 12, 1952, Jackson received the following letter:

> Dear Sir,
> As private citizens, we urge you to disqualify yourself in the forthcoming vote on the interpretation of presidential powers. According to newspaper accounts we have read, you are previously on record as believing the powers of the president are limitless. We do not believe this conviction is shared by the average American, nor do we believe the founders of our way of life had any such drastic conceptions. Two of the signers here are ex-veterans who fought against governments of unlimited power to preserve a Government of limited power in the United States.
> Signed, Marion Thrash, John Schalek, Myra Ripley (Pennsylvania).[4]

The concerns of these citizens can be exemplified by reading Jackson himself. In a *New York Times* article from June 10, 1941, Jackson, in defense of President Roosevelt's seizure of the North American Aviation Plant, stated that the "President's proclamation 'rests upon the aggregate of the presidential powers derived from the constitution itself and from the statutes enacted by Congress.' Moreover, [Jackson] said, 'the Constitution vesting in the President the Commander-in-Chief of the Army and Navy, awarded him additional authority.'" In the same article Jackson further observed that "there can be no doubt that the duty constitutionally and inherently rested upon the president to exert his civil and military as well as his moral authority to keep the defense effort of the United States a going concern."

Jackson recognized the concern about his involvement in the case. Jackson started making notes about the case on May 7, 1952, before oral arguments were made before the Court on the 12th and 13th, justifying his decisions to not recuse himself:

> Candor requires me to state that I have considered whether I should sit in this case, in view of having acted as an advisor to a dynamic President in time of crisis . . . I have concluded that my experience is too remote to carry any insurmountable predilections that warrant withdrawal and that practical experience with the problems of this case may contribute something to the debate as to the President's powers which extends backwards to beginning and likely forward to end of the Republic (Jackson's papers, Box 174).

Jackson saw little relation between the seizure of the steel mills and the situation in 1941. Jackson believed that the North American Aviation Plant seizure "more nearly resembles an insurrection than a labor strike. The president's proclamation recites the persistent defiance of governmental efforts to mediate any legitimate labor differences" (Jackson's papers, Box 175). In fact, on a piece of scrap paper, Jackson noted how the two situations bore little resemblance:

1. direct contract vs. no contract
2. breach, i.e. strike no excuse vs. no breach
3. government owned machinery = planes vs. no government property
4. violation agreement vs. legislative stretch
5. political—destroy collective bargaining vs. economic by collective bargaining
6. statutory solutions (1940 and 1916 acts) vs. inherent power.

Unlike Truman, Roosevelt had defense contracts with the aviation plant. As such, legislative authorization did exist for FDR to seize the plant. Two acts of Congress, the *National Defense Act* of 1916 and the *Selective Training and Service Act* of 1940, provided the president with authority to seize property if contracts existed between the government and private property to make military equipment for the defense of the country. As a result, when the aviation plant workers went on strike, there was a breach of contract which needed to be fulfilled. Furthermore, government property was involved in the 1941 case, but not in 1952. Having distinguished the steel seizure case from the North American Aviation Plant seizure in 1941, Jackson heard the case. Jackson's concurrence took into account a full range of possibilities that Black's either/or dichotomy of presidential authority did not address.

Jackson framed the question as one that examines when the Executive should receive leeway from the federal courts and when the actions of the Executive should be carefully scrutinized. Dividing executive authority into three categories, Jackson offers a framework for the courts to consider when deciding if the Executive has authority to act, a framework that can guide the courts in adjudicating war powers claims when the Executive limits individual liberties.

After noting that 150 years of constitutional law has furnished precedents for both sides of a debate, Jackson argues the "actual art of governing under our Constitution does not . . . conform to judicial definitions of the power of any of its branches based on isolated clauses, or even single Articles torn from context." Jackson's vote at conference sums up his position adequately. He "would affirm doing as little damage as possible." Jackson did not elaborate what this meant, but when reading drafts of the concurrence, his concern for not limiting executive authority in future cases becomes apparent. Jackson deleted restrictions to inherent power originally written after footnote 13, stating that "[t]he absence of any express power to use military force to carry out internal policies of the Executive and the denial by Congress of implied powers to do so, if Constitutional, precludes the claim that the President has military powers over our economy greater than his civil powers." He further deleted a statement in which he had indicated that while many presidents have made broad claims, they "did it with less aggression" (Jackson Papers, box 175).[5] Jackson was trying to protect President Truman and future presidents from restrictions on their authority by allowing for cooperation among the branches of government to allow expanded authority to the Executive, if delegated by Congress. At the same time, Jackson was concerned with protecting the American regime from encroachments of individual liberties by overzealous officeholders, acknowledging "the difficulty of divorcing issues of power from the personalities and parties immediately involved." Jackson's concern over Truman's actions was that presidential powers confirmed by the Court "will not expire with the current term, nor be exhausted when the present occasion passes."

Jackson puts together his framework for deciding cases that would "integrate the dispersed powers into a workable government." Quoted at length Jackson holds that:

1. When the President acts pursuant to an express or implied authorization of Congress, his authority is at its maximum, for it includes all that he possesses in his own right plus all that Congress can delegate. In these circumstances, and in these only, may he be said (for what it may be worth) to personify the federal sovereignty. . . . A seizure executed by the President pursuant to an

Act of Congress would be supported by the strongest of presumptions and the widest latitude of judicial interpretation, and the burden of persuasion would rest heavily upon any who might attack it.

2. When the President acts in absence of either a congressional grant or denial of authority, he can only rely upon his own independent powers, but there is a zone of twilight in which he and Congress may have concurrent authority, or in which its distribution is uncertain. Therefore, congressional inertia, indifference or quiescence may sometimes, at least as a practical matter, enable, if not invite, measures on independent presidential responsibility. In this area, any actual test of power is likely to depend on the imperatives of events and contemporary imponderables rather than on abstract theories of law.
3. When the President takes measures incompatible with the expressed or implied will of Congress, his power is at its lowest ebb, for then he can rely only upon his own constitutional powers minus any constitutional powers of Congress over the matter. Courts can sustain exclusive presidential control in such a case only by disabling the Congress from acting upon the subject. Presidential claim to a power at once so conclusive and preclusive must be scrutinized with caution, for what is at stake is the equilibrium established by our constitutional system.

When the president acts in direct violation of a congressional statute, his actions fall into the third prong of the Jackson's framework. The Court must decide if the Executive is misconstruing the intent of Congress in its interpretation of congressional statutes.

Truman's actions fell under the third prong. Jackson points out that Truman himself offered no congressional authorization for the actions and relied on inherent executive authority, eliminating prong I. Because the Congress "did not leave seizure an open field," the president was not acting in the absence of or denial of congressional authorization, thus eliminating prong II. The case fell into prong III because Congress passed legislation designed to deal with situations that Truman confronted and not one Act called for the executive to seize private property unilaterally. The president, therefore, had to rely on his own enumerated constitutional powers. As a result of this analysis, Jackson found that Truman did not have the power to seize the steel mills. It was up to Congress to do so.[6]

Jackson, however, was not ready to accept Black's narrow definition of executive authority. Jackson expounded his own three prongs by noting that:

[H]istory leaves it open to question, at least in the courts, that the executive branch, like the Federal Government as a whole, possesses only delegated powers. The purpose of the Constitution was not only to grant power, but to keep it from getting out of hand. However, because the President does not enjoy

> unmentioned powers does not mean that the mentioned ones should be narrowed by a niggardly construction. Some clauses could be made almost unworkable.

While Jackson wants to leave open the idea of more broadly interpreted authorizations of executive authority when the situation calls for it, the Court's majority did not.

Jackson's three-pronged approach, which, in his own words, is "overly simplified," provides a framework for looking at how the federal courts view executive power. It may be more imperative for this element of cooperation to exist in times when threats to the nation exist. Rebuking the president for giving himself war powers, Jackson reminds the president that:

> Nothing in our Constitution is plainer than that declaration of a war is entrusted only to Congress. Of course, a state of war may in fact exist without a formal declaration. But no doctrine that the Court could promulgate would seem to me more sinister and alarming than that a President whose conduct of foreign affairs is so largely uncontrolled, and often even is unknown, can vastly enlarge his mastery over the internal affairs of the country by his own commitment of the Nation's armed forces to some foreign venture.

In this regard, Jackson concurs with those members of the Court who saw the issue as Truman claiming powers of foreign affairs and national security to control a domestic issue when in fact the president "was not confronted with a grave emergency in which there was no law for him to execute to meet the needs of national safety" (Richberg, 1952; 716).

An early draft of Jackson's concurrence included a more pointed criticism of the president's decision to go to war on his own. The opinion stated that "American troops in Korea, whose safety and effectiveness are so directly involved here, were sent to the field by an exercise of the President's constitutional powers. Thus it is said he has invested himself with 'war powers.'" Jackson deleted from the sentence: "that, having on his own sent American troops abroad, from that he derives 'affirmative power' to seize means for producing supplies for them" (Jackson Papers, box 174–175). Jackson implies that if Truman went to Congress for authorization for the war, the decision of the Court may have turned out differently. With authority from Congress to go to war, it could be implied the president has the authority to seize private property as an emergency measure, implicitly delegated by Congress with its declaration of war or other emergency statutory measures placing the Executive from prong III to one of the other prongs that enjoy a lessened standard of scrutiny toward executive actions.

It makes sense for Jackson to notice and to advocate that the courts use a separation of powers framework in deciding war powers claims when individual liberties are limited by actions of the Executive, because Jackson sought to protect the Judiciary's integrity to uphold the Constitution by not deciding such cases squarely on the constitutional questions. After all, in his *Korematsu* dissent, Jackson had urged the Supreme Court to avoid establishing constitutional precedents under the pressure of emergencies. Jackson held "[O]nce a judicial opinion rationalizes such an order to show that it conforms to the Constitution, or rather rationalizes the Constitution to show that the Constitution sanctions such an order, the Court for all time has validated the principle of racial discrimination in criminal procedure and of transplanting American citizens." Jackson recognized that while military officers may "overstep the bounds of the Constitution," to decide the constitutional issues would result in the wartime incident becoming part of the Constitution in times of peace as well as armed hostilities. This point cannot be stressed enough.

The Applicability of Jackson's Concurrence to War Powers Cases

The *Youngstown* decision has its critics, and its relevance to judicial decision making today is not assumed. In fact, there are many arguments as to why the Jackson framework should not be looked to for guidance today. That troops have been committed abroad without any congressional or judicial sanctions is said to show the limited impact the *Youngstown* decision has had constraining presidents after Truman left office (Irons, 2005; 17). Others argue that Congress now steps aside in war powers controversies, staying out of the Executive's way altogether. Devins and Fisher point out that the *Youngstown* decision made sense at the time because Congress was expected to play a more decisive role in foreign affairs (2002; 72). This apparent unwillingness on the part of Congress to get involved in the crafting of war-powers policies would leave Jackson's framework perpetually stuck in the second prong at best, and inapplicable at worst. Either way, *Youngstown*'s famous concurrence becomes a "relic of the past" (Devins & Fisher, 2002; 80) as it has no value in categorizing war-powers claims. H. Jefferson Powell suggests that the concurrence is often misunderstood, claiming that Jackson had no intention of limiting external presidential authority but is meant to limit the president in regard to internal affairs alone (Powell, 2002; 129). Evidence for this claim is found in Jackson's concurrence itself when he states that "military powers of the Commander-in-Chief [are] not to supersede representative government of internal affairs;' it is 'the Constitution's policy that Congress, not the Executive, should control utilization of the war power as an instrument of domestic policy" (Jackson's concurrence as quoted in Powell; 129).

Early criticisms of *Youngstown* also existed, believing the case was "destined to be ignored" (Schubert, 1953; 64). Schubert "predicted that the majority's evasion of the question of the existence of a national emergency, coupled with its failure to recognize a real conflict among statutory policies, would confine the decision 'to its very special facts'" (Harbaugh, 1978; 1272). Corwin added the decision's concurring opinions acknowledged an inherent power for the president, and that "the doctrine of the case, as stated in Justice Black's opinion of the Court, while purporting to stem from the principle of separation of powers, is a purely arbitrary construct created out of hand for the purpose of disposing of this case, and is altogether devoid of historical verification" (Corwin, 1953; 64–65).

There is also recent literature that coincides with the case's early critics, suggesting the federal courts do not take into account the *Youngstown* decision or its concurrences when deciding war-powers claims. Henkin points out that traditionally, the Executive's actions are considered suspect, judged against what Congress has allowed or delegated to the president. However, while it is indeed the case that presidential power is assumed when Congress does not act, Congress has acted in a variety of ways, regulating "the executive in regard to the use of force, 'covert activities,' the sale of arms to terrorist states, and foreign aid to governments guilty of gross violations of human rights" (Henkin, 1990; 30). Henkin points out that along with congressional actions in the area of foreign affairs comes the Executive's position that Congress is encroaching on its inherent power to act on behalf of the nation internationally (Henkin, 1990; 30). This argument is in direct contradiction to what Jackson's concurrence alleges historically to be the case and to what my analysis reveals. Yet, Henkin is not alone in claiming the aggrandizement of executive authority over the last several decades has proven any framework put forth in *Youngstown* to be unworkable. This claim of Youngstown being outdated became more relevant since 2001 as the Executive is now expected to defend the State against non-state actors threatening international security today, and must do so with the inherent powers that the Court rejected in the 1952 case (Sidak, 2002; 37). This final critique of the *Youngstown* framework is most striking for cases when the president initiates hostilities. These cases are not included in this analysis because they have historically been decided based on a separation of powers framework since the question in front of the courts is specifically which branch of government can authorize hostilities.

Contrary to the view that the *Youngstown* decision itself would be ignored because of its lack of emphasis on the Korean War or as being outdated due to technological advancements and the ever aggrandizing of presidential power, Mark Rosen has recently made the argument that Jackson's concurrence is flawed because it assumes the decisions of Congress are supreme when the two elected branches of government share overlapping powers. Rosen points out that several conflict-sorting rules exist and Jackson never justifies why "categorical congressional supremacy" makes a better choice over the other sorting techniques (Rosen, 2007a; 4). Rosen's critique rests on the assumption that Jackson's concurrence does not justify its decision to choose the categorical congressional supremacy rule over the other possibilities of conflict-sorting rules, including time-based sorting rules, multifactor sorting rules, and no sorting rules. Rosen presents several possible conflict-sorting rules which are not based on the supremacy of one institution over the other. For example, time-based sorting rules dictate that whichever branch of government acts first is the branch which has authority to make policy when the branches share overlapping powers. Of course this view of conflict sorting suggests that the government has a strict separation of powers and that overlapping or concurrent powers are not conducive to this sort of regime. In fact, the way the American regime is set up is one that makes time-based sorting rules hard to justify. *The Federalist Papers* teach us that governmental authority is to be separated into distinct branches of government but that the powers while separated are in fact interdependent (*Federalist #51*). Another conflict sorting rule is a multifactor sorting rule which looks to see which branch of government has "an overwhelming interest in having its law applied" (Rosen, 2007; 24). What is telling and should be noted is that Rosen does not present any hypothetical situation as to how these sorting rules could possibly be applied in regard to the war powers where authority between the Congress and the Executive has to be sorted.

The critique of *Youngstown* continues by suggesting that scholars blindly accept as a "truism" Jackson's separation of powers framework, providing "first-rate analytics to arguing that a given presidential action is unconstitutional insofar as it is inconsistent with a statute" (Rosen, 2007a; 14). Rosen's lack of a systematic historical verification of Jackson's concurring tripartite system weakens his claim that "Jackson's concurrence is best interpreted as not having definitely resolved the relationship between Congress's powers and the president's commander-in-chief powers" (Rosen, 2007a; 7). After all, the federal courts, including the Supreme Court, have historically found that when the president creates war-powers policies contrary to the wishes of Congress, those actions will only be allowed if Congress lacks authority to act. It is not the case, then, that the president requires congressional authority before or after acting in said cases when they reach the federal courts.

Despite the numerous criticisms to the contrary, the framework in Jackson's concurrence is still useful today to guide judicial decision-making during war. In contrast to seeing *Youngstown*'s time as having come and gone, or worse yet still having never been, the critics of *Youngstown* miss a relevant element of analysis—where the Executive implements policies that limit individual liberties, the federal courts have not stepped aside from making decisions on the constitutionality of such actions, whether or not Congress is involved.

Jackson's concurrence is often heralded in casebooks as a landmark decision with a lot of impact (Brest et al, 2000; 707). Sanford Levinson went so far as to say that Jackson's concurrence is "the greatest single opinion in the history of the Supreme Court," being "intellectually satisfying" and as a result "in some sense persuasive." Jackson's concurrence was "well aware of the limitations of ordinary legal materials in providing answers to difficult problems" (Levinson, 1996; 202). Levinson believed that Jackson, being the last Justice with no formal legal training, understood the nature of the legal system, thus suggesting that in the real world, real solutions would be required in cases, acknowledging that formal legal rules would not work in adjudicating all cases before the courts.

Louis Fisher suggests that Jackson's concurrence specifically "remains the most perceptive advice to Congress: the political dynamics of presidential power are such that Congress must invoke the institutional tools at its command rather than expect assistance from the federal judiciary" (2004; 117). Others hail the *Youngstown* decision in general for being "illustrative of the Court's recognition of Congressional predominance" in the war powers (Wormuth and Firmage, 1986; 244).[7] Rudalevige even argues that *Youngstown* is a protector of individual liberties in a post-9/11 world. In contrast to critics who suggest the tenets of the case are useless in a day and age when the Executive needs to act fast and without constraint to protect the State from unconventional threats, Rudalevige points to the Second Circuit Court of Appeals decision in *Padilla v. Rumsfeld,* 352 F.3d 695; 2003, which references *Youngstown* to show that because "the *Non-Detention Act* explicitly denied presidents the power to detain American citizens on American soil" (2005; 251), the Executive would have to release the detainee. Although the Supreme Court reversed the lower court's decision in *Padilla,* it reaffirmed its adherence to the principles put forth in *Youngstown.* The Supreme Court would also mention the need for congressional authorization in connection to setting up military commissions two years later in 2006 when it decided *Hamdan v. Rumsfeld,* 126 S. Ct. 2749; 2006.

While scholars may not agree, the federal courts have in fact embraced the Youngstown framework as valuable in articulating the "concept of balanced institutional participation that underlies the national security constitution" (Koh, 1990; 105). Similarly, Silverstein shows that the federal courts continue to subscribe to Jackson's framework, short of a direct conflict between the two elected branches of government (Silverstein, 1997; 176). Koh and Silverstein look at *Youngstown* through the lens of the initiation of hostilities and both acknowledge that the Executive's powers have taken a unilateral turn in recent decades. While the reasons for its influence vary, the point remains firm. The *Youngstown* decision and its concurrence by Jackson both reject presidential claims of authority to write and execute legislation without having Congress delegate the authority to the president.

Proponents of *Youngstown* are united in their belief that Jackson's concurrence, if not always effective, at least provides a place "to begin analysis" (Levinson, 1996; 202). The concurrence is believed to act as a useful guiding post in adjudicating war-powers claims, attempting to tell the elected branches of government that there is a serious role for the Congress to play in making war-powers policies. Proponents of *Youngstown* see the Executive as being out of control today in its use of the war powers and see the decision as a way for the courts to acknowledge that Congress has the ability to put a check on presidential power. My analysis mirrors the theoretical thinking of Silverstein and Koh, but for different reasons. When it comes to individual liberties being limited by executive policies, the federal courts also and already follow a separation of powers framework for deciding such cases, limiting the executive's abilities when it acts without proper authorization.

Jackson's framework does not sort out anything about ambiguously delegated war powers. When the Constitution is ambiguous on institutional roles, Bickel suggests that the only assurance there is that the war powers are being implemented properly "lies in process, in the duty to explain, justify and persuade, to define the national interest by evoking it, and thus to act by consent" (Bickel, 1972; 18). In other words, if Congress and the Executive are working together, as Jackson's first prong exemplifies, the Court will be most lenient towards these federal government initiatives during war. As such, Jackson's paradigm for thinking about executive power during armed hostilities does so in the way Bickel promotes. For half a century, Jackson's concurrence has been "the starting point for judicial reasoning and academic conjuring about the separation of powers between Congress and the President and, more specifically, presidential prerogative asserted in the name of national security" (Sidak, 2001; 36).

While it is not entirely clear if Jackson's concurrence is meant to be descriptive as well as prescriptive, I believe it is both. There is a fair amount of historical accuracy in the reasoning of federal court opinions dealing with individual-rights abuses by the Executive under the rubric of the war powers. Looking at the language the justices use in framing their opinions, which subsequently becomes the law of the land, does not take into account the intentions or exogenous reasoning behind federal court decisions. However, the legal reasoning itself is important for the future integrity of the Judiciary as an institution. The use of the separation of powers terminology in deciding war powers cases provides for a principled approach to judicial decision making in times of war that allows the Court to consider its institutional role in such trying times. The remainder of the chapter will explain why this is the case.

LEGITIMACY OF THE JUDICIARY AND THE WAR POWERS

The Constitution distributes the war powers among the elected branches of government which in turn are encouraged and in fact required to work together in times of national crisis. During war, it thus makes sense for the courts to use the separation of powers to adjudicate claims before it. The Constitution was arguably more concerned with the defense of the nation than with meticulously dividing powers between Congress and the president. Starting with the Preamble, the Constitution is set up to provide for the common defense. The president's oath is to defend and protect the Constitution. The supremacy clause means that the laws passed by Congress are the laws of the land, thus allowing Congress to place restrictions on the Executive's ability to act in contrast to the wishes of Congress.

If the war powers are shared powers between the elected branches of government, Jackson's framework is a viable option for guiding the federal courts in their war powers jurisprudence. I am not alone in asserting that the separation of powers drives war powers cases. As Gordon Silverstein notes, "[f]rom the beginning, the Court has maintained that one of its primary obligations in foreign and domestic policy disputes is to police the separation of powers" (Silverstein, 1997; 22). Silverstein suggests that the courts decide war powers cases in three waves. The first wave, which consists of the time period from the founding to the world wars, finds the courts deciding cases by looking at whether or not the two elected branches of government were working together. This, of course, is how I suggest the courts decided cases not only historically, but still today in regard to war powers controversies where the Executive limits individual liberties. The federal courts interpreted these first-wave cases by looking at what the national government as a whole was constitutionally authorized to do. Even *United States v. Curtiss-Wright Export Corp.,* 299 U.S. 304; 1936, which is often cited as expanding executive authority as the "sole organ" in foreign affairs, in fact determines how broad the powers of the national government are in their entirety. The concept of the sole organ in this case was in regard to the president's authority to communicate with other nations, not to make foreign policy without consultation from Congress as is often suggested.[8] Justice Sutherland, in his 1919 book *Constitutional Powers and World Affairs,* explains, as he also points out in his 1936 *Curtiss-Wright* opinion, that in foreign affairs the Constitution is largely silent, or at least vague, and as such the courts must interpret what the government as a whole is allowed to do, not just the Congress and not just the Executive (Silverstein, 38).

I believe that the Court is consistent in its decision-making concerning the war powers. Silverstein backs this argument when he suggests that "a close examination of the evolution of the judicial [war powers] doctrine reveals it to be surprisingly consistent and coherent" (Silverstein, 7). While we agree on the consistency and coherency of the courts' war powers philosophy, we differ on what is consistent and how it is coherent. As such, Silverstein's second and third waves suggest this consistency is found in the courts' continued and growing deference to the Executive. From the Second World War until the 1950s, the courts face what Silverstein terms the "emerging executive prerogative interpretation" where it granted the Executive great latitude in its actions unless clear and explicit congressional opposition existed. The third wave of constitutional interpretation for foreign policy cases started in the 1970s and insisted on explicit actions on the part of Congress before the courts would take action against the Executive (Silverstein, 24).

In contrast to Silverstein's arguments, the courts actually defer to Congress, which in turn often defers to the Executive. Congressional authorization in even the broadest terms accepted by the courts is still essential to expanding executive authority during armed hostilities. As such, Silverstein's first wave is the correct and consistent way the courts have interpreted war powers cases, and further, Silverstein's first and second wave actually collapse into one. This view is also consistent with Jackson's first and second prongs of the three-pronged framework put forth in *Youngstown.* I believe that Silverstein's third prong requiring explicit congressional disapproval of the Executive's action before the courts will deny the Executive the ability to act is too narrow a construction of constitutional interpretation. When legislation is in place that conflicts with some action of the Executive, the federal courts decide that the Executive is out of line if the Executive does not possess the authority to act under its own powers enumerated in the Constitution. This has historically been the case as examples from the Quasi War with France to the recent conflict over detainees suspected of being terrorists show. Silverstein expects Congress to explicitly say something about the specific act of the Executive making its way through the federal courts system before the courts will take action. While this position is common and accurate in regard to the initiation of hostilities since the Vietnam War, when individual liberties are at stake, the courts are still very active in answering claims of unconstitutionality.

In recognizing the importance of consensus from our national leaders in times of armed hostilities, the fact remains, however, that scholars have not championed a framework calling for rights-based litigation to be adjudicated under such rigid guidelines as the separation of powers. Issacharoff and Pildes have noted that much of the scholarly debate surrounding the curtailment of individual liberties during armed hostilities is centered on rights discourse, though the cases that are the focus of the debate themselves are decided in the language of institutional roles and rules (Issacharoff and Pildes, 2003; 7). This lack of rights discourse may partly be explained by the fact that the first 140 years of the Republic rested on using institutional language to decide most cases coming before it. In fact, during the first century of American history after the ratification of the Constitution, the Bill of Rights had little impact on the daily lives of American citizens and was not given much thought as a document to protect individual liberties.[9] The emphasis on individual liberties started after World War I with the aftermath of the Palmer Raids, and did not gain serious momentum until after World War II (Brinkley, 2003; 24-25), with the courts shifting largely to focus on civil liberties protections for the people living within the United States (McMann, 1999; 69).

The rights revolution experienced in the 1960s and 1970s saw new issues come to the courts with old laws being challenged. When the Executive's policies curtailing rights during armed hostilities were before the courts, courts emphasized precedents requiring cooperation between the elected branches of government that already existed. As far back as the Civil War, Justice Salmon Chase, in his *ex parte Milligan* dissent, argued that it is a mistake to frame questions in rights-based language. As further discussed in Chapter 3, Chase and three of his colleagues agreed that the military tribunals set up by the president were unconstitutional, not because citizens have a right not to be tried by them, but because Congress did not authorize them. Making rules concerning the government of the armed forces cases "arising in the land and naval forces, or in the militia in actual service in time of war or public danger, are expressly excepted from the fifth amendment . . . and it is admitted that the exception applies to the other amendments as well as to the fifth" (Chase's *Milligan* dissent). My analysis shows that the courts have largely followed Justice Chase's lead. Using rights-based language would be legitimate because the cases concern violations of liberties, but the separation of powers framework offered by Jackson offers something more to war-powers adjudication that language in the Bill of Rights does not. Simply because a rights claim is made does not mean that the federal courts, even if they decide the case using rights-based language, will protect the rights in question. The language found in the Bill of Rights is not only interpreted by nine justices with different philosophies on the law, but is also malleable. Since no right is absolute, it is entirely possible for the courts, when using rights-based language, to limit a constitutionally protected right in such a way that when the emergency subsides, the limit placed on the right in question could remain.

Most of the chapters that follow show how the courts often decide rights-based war powers cases using a separation of powers rationale rather than rights-based language. Of course, this is not always the case. In fact, to show the problems that arise when deciding these cases using the constitutional arguments themselves, I highlight cases concerning free speech. It could be argued that it is not the president initiating these rights-based limitations, but rather Congress. However, it is also the case that the president asked for legislation that would limit free speech in times of war. Regardless of the reasoning, deciding the cases based on whether or not the Bill of Rights limits the government during World War I actually resulted in limits to speech that would persist in times of perceived peace. This brings to mind Jackson's dissent in Korematsu, suggesting that the federal courts should stay out of these cases as a way to protect rights when the hostilities end. The courts looked at cases challenging the validity of the *Espionage Act* through the lens of whether Congress could pass the Act, not whether the Executive could restrict free speech. In *Schenck v. United States,* 249 U.S. 47; 1919, the defendant was accused of distributing a pamphlet that argued the draft was unconstitutional. The Court states that some speech permissible in time of peace may be limited in a time of war by Congress, despite the language of the Constitution which states "Congress shall make no law abridging the freedom of speech or of the press." Holmes writes that "the most stringent protection of free speech would not protect a man in falsely shouting fire in a theatre and causing a panic." Holmes creates the clear and present danger test, shaping First Amendment restrictions in times of peace for decades to come.

Chapter 5 highlights that the separation of powers is not the only way the courts decide war powers cases limiting individual liberties. It is an important case study to show how answering the constitutional questions rather than questions of federalism does not always lead to a desired, and expected, result. By leaving the language of the Bill of Rights alone, the courts are in a way actually protecting our rights already in place before the start of the hostilities. At the very worst, when the emergency situation is over, rights limited will not face a continued encroachment. By looking for agreement between the elected branches of government, the federal courts allow the government to satisfy the requirements of national security without weakening the rights enjoyed before the armed conflict began. This approach to judicial decision making protects the Constitution from the federal courts' own inclinations to make broad constitutional claims of executive authority, which they will regret later, or to be used in a domestic policy setting to limit rights further. Silverstein argues:

> If the justices choose to base their justification on a broad reading of the Constitution, they take the risk that this reading will return to haunt them later. Since the American judicial system relies heavily on *stare decisis,* where the case law is built upon precedent, broad readings in foreign policy cases can become precedents for equally broad readings in domestic policy cases drawing on the same constitutional phrases (Silverstein, 1997; 23).

Alternatively, if the courts limit executive power in a way that elected officials believe is too detrimental to society, the courts could be ignored. The fear is that this would cheapen or weaken the overall strength of the world's oldest working Constitution. In no way does this suggest there are two constitutions, one in peace and another in war. Essentially, the individual liberties that we enjoy in peace could be limited during armed hostilities in a way that such limits would remain at the end of hostilities if rights-based language was used to adjudicate the cases.

Institutional integrity is important for the courts because if the courts have the force of the federal government behind them, the courts will also have the people and "[a]pproval of the Court within the mass public leads to better implementation of its decisions, reduces chances that the other branches will limit or reverse those decisions, and deters action by the legislature and executive against the Court itself" (Baum, 2006; 63). The Judiciary is concerned, therefore, with "making sure the Court remains a credible force in American politics" (Epstein and Knight, 1998; 46). While the Judiciary is looked to for settling societal disputes, both legal and political, when it comes to the war powers, the courts are careful not to jeopardize its institutional integrity that it could lose if it makes a ruling that the elected branches of government found unacceptable for the defense of the nation.

Instead of having the legitimacy of the Judiciary or the Constitution called into question, the courts create a principled approach to judicial decision making that places the onus on the elected branches to justify the curtailment of liberties and at the same time creates less jeopardy of individual liberties being limited in times of peace based on decisions made during times of armed conflict. In other words, agreement by the elected branches of government during armed hostilities does not necessarily create legitimacy, but rather protects it. Legal reasoning matters because no matter what the issue and how the federal courts go about making its war-powers decisions, the effort is constant with the courts looking for agreement between Congress and the Executive and the Constitution is protected.

CONCLUSIONS

The federal courts are most lenient toward the actions of the Executive when Congress has given authorization to limit individual liberties during times of war. One reason for this leniency on the part of the courts is because war-powers cases dealing with the limits to individual liberties present situations where values conflict and the courts must settle disputes where national security is pitted against the liberty of the people. The result is that when values do conflict and cases arise in front of the courts, they "must proclaim one as overriding, or find an accommodation among them. The result is a principle, or a new value, if you will, or an amalgam of values, or a compromise of values; it must in any event also have general significance and even-handed application" (Bickel, 1986; 58). Furthermore, for Bickel, a decision of the Court has to be "self-conscious: it must be intelligible, rational, candid. In no circumstances can it begin to be justifiable unless it meets the irreducible implications that the very words 'court' and 'judge' have for centuries conveyed in our tradition; unless, in short, it is disinterested" (Bickel, 1986; 205).

Looking for agreement between the branches of government in regard to the war powers is one way of creating a new value of compromise between the two competing values, security and liberty. This is to protect the legitimacy of the Court's decisions as well as protect the Constitution itself from overzealously declaring war powers policy too broad or too narrow. As I have suggested, if cases concerning individual liberties are answered squarely on the constitutional questions when the nation is engaged in hostilities, and if the rights are limited, that particular limit may do more damage to the Amendment in question than if the violation was justified or not on the statutory grounds.

Finally, by emphasizing the separation of powers when deciding rights-based war powers claims, the courts do not defer to the Executive with a blank check. The courts offer some protection to individual liberties during armed hostilities by looking for congressional authorization for executive actions. Therefore, the courts actually defer to Congress. Since the federal courts are concerned about their institutional legitimacy, it makes sense for them to employ the separation of powers framework. Such an approach may not only protect the courts and the Constitution, but it might also protect individual liberties during armed hostilities.

ENDNOTES

1. The judges themselves decide which level of analysis each case falls under, just as is the case for rights-based litigation in peacetime today.

2. Truman's letter to Congress stated:

The Congress is undoubtedly aware of recent events which have taken place in connection with the management-labor dispute in the steel industry. These events culminated in the action which was taken last night to provide for temporary operation of the steel mills by the Government.

I took this action with the utmost reluctance. The idea of Government operation of the steel mills is thoroughly distasteful to me, and I want to see it ended as soon as possible. However, in the situation which confronted me yesterday, I felt that I could make no other choice. The other alternatives appeared to be even worse–so much worse that I could not accept them.

One alternative would have been to permit a shutdown of the steel industry. The effects of such a shut-down would have been so immediate and damaging with respect to our efforts to support our armed forces and to protect our national security that it made this alternative unthinkable.

The only way that I know of, other than Government operation, by which a steel shutdown could have been avoided was to grant demands of the steel industry for a large price increase. I believe and the officials in charge of our stabilization agencies believed that this would have wrecked our stabilization program. I was unwilling to accept the incalculable damage which might be done to our country by following such a course.

Accordingly, it was my judgment that Government operation of the steel mills for a temporary period was the least undesirable of the courses of action which lay open. In the circumstances, I believed it to be, and now believe it to be, my duty and within my powers as President to follow that course of action.

It may be that the Congress will deem some other course to be wiser. It may be that the Congress will feel we should give in to the demands of the steel industry for an exorbitant price increase and take consequences so far as resulting inflation is concerned.

It may be that the Congress will feel the Government should try to enforce the steel workers to continue to work for the steel companies for another long period, without a contract, even though the steel workers have already voluntarily remained at work without a contract for 100 days in an effort to reach an orderly settlement of their differences with management.

It may even be that the Congress will feel that we should permit a shut-down of the steel industry, although that would immediately endanger the safety of our fighting forces abroad and weaken the whole structure of our national security.

I do not believe that Congress will favor any of these courses of action, but that is a matter for the Congress to determine.

It may be, on the other hand, that the Congress will wish to pass legislation establishing specific terms and conditions with reference to the operation of the steel mills by the Government. Sound legislation of this character might be very desirable.

On the basis of the facts that are known to me at this time, I do not believe that immediate congressional action is essential; but I would, of course, be glad to cooperate in developing any legislative program which the Congress may wish to consider.

If the Congress does not deem it necessary to act at this time, I shall continue to do all that is within my power to keep the steel industry operating and at the same time make every effort to bring about a settlement of the dispute so the mills can be returned to their private owners as soon as possible. http://steelseizure.stanford.edu/Truman/harry.truman.1952.april9.html (May 9, 2007).

3. On Friday, April 25th, the *Washington Post* ran a story describing the previous day's courtroom activity: "[Judge David A. Pine] repeatedly interrupted [Assistant Attorney General Holmes] Baldridge as the government attorney claimed broad 'inherent' powers in the President. 'Are you saying that the President claims no statutory power for this seizure?' Pine asked, and Baldridge acknowledged this was true. 'When an emergency situation in this country arises which is so important to the public welfare that something had to be done now, it is the President's duty to step in,' Baldridge replied. Then, the judge asked, 'Do you mean that the President can determine whether an emergency exists and that the court cannot review it to see whether there is really an emergency?' 'That is correct,' Baldridge said" (as quoted in Rehnquist, 2002; 159).

4. The material for this section was viewed at the Library of Congress in Washington, DC in June, 2006. I had the opportunity to go through the papers of Justice Robert H. Jackson. The materials included in the following pages come from boxes 174, 175, and 176.

5. Jackson left footnote 13 to cite only the congressional statue to which he referred, 20 Stat. 152, 10 U.S. C § 15.

6. Roche notes that prong III may not be a useful prong on which to base a framework for judicial decision-making because "with the exception of the seizure of the steel industry, there has not been one single instance of a President actually taking prerogative action in a domestic crisis against the wishes of Congress" (Roche, 1952; 611). I question this assertion. If we include cases where the courts suggest the Executive misinterprets the intent of Congress and thus violates legislation, prong III is a viable option.

7. Richard Posner, a judge for the Seventh Circuit in Chicago, seconds this sentiment and uses the example of conscription to illustrate the point. Posner argues that from *Youngstown*, we get the position that if the president puts in place the draft without congressional authorization, his authority to do so must come elsewhere in the Constitution. Posner confirms that *Youngstown* points out there is no such elsewhere for the Executive to draw upon (Posner, 2006; 68).

8. In the 10 Annals of Cong. 611, Marshall's quote in its proper context is as follows:

> The President is the sole organ of the nation in its external relations, and its sole representative with foreign nations. Of consequence, the demand of a foreign nation can only be made on him.
>
> He possesses the whole Executive power. He holds and directs the force of the nation. Of consequence, any act to be performed by the force of the nation is to be performed by him.
>
> He is charged to execute the laws. A treaty is declared to be a law. He must then execute a treaty, where he, and he alone, possesses the means of executing it.
>
> The treaty which is a law, enjoins the performance of a particular object. The person who is to perform this object is marked by the Constitution, since the person is named who conducts the foreign intercourse, and is to take care that the laws be faithfully executed. The means by which it is to be performed, the force of the nation, are in the hands of this person. Ought not this person to perform the object, although the particular mode of using the means has not been prescribed? Congress, unquestionably, may prescribe the mode,

and Congress may devolve on others the whole execution of the contract; but, till this be done, it seems the duty of the executive department is to execute the contract by any means it possesses (613–614).

9. The Bill of Rights was added during the first Congress and was promised to the anti-federalists as an assurance of individual liberties to be protected from encroachments by the federal government. However, its passage did not "quickly convert the Constitution into a bulwark for individual liberties, or transform the content of constitutional jurisprudence...." Violations of rights and liberties were inflicted upon several groups of society including African Americans, Native Americans, a variety of immigrant groups including Mexicans and Chinese, as well as rights infringements of women and criminals and religious groups such as the Jewish community and Catholics (Brinkley, 2003; 25). As an example, Brinkley highlights the fact that the protections in the Fourth, Fifth, and Sixth Amendments afforded to criminal suspects were "often token or nonexistent" (Brinkley; 25). In fact, according to Henkin, the only case to reach the Supreme Court before the Civil War that pertained to civil liberties was *Dred Scott*, invalidating the Missouri Compromise because it denied the slave owner his property rights (Henkin, 1996; 278). While I contend and show in my four case studies that cases dealing with individual liberties reached the Supreme Court as early as the Quasi War with France, Henkin's point is duly noted.

Chapter 3

Military Detentions

Two interrelated, and often inseparable, issues are repeatedly decided when cases concerning military detentions reach the federal courts. The first issue revolves around the threshold question concerning where to try suspects. Does authority exist for detainees to be tried by military commission set up by executive order alone or is it necessary for the Executive to have congressional authorization? Alternatively, are military commissions illegitimate avenues for dealing with captives in military custody when the civilian courts are open and functioning? The second issue concerns determining when the writ of habeas corpus can be withheld from a detainee. Often, the two issues are determined simultaneously, with detainees challenging the authority of the trial's forum through a petition for the writ. Yet today, and in a small number of circumstances in the past, the applicability of the writ itself has been called into question. Stated under the limits to the powers of Congress in Article 1, section 9 of the Constitution, "[t]he privilege of the Writ of Habeas Corpus shall not be suspended, unless when in Cases of Rebellion or Invasion the public Safety may require it."[1] This chapter questions how the federal courts have historically decided these two issues stemming from military detentions during times of war.

When deciding issues concerning due process of detainees and the writ of habeas corpus, a rights-based discourse could be used. However, the federal courts place emphasis first on the separation of powers, only after which addressing the rights issue, if not rejecting it altogether. The federal courts look for congressional authorization of Executive actions, deciding cases on statutory grounds rather than constitutional ones.

Again, this is articulated in Justice Robert Jackson's concurring opinion to *Youngstown Sheet & Tube v. Sawyer,* 343 U.S. 579; 1952, a three-pronged approach to judicial decision is put forward where the Executive and Congress share authority in the domain of the war powers.[2]

The federal courts admittedly do not feel competent in passing judgment on essentially military policies. However, such cautionary judicial decision-making also maintains the courts' institutional duty to uphold the Constitution by providing limited protection to individual liberties by ensuring the elected branches of government are working together before limits to our freedoms are upheld. It follows that in relation to military detentions, the courts defer to both elected branches of government in times of war, but defer to Congress over the Executive if Congress has spoken on the issue or has the constitutional authority to act where the Executive is limited in doing so.

This chapter proceeds in the following fashion. I first briefly examine the history of the writ of habeas corpus and of military commissions to put my analysis into context. Second, I examine the Civil War and World War II precedents, putting to the test Jackson's framework. Third, I look at the federal courts today in regard to the current armed hostilities in Afghanistan and Iraq, examining whether the courts expect the Executive and Congress to work together in a similar fashion as in the past.

HISTORICAL BACKGROUND

The writ of habeas corpus allows anyone held in detention to challenge the lawfulness of that detention before a court, so that a judge may determine whether the detention is lawful. If the imprisonment is without cause or otherwise illegal, the detained is to be set free. The privilege is "perhaps the most cherished remedy in Anglo-American jurisprudence" (Freedman, 2001 as quoted in Baker, 2003; 558), and has become known as "the Great Writ of Liberty" (Freedman, 2001; 1). The Supreme Court itself has touted the writ as "the best and only sufficient defense of personal liberty" (*ex parte Yerger,* 75 U.S. 85, 1868).

The writ originated from English jurisprudence, with aspects found as early as 1215 in the Magna Carta. Known today also as the Charter of Freedom, the Magna Carta states that "no free man shall be seized or imprisoned, or stripped of his rights or possessions . . . nor will we process with force against him, or send others to do so, except by the lawful judgment of his equals or by the law of the land."[3] It was not until the late 16th century, under Elizabeth I, that habeas corpus first found legal footing in English common law. However, this legal footing would not last. Less than three years on the throne, by 1628 Charles I led the British into disastrous warlike expeditions against the Spanish and the French. This resulted in a clash between the Monarch and Parliament. The king forced citizens to loan money to the Crown and quarter troops in their homes. The king also authorized arbitrary arrests in violation of the Magna Carta. The Petition of Right was delivered to the Crown demanding that "no one be imprisoned without a showing of cause, that habeas corpus be available in all cases . . . and, if a writ were returned without cause, that the prisoner be released" (Robertson, 9). Charles I, though agreeing to the petition, would later disavow it, and in fact would dissolve Parliament for eleven years. Parliament would not be called back into session until the king ran out of money.

Upon returning to power, the English Parliament passed the *Habeas Corpus Act* in 1641, codifying the Petition of Right into law. King Charles I was beheaded and the monarch temporarily eliminated under the rule of Oliver Cromwell. However, Cromwell, too, dissolved Parliament and was dismissive of the writ. After Cromwell's death, Parliament and the monarch were restored. Under the reign of Charles II, Parliament would be dissolved another four times, but not without it being able to pass the *Habeas Corpus Act* in 1679. The Act would protect the people from monarchs that might be inclined to ignore the legal processes guaranteed by the writ. The Act ensured that "unless it appeared from the return that the prisoner was 'detained upon a legal process, order or warrant, out of some court that hath jurisdiction of criminal matters,' the petitioner was to be discharged—that is set free" (Robertson, 2008; 12).

The right to the writ of habeas corpus was extended under British law to the colonies on August 9, 1722. A Privy Council Memorandum stated that laws of the conquering country would be transferred to the new world.[4] By time of the American Revolution, the writ of habeas corpus was already entrenched in colonial law. On August 28, 1789, there were concerns raised at the Constitutional Convention about including a clause in the Constitution that would allow for the suspension of the writ even in times of rebellion or insurrection. John Rutledge suggested declaring the writ inviolable so that no branch of government could suspend it regardless of circumstances (Farrand, Vol. 2; 438). In the end, the proposed Constitution was ratified with no effort to amend the suspension clause.[5]

The writ of habeas corpus is presented in the Constitution under the limitations to the powers of Congress, yet it is unclear whether the framers intended the Congress alone to have the ability to suspend the writ or if the Executive also was granted authority. Despite the vagueness on part of the founding generation, the federal courts have come to interpret the Constitution's suspension clause as requiring the authorization of Congress for the Executive to suspend the writ of habeas corpus.

Questions that concern the type of court used to try military detainees arise in challenges made to the legality of military commissions. The establishment of military commissions to try violators of the law of war was provided for indirectly in the Constitution. Article 1, section 8, vests the power in Congress to "constitute Tribunals inferior to the supreme Court." This means Congress has constitutional authority to set up courts, including military commissions. It does not necessarily mean that such authority is automatically denied to the Executive. There are times when the Congress and the Executive have congruent powers and the courts acknowledge that military commissions are created out of military necessity. The courts' recognition of this in fact may lend credibility to the Executive's claim of having the inherent authority to set up military commissions as part of the president's duty as commander-in-chief of the Armed Forces.

Congruent powers may exist, but Congress has utilized its authority in this regard. Laws establishing rules concerning the military even predated the Constitution. In 1775, the Second Continental Congress passed a set of 69 enumerated articles for the regulation and governance of the newly formed Continental Army. These articles included prohibitions against mutiny, striking a superior officer and desertion. In 1806, the first Congress enacted the Articles of War, a set of 101 rules defining both procedures and punishments for the military.

The Articles of War were not an American idea, with governments for nearly a thousand years having "codes and principles to maintain order and discipline among soldiers and sailors to protect civilians and their property" (Fisher, 2005; 1).[6] Initially, American rules concerning military law were based on the British Articles of War written in the 1650s and amended in 1749 and in 1757 (Fisher; 485). Serving the purpose of governing the conduct of soldiers and sailors as well as to establish procedures for courts-martial, the Articles were rarely revised during the next century.[7]

The Lieber Code, written by Francis Lieber, an immigrant to the United States from Germany who had served with the Prussian troops against Napoleon, was "the first codification of the laws of war issued to a national army for its guidance and compliance" (Lieber Code, Dec. 31, 1863 General Orders No. 100. at 162), and included 157 articles subdivided into sections "dealing with such topics as military necessity, retaliation, prisoners of war, hostages, spies, exchanges of prisoners, and flags of truce" (Sec. V, art 88 as quoted in Hardaway, 2005; 191). The Lieber Code defines martial law as "the suspension by the occupying military authority of the criminal and civil law" but was qualified by following up with martial law being application as far as the military required it (Fisher, 2005; 77). According to Fisher, the implication was that "civil courts could continue to operate in some capacity" (Fisher, 2005; 77).

By time the legality of military commissions became an issue in front of the federal courts, rules were in place, as passed by Congress, to govern the various branches of the American Armed Forces, including military courts. Military commissions are used when civil courts are not functioning or considered unsuitable to handle a specific case. Justice Anthony Kennedy's concurring opinion in *Hamdan v. Rumsfeld,* 548 U.S. 507, 2006, notes that a military commission was first convened in the United States in 1847.[8] During the Mexican War, General Winfield Scott lacked both a judicial tribunal to try violators of ordinary crimes in the occupied territory as well as a tribunal to try violators of the law of war. General Scott set up two courts. The first was a military commission to try suspected perpetrators of crimes that would be tried in civil courts during times of peace. Scott also set up what was called a "council of war" to try violators of the law of war. Yet even when created out of necessity, General Scott issued an order of martial law only "until Congress could be stimulated to legislate on the subject (Scott, 1864, 2; 392, as quoted in Fisher, 2003; 486).[9] Offenses before the military commission were classified as follows: "(1) Crimes and statutory offenses cognizable by State and U.S. courts, and which would properly be tried by such courts if open and acting; (2) Violators of the laws and usages of war cognizable by military tribunals only; (3) Breaches of military orders or regulations for which offenders are not legally triable by court-martial under the Articles of War" (Winthrop, as quoted in Stone's *In re Yamashita* Court opinion).[10]

Further evidence that the constitutional authority to create and regulate military tribunals was with Congress is the legal memorandum issued by the Attorney General in 1818. William Wirt wrote that:

> the President is the national and proper depositary of the final appellate power, in all judicial matters touching the police of the army; but let us not claim this power for him, unless it has been communicated to him by some specific grant from Congress, the fountain of all law under the constitution (Fisher quoting Wirt, 2003; 486).

Yet proponents of a strong Executive still maintain that the president has authority to set up commissions on his own accord, without authority delegated by Congress.

Presidents seem to believe that the term executive power is "a general term and therefore a grant of power in itself," growing when "considered in the aggregate" (Pious, 71). When thought about in this way, so long as the federal government has authority to act, the president can act accordingly to protect national security.[11] Over two centuries of American history show the use of military commissions set up by the Executive to try enemy combatants, from president Washington to Roosevelt.[12] Establishing commissions by executive order is what the Justice Department refers to as "traditional hands-off approach to military commissions (in contrast to courts-martial)" (U.S. Justice Department, 2006; 7), by Congress. As Jackson's second prong of the *Youngstown* framework notes, when Congress does not act on an issue, this may invite the Executive to do so. As is the case with the writ of habeas corpus, though it is clear that Congress can establish military commissions and rules to govern the armed forces, it is not clear if this limits or excludes the Executive from having congruent power with Congress.

The first time the legality of military commissions came before the federal courts was during the Civil War.[13] The dual system of one court for civilian and another for war crimes used during the Mexican War was gone. Taking the place of the dual-court system was a united system called the war court, or military commission, and was set up to try all crimes committed during the war. With this brief history of both the writ of habeas corpus and the limited use of military commissions and rules for military detentions in front of the federal-courts system before the Civil War, the development of these issues during the Civil War, World War II, and the "war on terrorism" shows how the separation of powers rather than rights-based language governs federal-court decision making and will even at times offer protection to individual liberties.

THE CIVIL WAR

On April 27, 1861, Abraham Lincoln suspended the writ of habeas corpus and declared martial law in Maryland. The president's actions were an attempt to restore order after Confederate sympathizers attacked Union soldiers and Baltimore's mayor ordered bridges to be burnt down, isolating the North (Stone, 2003; 220). Lincoln ordered a blockade of southern ports, spent public funds, expanded the Army and Navy, confiscated property of the enemy, commissioned trial by military courts where civil courts were still open and operating, suppressed newspapers, and ordered conscription by presidential legislation. Congress was not consulted on Lincoln's decisions and therefore all of these actions were committed without a declaration of war or statutory authorization from Congress.

In *ex parte Merryman,* 17 F. Cas. 144; 1861, the federal courts questioned Lincoln's authority, but were met with hostility from the Executive branch itself. After Lincoln suspended the writ of habeas corpus and replaced Maryland's civilian courts with military commissions, John Merryman was arrested without warrant and confined in Baltimore, Maryland at Fort McHenry. A trial for treason took place, despite there being no proof or witnesses presented against Merryman. The circuit court ruled that the writ of habeas corpus could not be suspended without congressional authorization.

Lincoln refused to comply. Roger Taney attempted to serve the writ, but being unsuccessful, the Chief Justice wanted to have the commanding general arrested for contempt of court. Taney was again unsuccessful, and wrote that the president violated his oath to uphold the Constitution. Taney argued that the Constitution is "expressed in language too clear to be misunderstood by any one" and that there was "no ground whatever for supposing that the president, in any emergency, or any state of things, can authorize the suspension of the privileges of the writ of habeas corpus, or the arrest of a citizen, except in aid of the judicial power." In this case, the president, "does not faithfully execute the laws, if he takes upon himself legislative power, by suspending the writ of habeas corpus, and the judicial power also, by arresting and imprisoning a person without due process of law."

The federal-courts system could not go head-to-head with the Lincoln administration. The Court was vulnerable after the *Dred Scott* decision and its influence was at a "historic low point" (Robertson, 2008; 23). Lincoln was able to ignore the court's decision, and in *Merryman,* Taney could only verbally rebuke the president, with no practical effect. Taney added:

> I have exercised all the power which the constitution and laws confer upon me, but that power has been resisted by a force too strong for me to overcome . . . I shall, therefore, order all the proceedings in this case, with my opinion, to be filed and recorded in the circuit court of the United States for the district court of Maryland, and direct the clerk to transmit a copy, under seal, to the president of the United States. It will then remain for that high officer, in fulfillment of his constitutional obligation to 'take care that the laws be faithfully executed,' to determine what measures he will take to cause the civil process of the United States to be respected and enforced (Taney's *Merryman* opinion).

Taney was sending a message to Lincoln that the court fulfilled its constitutional obligation by upholding the right to the writ of habeas corpus and it was now up to the president to do the same. The president did not and Congress would retroactively approve of all Lincoln's wartime measures.

The legality of Lincoln suspending the writ of habeas corpus was also dealt with in several other district and circuit court rulings. The courts would offer similar protections to the writ based on a separation of powers framework. In *The United States, ex rel John Murphy v. Andrew Porter, Provost Marshal,* 2 Hay & Hays 395; 1861, the court held that the writ must be delivered to release a young boy from military duty. The Provost Marshal refused to deliver the writ, delivering another blow to the authority of the federal courts. The same issue resurfaced the next year when military officers made it impossible for a district court-ordered writ to be issued (*In re Winder,* 30 Fed. Cas. 288; 1862). Despite the rulings to protect the rights of the detained, the outcomes did not match the support for the petitioner's rights that the courts in fact attempted to guarantee.

In 1862, a district court held in *ex parte Benedict,* 3 Fed. Cas. 159 (D. N.Y. 1862) that Lincoln did not have the ability to suspend the writ of habeas corpus without being authorized by Congress. A circuit court in Vermont similarly held that the War Department lacked authority to issue an order suspending the writ of habeas corpus (*ex parte Field,* 9 Fed. Cas. 1, 3 (C.C. Vt. 1862). Congress did not declare martial law, did not suspend habeas corpus and it was therefore unnecessary to do so in states remaining loyal to the Union. The courts were clear; the writ of habeas corpus was only to be suspended if Congress passed a law providing for its suspension.[14] Once Congress passed a statute authorizing Lincoln's actions in March 1863, two district courts upheld Lincoln's actions as they were based on "valid and efficient in law."[15]

Shortly after the end of the Civil War, the legality of the establishment of military commissions was considered. Lincoln's attorney general, Edward Bates, thought military commissions were unlawful and "a gross blunder in policy." Continuing, Bates argued that "ours is a government of *Law,* and that the law is strong enough, to rule the people wisely and well; and if the offenders be done to death by that tribunal, however truly guilty, they will pass for martyrs with half the world" (Beale, 1933; 483). Despite Bates' position, commissions were set up and their legality challenged in *In re Egan,* 8 Fed. Cas.; C.C.D.N.Y.; 1866. Five months after the end of the war, Egan, a civilian, was tried by military commission and convicted of murder. The court, in echoing Bates, held that the military commission is "neither more nor less than the will of the general who commands the army. It overrides and suppresses all existing civil laws, civil officers, and civil authorities" (Nelson's *Egan* opinion). The *Egan* court held that martial law "can only be indulged in case of necessity . . . [W]hen the necessity ceases, martial law ceases' . . . Such necessity exists when war or rebellion prevents the civil courts from exercising their normal functions, but necessity ends when the war ends and the courts resume their normal function." The civil courts of South Carolina were open and functioning at the time of Egan's trial. As a result, the military commission lacked the jurisdiction to try Egan for murder.

Rights-based discourse is prevalent in this case. However, Judge Nelson, first and foremost notes that the trial was not set up "under the rules and articles of war, as established by the United States in congress assembled, for, they are limited to the government of the land and naval forces of the United States, and of the militia when in actual service, in time of war or public danger." The Executive lacked the legal footing it needed because Congress did not set up the military commission.

The same year, in *ex parte Milligan,* 71 U.S. (4 Wall.) 2; 1866, the Supreme Court also reversed the ruling of a military commission used to try a civilian. The Court held that when civil courts are operational, the military courts have no jurisdiction to try citizens unconnected to the Armed Services. It was irrelevant that Milligan was planning to free soldiers of the Confederacy and was arrested to thwart the rescue mission. Justice David Davis held that "the Constitution of the United States is a law for rulers and people, equally in war and in peace, and covers with the shield of its protection all classes of men, at all times, under all circumstances." Davis acknowledged it was easy to look at the issue passionlessly as the hostilities ended by time the case reached the Court, recognizing further that when the war was ongoing, the Judiciary was not necessarily the proper place to pass judgment on military initiatives.

In his dissent, Chief Justice Salmon Chase's argued that military commissions could have been set up if both elected branches of government agreed on the issue. Chase clarified:

> Congress . . . did not see fit to authorize trials by military commission in Indiana, but by the strongest implication prohibited them. With that prohibition we are satisfied, and should have remained silent if the answers to the question [from the majority of the Court] had been put on that ground, without denial of the existence of a power which we believe to be constitutional and important to the public safety—a denial which . . . seems to draw in question the power of Congress . . . .

Chase reiterates that the text of the Constitution grants Congress the authority to make rules concerning the Army and Navy, as well as the authority to set up courts inferior to the Supreme Court. Chase suggests that "it is within the power of Congress to determine in what states or districts such great and imminent public danger exists as justifies the authorization of military tribunals for the trial of crimes and offences against the discipline of security of the army against the public safety." If Congress authorized the commission, according to Chase, the Court would be compelled to uphold the actions of the Executive in the *Milligan* case. Chase's reasoning suggests that any war powers that Congress decides to delegate to the president is therefore permissible. The *Milligan* decision is heralded as an example of the federal courts rebuking executive war-making authority. Since the Civil War, however, the federal courts have decided cases in line with Chase's dissent rather than the Court opinion.[16]

Though the number of cases is limited, both the circuit court and the Supreme Court decisions produced similar rulings. Lincoln did not have authority alone to limit individual liberties by establishing military commissions or by limiting the right of detainees to petition for the writ of habeas corpus. If Congress authorized these executive initiatives, the patterns of judicial decision making during the Civil War, given the rationale used in the court opinions suggest that the federal courts would have upheld the detentions, with the possible exception of *Milligan.* However, even in *Milligan,* Chase's dissent suggests if Congress established the military commissions, at least four members of the Court would have been inclined to uphold the conviction.[17]

Restrictions placed on granting habeas corpus for those in military detention reached the Supreme Court after the Civil War. In *The Mayor v. Cooper,* 73 U.S. 247, 1868, the Court decided whether a habeas petition could be withheld from individuals in the South who were arrested for acts committed under presidential orders. Congress passed an Act on May 11, 1866 establishing that orders of the Executive constituted a legal defense to charges brought against those being held accountable. The Court granted the habeas claim based on this Act of Congress. A year later, however, the Court would rule that it lacked jurisdiction to hear a habeas petition, also based on congressional action.

William McCardle, opposing the military presence in the South, encouraged active resistance to the military's presence in the area in the local newspaper. Having been arrested for his protest and scheduled to be tried by military commission, McCardle petitioned for a writ of habeas corpus arguing his detention was illegal. McCardle was a civilian and not a member of the military, and argued he should be tried in the civilian not military court. Congress passed an Act that repealed the 1867 *Habeas Corpus Act* which McCardle used to back his claim that the Court could grant him relief under the writ. The Act allowed any federal judge the ability to grant habeas corpus to any person being held contrary to the Constitution. In April, 1869, Chief Justice Chase held in *ex parte McCardle,* 74 U.S. 506, 1869, that "[w]ithout jurisdiction the court cannot proceed at all in any cause. Jurisdiction is power to declare the law, and when it ceases to exist, the only function remaining to the court is that of announcing the fact and dismissing the cause." McCardle's case was argued in March, 1869. Before the Court handed down its decision, the act repealing the jurisdiction of the Court passed Congress. The Court held that "the effect of the act was to oust the court of its jurisdiction of the particular case then before it on appeal, and it is not to be doubted that such was the effect intended." The acts of Congress prior to 1867 authorizing the Court to exercise appellate jurisdiction in regard to the writ of habeas corpus were in fact repealed by the Act of 1869.

Six months after *McCardle,* the issue of Congress taking away the jurisdiction to hear habeas corpus claims from the federal courts once more reached the Supreme Court in *ex parte Yerger,* 75 U.S. 85, 1869. Chief Justice Chase, again writing for the Court, asked whether the Court could look into the lawfulness of detention, and offer relief from it if found unlawful. The section of the Act repealing the courts' jurisdiction to hear cases concerning the writ was "limited in terms, and must be limited in effect to the appellate jurisdiction authorized by the act of 1867," not extended to military tribunals. Through a narrow reading of the 1869 statute, the Court maintained jurisdiction over habeas corpus claims and based its argument on previous congressional acts which previously broadened who could access the writ.[18]

As Table 3.1 indicates, the Civil War produced no instances where the courts found that Congress authorized the Executive's action but determined that the federal government as a whole lacked the power to act. Furthermore, there are no circumstances where the Executive had its actions declared constitutional without either having or getting congressional authorization, implicit or explicit. *McCardle* is a special circumstance. I place the case in the first prong of Jackson's framework because with Congress removing jurisdiction of the courts, it is implicitly intending for the actions of the Executive to be upheld. In regard to the establishment of military commissions, the first prong of Jackson's framework can mostly be eliminated. The two elected branches of government did not work together. Congress did not authorize the tribunals set up by Executive Order. Furthermore, the courts denied that setting up the military commissions by executive order alone was permissible under the circumstances brought before the courts.

Whether or not military necessity called for the commissions to be set up was left undecided. Because the civil courts were functioning, the courts saw the authority to try citizens by military commission outside the realm of executive power. Furthermore, though the Constitution is not clear on which branch of government has the power to suspend the writ, the federal courts held during the Civil War that it was a necessity for Congress to do so. As such, Lincoln's initiatives were in the third prong of Jackson's framework as he acted without congressional authority and in fact actually usurped what the courts decided was within the enumerated powers of Congress to do. The courts repeatedly held that the president was out of line, as is indicative of Jackson's third prong which holds that if the courts allow the president the power to act in said cases, the courts necessarily must conclude that Congress is without the power to act. When Congress retroactively approved Lincoln's wartime measures, the courts upheld the Executive's initiatives.

Table 3.1 further shows that during the Civil War, the federal courts offered protection for individual rights by refusing to defer to the Executive in its war-powers initiatives. Instead, the courts looked for congressional authorization of executive initiatives. With the exception of *Milligan,* the courts based their decisions on a separation of powers framework, looking for

Table 3.1. Judicial Deference to Congress During the Civil War

	Court upheld executive action	*Court struck down executive action*
Congressional authorization	*In In re Dunn,* 1863 *In re Fagan,* 1863 *The Mayor v. Cooper,* 1868 *ex parte McCardle,* 1869	
No Congressional authorization/ contrary to the wishes of Congress		*ex parte Field,* 1861 *ex parte Merryman,* 1861 *US ex rel John Murphy,* 1861 *ex parte Benedict,* 1862 *ex parte Field,* 1862 *In re Winder,* 1862 *ex parte Milligan,* 1866 *In re Egan,* 1866 *ex parte Yerger,* 1866

cooperation amongst the elected branches of government rather than using a rights-based discourse. Of course, this is not surprising, considering the rise of rights-based litigation did not come to the forefront of the courts until the end of World War I. The emphasis on the separation of powers remains interesting to note because these cases concern the curtailment of rights, but the separation of powers framework continues to be used even after the rights revolution of the early 20th century.[19]

WORLD WAR II

During the Second World War, military detentions became an issue before the federal courts on a number of fronts. The executive orders and subsequent legislation that placed curfews on, detained, and relocated American residents and citizens were legally challenged, as well as trials by military commission when the civilian courts were open and functioning. During and after hostilities, the Court rationale for upholding or striking down government encroachments on individual rights was based on a separation of powers framework as done during the Civil War. Rationales for deciding cases remained consistent with the courts requiring congressional authorization of executive actions. The Court found authorization for presidential initiatives during WWII that the Executive lacked during the Civil War. Congress was more generous in its delegation of war powers to the Executive early on during the Second World War. As a result, policies that were struck down during the 1860s were upheld during WWII.

In June, 1942, eight German spies entered the United States on a submarine in two groups of four. One group arrived on Long Island, the other in Florida. The goal of the saboteurs was to blow up critical infrastructures for the war effort, with the intention of conducting "terrorist activities" (Hardaway, 2005; 179). The men entered the country wearing German Marine Infantry uniforms, but went inland wearing civilian clothing. George John Dasch, one of the German spies, turned himself in. Dasch acted as an informant for the FBI, divulging the whereabouts of the other Germans in question (Fisher, 2003; 489). All eight men were successfully detained by the government as a result of the informant.

On July 2, 1942, President Roosevelt set up a military commission, by Executive Proclamation 2561, to try the alleged spies. The same proclamation also closed access to the federal courts to "persons who are subjects, citizens or residents of any nation at war with the United States . . . and are charged with committing, or attempting or preparing to commit sabotage, espionage . . . or violations of the law of war" (Proclamation No. 2561). Roosevelt cited the law of war and his ability as commander- in-chief of the Army and Navy as Constitutional authority to try the accused spies by military commission. Despite claims of inherent power, the commission was authorized by Congress pursuant to Article 15 of the 1920 Articles of War that granted "jurisdiction over such offenses to 'military commissions, provost courts, and other military tribunals" (Hardaway, 2005; 179).

The month-long trial was conducted in secrecy, running from July 8 through August 1, 1942. Nearing the end of the trial, Col. Royall petitioned for a writ of habeas corpus in federal court, challenging the jurisdiction of the commission (Fisher, 2003; 490). The Supreme Court scheduled oral hearings before action was taken at the district court level. The District Court turned down the petition. Before the D.C. Circuit Court of Appeals made a ruling on the matter, the Supreme Court heard oral arguments for nine hours over a two-day period. Royall cited the 38th Article of War, arguing that it was Congress that possessed the power to establish military commissions and that for any actions of the president to be valid he would need explicit action taken on their part (Fisher, 2005b; 84). The Administration argued that it was just confirming a policy already set up by Congress (Fisher, 2005b; 87). The Court would agree.

On the third day, before issuing their opinion, the papers were received from the D.C. Circuit giving the Supreme Court official jurisdiction to hear the case (Fisher, 2003; 491). The jurisdiction of the military commission of the convicted spies was upheld by the Supreme Court. A short per curiam was issued, stating that a full opinion would be released at a later date. Six of the eight saboteurs were executed. Three months later *ex parte Quirin,* 317 U.S. 1, 1942, was released.

On an institutional level, Fisher argues that it was important for the Court to avoid any concurring opinions that could potentially raise doubts about the executions (Fisher, 2005b; 95). The Court held that "citizens who associate themselves with the military arm of an enemy government, and with its aid, guidance, and direction enter this country bent on hostile acts are enemy belligerents within the meaning of the Hague Convention and the Law of War." The Court makes a distinction between lawful and unlawful combatants. Lawful combatants are soldiers dressed in uniform. Unlawful combatants are typically dressed in civilian clothes. The Court argued that lawful combatants must be held as prisoners of war when captured, denying similar protections to unlawful combatants. Furthermore, unlawful combatants could be tried by military commissions because the president's proclamation that set up the commissions were in fact recognized by Congress in Articles 15, 38, and 46 of the Articles of War. In explaining the role of Congress, Chief Justice Harlan Stone held that:

> Congress, in addition to making rules for the government of our Armed Forces, by the Articles of War has exercised its authority under Art. I, s 8, cl. 10 of the Constitution to define and punish offenses against the law of nations, of which the law of war is a part, by sanctioning, within constitutional limitations, the jurisdiction of military commissions to try persons for offenses which, according to the rules and precepts of the law of nations, and more particularly the law of war, are cognizable by such tribunals. And by Article of War 15, Congress has incorporated by reference, as within the jurisdiction of military commissions, all offenses which are defined as such by the law of war and which may constitutionally be included within that jurisdiction (Stone, *ex parte Quirin*).

American citizenship did not preclude a captured combatant from being declared unlawful. Justice Stone held that "even if it is assumed that Burger and Haupt are citizens of the United States, this does not change their status as 'enemies' of the United States. . . . This rule applies to all persons living in enemy territory, even if they are technically . . . citizens."[20] Enemy combatants are tried by rules stipulated in the law of war, which do not require a trial by jury as does the Constitution. Stone concludes that the Bill of Rights was not intended to be extended to violators of the laws of war when it was drafted.

It is important to note that Jackson originally had written a concurring opinion where he makes his arguments about the judiciary staying clear of judging military initiatives known, an argument that would be made again and one that brings keeping the integrity of the judiciary to forefront. Jackson had written that combining the courts with the military "is the end of liberty as we in this country have known it. . . . If we are uncompromisingly to discountenance military intervention in civil justice, we would do well to refuse to meddle with military measures dealing with captured unlawful enemy belligerents" (Fisher, 2005b; 97).

The question of whether or not military commissions were a constitutional venue to try violators of the law of war again reached the Court when the commanding general of the Japanese Army in the Philippine Islands contested their jurisdiction. General Tomoyuki Yamashita was charged with "failing to control the operations of his troops, allowing them to commit specific atrocities against the civilian population and prisoners of war" (Fisher, 2003; 498). The Court upheld Yamashita's conviction, partly based on the precedent of *ex parte Quirin,* stating that there was "congressional recognition of military commissions and its sanction of their use in trying offenses against the law of war."

The Court made it clear that it lacked jurisdiction to reconsider the decisions of military commissions. However, the federal courts could ensure the reasons for the restraint of liberty was lawful. The Articles of War, argued to protect the Japanese General, were intended for the protection of American soldiers alone.[21] As Stone further points out, "[T]he extent to which the power to prosecute violations of the law of war shall be exercised before peace is declared rests, not with the courts, but with the political branch of the Government, and may itself be governed by the terms of an armistice or the treaty of peace" (Stone's *Yamashita* opinion). In this case, there was no peace formally declared and the military commissions in question had authorization from both elected branches of government.

Dissenting opinions called for the rights of the individual to be recognized over the statutory authorization of Congress, citing Yamashita's rights of due process under the Fifth Amendment. Justice Frank Murphy argued that Yamashita was "rushed to trial under an improper charge, given insufficient time to prepare an adequate defense, deprived of the benefits of some of the most elementary rules of evidence and summarily sentenced to be hanged" (Murphy's *Yamashita* dissent). While Murphy's dissent focused on his substantive rights as a man on trial, Justice Wiley Rutledge added in his dissent that the proceedings held against Yamashita were in violation of the congressionally enacted Articles of War, disagreeing that they were established for the protection of American soldiers alone. Rutledge added the American tradition is one that "does not allow conviction by tribunals both authorized and bound by the instrument of their creation to receive and consider evidence which is expressly excluded by an Act of Congress or by treaty obligation."[22]

The denial of habeas corpus also presented itself in front of the federal courts. Again, the role of Congress was often prevalent. The writ was denied to a Japanese General in *Hirota v. MacArthur,* 338 U.S. 197; 1948. Lawyers for Hirota claimed that the military commission that tried the General was unlawfully constituted. The Court held that the federal courts lacked jurisdiction to review the detention and trial of the military commission because it was an international tribunal set up by the Allied Powers, not the Americans alone. Furthering the view that the Judiciary is no place to review military decisions, Justice Douglas wrote a concurring opinion, stating that agreements with allies are to be made by the Executive and "[w]hether they are wise or unwise, necessary or improvident, are political questions, not jusdiciable ones . . . Agreement with foreign nations for the punishment of war criminals, insofar as it involves aliens who are the officials of the enemy or members of its armed services, is a part of the prosecution of the war" (Douglas' *Hirota* opinion).

Other cases also show the need for congressional authorization of executive initiatives to limit individual liberties during WWII. In *Ahrens et. al. v. Clark,* 335 U.S. 188; 1948, the Court stated that because an executive removal order for 120 Germans has legal footing in the *Alien Enemy Act* of 1798, it was valid. In *Humphrey, Warden v. Smith,* 336 U.S. 695; 1949, an American soldier was convicted of rape. Article 70 of the Articles of War requires that an impartial investigation of the alleged event take place. Smith claimed no impartial investigation occurred. However, the Court held that the petitioner could not be released on a writ of habeas corpus because Congress did not intend to make judgments void when one of the articles was not fully followed. The evidence the Court used to back this claim was that no pretrial investigations were necessary in Navy proceedings, and Congress made the rules for both the Navy and the Army. The Court also pointed out that the Army itself asked for Article 70 to be included in the Articles of War, so army officials would ensure an impartial investigation would be held when it was feasible.

In 1950, twenty-one German citizens held in custody of the U.S. Army were tried and convicted by military commissions for war crimes in China against the United States after Germany's surrender. Those convicted claimed being civilian members of the German government, and not soldiers. Filing a petition for the writ of habeas corpus, the prisoners argued their convictions and detentions violated Articles I and III of the Constitution as well as the Fifth Amendment and the Geneva Conventions. In *Eisentrager v. Forrestal,* 174 F.2d 961, 1949, the Court of Appeals answered the constitutional questions and held that when actions of the government are contrary to the tenants of the Constitution, those actions will be declared void. The Fifth Amendment guarantees the writ will be delivered to those who request it, no exceptions. It followed that even with congressional sanction, denying the writ to those in American custody would not be tolerated and the federal government as a whole lacked such power. Jackson's Youngstown concurrence, too, reminds us that it is not guaranteed the courts will allow for the political branches of government to do anything when they cooperate, just that the courts will be much more lenient in their decisions. We see the lower courts, at times, are willing to knock down the actions of the federal government as a whole when Congress and the Executive are both on board, and as we will see again during the war on terrorism cases, such rulings are often times short-lived.

The Court's decision in *Johnson v. Eisentrager,* 339 U.S. 763; 1950, reversing the lower court, noted that it would seem wrong for the Fifth Amendment which is not guaranteed to American soldiers to be guaranteed to its enemies. The Court further held that the writ has not been extended to individuals who have never been within American territorial jurisdiction. Furthermore, "if the Fifth Amendment confers its rights on all the world . . . [it] would mean that during military occupation irreconcilable enemy elements [and] guerilla fighters . . . could require the American Judiciary to assure them freedoms of speech, press, and assembly as in the First Amendment, right to bear arms as in the Second, as well as rights to jury trial as in the Fifth and Sixth Amendments" (Jackson's *Eisentrager* opinion). Jackson continued:

> To grant the writ to these prisoners might mean that our army must transport them across the seas for hearing. . . . It might also require transportation for whatever witnesses the prisoners desired to call as well as transportation for those necessary to defend legality of the sentence. . . . Such trials would hamper the war effort and bring aid and comfort to the enemy. They would diminish the prestige of our commanders, not only with enemies but with wavering neutrals.

Jackson also contends that there are no statutes of Congress that extends the Bill of Rights to alien enemies.

The military commissions were held Constitutional during the Second World War because they were sanctioned by Congress, and in the case of *Eisentrager,* no law extended the Bill of Rights to alien enemies. The Court saw the Executive making decisions within the separation of powers framework set up by the framers. Incidentally, this vision is in accordance with Jackson's first prong of the *Youngstown* framework, with the federal courts showing leniency towards the Executive's initiatives because the Executive and Congress were working together.

Military commissions were not the only curtailment of individual liberties in regard to military orders during WWII. In 1943, the issue of whether or not a curfew could be placed on Japanese Americans went before the Supreme Court. The curfew was upheld in *Hirabayashi v. United States,* 320 U.S. 81; 1943. More than 100, 000 individuals were affected and roughly two-thirds were natural-born American citizens. Stone, writing for the Court, held that the military's imposed curfew on those living in the United States of Japanese ancestry, alien or citizen, was a constitutional delegation of power from Congress to the Executive. With the authorization, the Court did not need to consider whether the Executive had the authority on its own to order the curfew. The Court's rationale was that the war power is "the power to wage war successfully," quoting former Chief Justice Charles Evans Hughes,[23] and it includes winning the war not only on the battle field but also in protecting the Armed Forces as well as war materials to make success on the battlefield a possibility.

The lower (*United States v. Hirabayashi,* 46 F.Supp. 657; 1942) and Supreme Court both questioned the proper role of the federal courts in second guessing military policies, and came up with the same answer. Writing for the Supreme Court, Stone points out that the current "conditions call for the exercise of judgment and discretion and for the choice of means by those branches of the Government on which the Constitution has placed the responsibility of war-making, it is not for any court to sit in review of their wisdom of their action or substitute its judgment for theirs" (Stone's *Hirabayashi* opinion). The Court further concludes the curfew would not be invalid due to an infringement on the liberty of some citizens because "like every military control of the population of a dangerous zone in wartime, it necessarily involves some infringement of individual liberty." Stone concludes that the Fifth Amendment restrains Congress only insofar as it legislates a denial of due process. We have an indication here that this standard of using what became Jackson's separation of powers framework to adjudicate individual liberties cases is a reaction to the federal courts being uncomfortable imposing its judgment over that of the elected branches of government and the military due to a lack of expertise in the area. However, Stone does point out that it is "the Constitution" that "commits to the Executive and to Congress the exercise of the war power in all vicissitudes and conditions of warfare." As such, it is therefore the duty of the courts to give the elected branches of government "wide scope for the exercise of judgment and discretion in determining the nature and extent of the threatened injury or danger in the selection of the means for resisting it" (Stone's *Hirabayashi* opinion).

Justice Douglas concurred in the Court opinion stating that, "We cannot sit in judgment on the military requirements of that hour" (Douglas *Hirabayashi* concurrence). Justice Murphy also concurs echoing what would become the logic of Jackson's framework. Murphy suggests that when the president and Congress act together they "may generally employ such measures as are necessary and appropriate to provide for the common defense and to wage war 'with all force necessary to make it effective.'" Murphy adds, however, that having the ability to wage an effective and successful war does not mean the Bill of Rights can be suspended. Murphy agrees with the Court opinion because of the agreement between both branches of government yet is acutely aware that this power of the federal government is not unlimited.

A year after the curfew was upheld, the Court, in a 6-3 split, upheld the conviction of Fred Korematsu. Korematsu was charged with staying in San Leandro, California, a military area contrary to a civilian exclusion order. An Act of March 21, 1942 authorized military orders, proclaimed by President Roosevelt in Executive Order No. 9066, calling for Japanese Americans to be excluded from certain military areas on the West Coast. Writing for the Court in *Korematsu v. United States,* 323 U.S. 214; 1944, Black held that the military found evidence of disloyalty among Japanese Americans. Thousands of Japanese nationals requested to be repatriated to their homeland and more than 5000 refused to denounce the Empire of Japan and swear allegiance to the United States. However, there was no widespread evidence to question the loyalty of Japanese Americans (Steyn, 2004; 2). In fact, Korematsu tried to join the army after the Pearl Harbor attack but was rejected due to health reasons. The Court held that "the military authorities considered that the need for action was great, the time was short. We cannot—by availing ourselves of the calm perspective of hindsight—now say that at that time these actions were not justified" (Black's *Korematsu* Court opinion). The military authorities concluded that having a curfew in place did not provide adequate protection and ordered the exclusion. The Court determined that the exclusion took place with congressional authority.

Black held that in light of *Hirabayashi,* the Court was "unable to conclude that it was beyond the war power of Congress and the Executive to exclude those of Japanese ancestry from the West Coast War area at the time they did" (Black's *Korematsu* opinion). The circuit court employed the same rationale in *Korematsu v. United States,* 140 F2nd 289; 1943. Judge Wilbur argued that "a great part of war action as is possible shall be under Congressional enactment and every President in every war we have ever prosecuted has adhered to this principle. The Congress controls the purse strings and this alone is sufficient to make cooperation between the executive and the legislative authorities absolutely necessary. . . . There is no sanction in our governmental scheme for the courts to assume an overall wisdom and superior virtue and take unto themselves the power to vise the Acts of Congress and the President upon war matters. . . ." Had the president made the decision on his own, it is unclear if the either the circuit or Supreme Court would offer the same amount of deference they showed. The courts deferred to Congress, having authorized the president's initiatives. The military acts as an extension of the Executive, with the president being the commander-in-chief of the Armed Forces. The Court emphasized that this extension of the Executive is "charged with the primary responsibility of defending our shores." Having acted "in accordance with Congressional authority," the Court is more likely to defer to the military's initiatives when the Court considers Congress to have authorized its actions as it is Congress which makes rules governing the Armed Forces.

Frankfurter's *Korematsu* concurrence is brief and rests on the congressional validation of the military order. In fact, by virtue of the war powers being constitutionally delegated in the first place "for safeguarding the national life by prosecuting war effectively," if Congress authorizes executive actions, so should the courts respect that decision as nothing in the Constitution prohibits the delegation of the war powers between the elected branches of government. Frankfurter again, as was the case in the *Hirabayashi* decision, placed emphasis on Chief Justice Hughes statement that the war power is, "the power to wage war successfully."

Jackson's *Korematsu* dissent points out that Korematsu was convicted of an action that is not usually a crime. Rejecting the Court's claim that Korematsu's conviction was grounded in an Act of Congress, Jackson argued it rests entirely on Executive and military orders. Furthermore, denying the Court position that "if the military commander had reasonable military grounds for promulgating the orders, they are constitutional, and become law, and the Court is required to enforce them," Jackson suggests that it is dangerous for the Court to uphold as constitutional military orders suggesting they should be left without official endorsement of the Court. Jackson acknowledges it is not practical for each military order to conform to the Constitution, but holds firm that neither should the Constitution be made to conform to military orders. In displaying both prudence in his judicial decision-making, as well as the vulnerability of the federal courts when deciding war-powers cases, Jackson claims that he could not tell "from any evidence before [him], that the orders of General [John] DeWitt were not reasonably expedient military precautions, nor could [he] say that they were." Despite the potential reasonableness of the military procedures, Jackson denied they were constitutional.

The legitimacy of the Judiciary is brought to the forefront in Jackson's dissent. Jackson believes that "military decisions are not susceptible of intelligent judicial appraisal. They do not pretend to rest on evidence, but are made on information that often would not be admissible and on assumptions that could not be proved." Jackson points out that while the military order is likely to only last as long as the emergency in question, once the Court gave it constitutional validity, the Court legalized racial discrimination. The Court being ill-equipped to judge the reasonableness of military orders, Jackson saw this job best being left to those who command the war powers. At the same time, Jackson still acknowledges the limits on the Executive and Congress. The "chief restraint upon those who command the physical forces of the country . . . must be their responsibility to the political judgments of their contemporaries and to the moral judgments of history." Jackson did not call for General DeWitt's orders to be struck down. Instead, Jackson believed the Court was in no position to make a decision on such military initiatives either way, similarly to the arguments he made in the *Quirin* concurrence he wrote but never published with the Court.

There are two cases where the Court upheld the rights of the litigants during World War II. However, the Court did not use rights-based language found in the Constitution in striking down these executive actions, or at the lower court levels upholding the executive actions in question. Instead, the Court's rationale in protecting individual liberties remained primarily a separation of powers framework. In *ex parte Duncan,* 146, F. 2d 576; 1944, the circuit court upheld two convictions by military commission in Hawaii during a time when martial law had been declared by the Governor, Joseph Poindexter. Though the court's analysis included whether or not the civilian courts could be said to be functioning or not, the key to the decision was the court's interpretation of the intention of Congress stating that "[p]resumably Congress intended to authorize the institution by the Governor, with Presidential approval, of such measures of military control as might be thought necessary to deal with any situation possible of occurrence in this remote archipelago, the turbulent history of which was fresh in the minds of the legislators."

The Supreme Court disagreed with the lower court's interpretation of congressional intentions, but also decided the case based on a separation of powers framework, with the constitutional rights of those convicted as a mere afterthought. In *Duncan v. Kahanamoku,* 327 U.S. 304; 1946, the Court overturned the military commission convictions because it concluded that the Hawaiian *Organic Act* did not allow for martial law to circumvent the authority of the civil courts, believing them to be operational. Justice Black stated that if "the *Organic Act,* properly interpreted, did not give the armed forces this awesome power, both petitioners are entitled to their freedom."[24] The Court concluded that the Act did not grant such authorization, with Congress intending for Hawaiians to be entitled to the same constitutional protections as the rest of the states.

Justice Black, who wrote the majority opinion in *Korematsu,* held in *Duncan* that "the phrase 'martial law' as employed in that Act, therefore, while intended to authorize the military to act vigorously for the maintenance of an orderly civil government and for the defense of the Islands against actual or threatened rebellion or invasion, was not intended to authorize the supplanting of courts by military tribunals." The petitioners, one charged with embezzling stock, the other with fighting a couple of marines, argued constitutional grounds, which the Court chose not to address. The case was decided based on statutes. The Court held that if the statutory authorization required from Congress was in place, martial law could have substituted its own courts in the place of civilian ones. The deference to Congress that the federal courts exemplify is striking in this case and can be likened to Chase's *Milligan* dissent where he states that it is because Congress has not authorized the actions of the Executive that they are not upheld by the Court.

Actions of the military and Executive are subject to review in the Supreme Court, but Justice Burton's dissent emphasizes that this responsibility "requires the courts to put themselves as nearly as possible in the place of those who had the constitutional responsibility for immediate executive action. For a court to recreate a complete picture of the emergency is impossible." For Burton, maintaining the legitimacy of the federal courts system as well as the institutional mission of the Judiciary results in the courts deference to Congress in times of armed hostilities, Burton argues that "for this Court to intrude its judgment into spheres of constitutional discretion that are reserved either to the Congress or to the Chief Executive, is to invite disregard of that judgment by the Congress or by executive agencies under a claim of constitutional right to do so." The *Duncan* decision shows what the chapter exemplifies, that there are boundaries the federal courts impose on the Executive's war-making efforts include the necessity of obtaining the authorization of Congress before implementing initiatives that curtail individual liberties during armed hostilities as well as viewing court intervention of military initiatives with a skeptic eye, being unwilling to suggest the courts know more about the needs of national security than do the military and political officials charged with making such decisions.

Similarly in protecting individual rights at the end of hostilities, in *ex parte Mitsuye Endo,* 323 U.S. 283; 1944, the Court held that "the War Relocation Authority is without power to detain in one of its relocation centers a Japanese citizen whose loyalty to the United States is unquestioned." The Court did not decide the issue on the constitutional grounds of whether or not a citizen could be detained without being charged with a crime. Nor did the Court suggest the congressional act the government used to justify its detentions was unconstitutional. The Court held that the purpose of the 1942 Act and Executive Orders No. 9066 and 9102 were to protect the United States against espionage and sabotage. When the War Relocation Authority classified Endo as loyal to the country and therefore able to temporarily leave the center, restricting her liberty would not further protect the nation against espionage and sabotage. Endo, being loyal to the United States, was therefore entitled to her freedom.

The Court made it clear that it was not passing judgment on any military rules or congressional laws implemented and brought before the Court in past cases like *ex parte Quirin* or *Hirabayashi.* The case at hand was different, Endo was being held by a civilian agency, the War Relocation Authority. The Court emphasized that neither the Act of Congress nor the Executive Order that the War Relocation Authority relied on for authorization used the language of detention. The absence of specific mention of detention did not necessarily mean the War Relocation Authority lacked the authorization to detain. However, a citizen determined to be loyal "presents no problem of espionage and sabotage" and must be outside the reach of such a law. Justice Douglas held that the Court must also look at the plain language of the Act of Congress and not assume more power than is "clearly and unmistakably" used. The War Relocation Authority, by detaining loyal citizens, overstretched its authority and misinterpreted the Act of Congress of March 21, 1942. Endo was to be released not because of her constitutionally protected freedoms, but because the "power to detain a concededly loyal citizen may not be implied from the power to protect the war effort against espionage and sabotage (Douglas' *Endo* Opinion)" as allocated from Congress to the Executive.

The federal courts were more inclined to uphold individual liberties during the Civil War than during World War II. However, the rationale for the decisions did not change, as is shown by Table 2. The federal courts based their decisions on whether or not statutory authorization was present for the executive action in question. The military commissions during the Second World War were upheld because they had legislation backing their creation

Table 3.2. Judicial Deference to Congress during World War II

	Court upheld executive action	*Court struck down executive action*
Congressional authorization	*ex parte Quirin,* 1942 *U.S. v. Hirabayashi,* 1942 *Hirabayashi v. U. S.,* 1943 *Korematsu v. U. S.,* 1944 *ex parte Duncan,* 1944 *In re Yamashita,* 1946 *Ahrens et al. v. Clark,* 1948 *Humphrey v. Smith,* 1949 *Johnson v. Eisentrager,* 1950	*Eisentrager v. Forrestal,* 1949
No Congressional authorization/ contrary to the wishes of Congress		*ex Parte Mitsuye Endo,* 1944 *Duncan v. Kahanamoku,* 1946

that was not present during the Civil War. This legislative action on part of the Congress accounts for the different outcomes from the federal courts despite consistent judicial language and reasoning being used.

The federal court cases from the Second World War demonstrate that overwhelmingly when cases concerning military commissions and requests for the writ of habeas corpus came before the courts, the courts looked to the intentions of Congress in making their rulings. Unlike during the Civil War, Table 3.2 does show one instance where the lower court found that Congress authorized the Executive's action but the federal government as a whole lacked the power to act, just to be overturned by the Supreme Court. The Supreme Court's *Eisentrager* reversed the lower court disagreeing that the Bill of Rights extended to alien enemies because no statute of Congress made it so. Also as was the case during the Civil War, there were no circumstances during WWII where the Executive's actions were declared constitutional without either implicit or explicit congressional authorization. During the Civil War, there are no cases at the Supreme Court level upholding the Executive's decisions in regard to military detentions and commissions. At the lower court level, there are a number of cases refuting the government's claim to deny the writ of habeas corpus. Though these decisions were often ignored by government officials, the decisions were based on the lack of statutory authorization of presidential actions. Once Congress passed legislation backing Lincoln's initiatives, the courts also backed the Executive as the district court cases show in *In re Dunn* and *In re Fagan*. During World War II, the Supreme Court rebuked the Executive in only two significant cases. Both issues dealt with interpreting congressional authorization to limit the rights of the citizens rather than using rights-based constitutional discourse.

THE WAR ON TERRORISM

An ongoing battle concerning the rights of captured suspected Taliban and al Qaeda supporters has occurred since the start of what has been called a war on terrorism in 2001 after the 9/11 attacks in New York and Washington. In the four cases before the Supreme Court concerning the writ of habeas corpus, the writ has yet to be denied to petitioners. In two of the cases (*Rumsfeld v. Padilla,* 542 U.S. 426; 2004, and *Hamdi v. Rumsfeld,* 542 U.S. 507; 2004), American citizens were involved, whereas the third and fourth cases deal with non-U.S. citizens (*Rasul v. Bush,* 542 U.S. 466; 2004, and *Boumediene v. Bush,* 553 U.S. ____; 2008). The Bush administration argued the detainees were not entitled to seek relief in the federal courts system because, as enemy combatants, they lacked the protections of both domestic and international law. Suspected terrorists are considered unlawful combatants and do not qualify under the domestic Uniform Code of Military Justice for trial by court martial. Under international law, "[t]he applicable principle . . . is that enemy prisoners of war who were legitimate combatants in the first place must be afforded the same form of due process as our own soldiers, but enemy war criminals are not so entitled" (Richardson and Crona, 2005; 142). The government was left to find another avenue to try suspected terrorists.[25]

The first of the four cases concerning the legality of the military detentions deals with an American citizen captured on American soil. Whether Jose Padilla could be held as an unlawful combatant depended on whether American citizens could be declared enemy combatants by their own government. Padilla was a convicted murderer and gang member who moved to Egypt and converted to Islam. He was accused of approaching Abu Zubaydah, the operational coordinator for al Qaeda in Afghanistan to discuss his plan to steal radioactive material for the purpose of building and detonating a dirty bomb in the United States. Padilla was arrested at the O'Hare International Airport in Chicago in May, 2002.

On June 9, 2002, Bush directed then-secretary of defense, Donald Rumsfeld, to detain Padilla as an enemy combatant for committing "hostile and warlike acts, including preparation for acts of international terrorism (Richardson and Crona, 2005; 144). Padilla was placed in military custody at the U.S. Navy brig in Charleston, South Carolina. His lawyer filed a habeas corpus petition two days later in the U.S. District Court for the Southern District of New York. The president, as well as the Secretary of Defense and the commander of the naval brig, Melanie A. Marr, were named as respondents.[26]

At the Supreme Court, lawyers for Padilla argued his detention violated the Fourth, Fifth, and Sixth Amendments. The Court did not rule on the merits of the case. Instead, by a 5-4 split, the Court decided the case on jurisdictional grounds. Chief Justice William Rehnquist stated that the petition for habeas corpus was filed in the wrong court. Rehnquist emphasized that federal habeas corpus statutes are straightforward and provide that the proper respondent is "the person who has [direct] custody [of the petitioner]" (Rehnquist's *Padilla* opinion). In 1867, Congress added the provision to the habeas statute requiring petitions to be filed by the person with proper custody in their respective jurisdiction to avoid judges everywhere hearing habeas claims from petitioners in other jurisdictions. As a result, Padilla's lawyers would have to file the petition for habeas corpus again, naming Marr as respondent in the case. Padilla's situation is reminiscent of *ex parte Vallandigham,* decided during the Civil War, where the Court ruled that it lacked jurisdiction to rule on the merits of the case because of a mistake in filing the application on the part of the petitioner. The Court did not need to consider whether Congress authorized the detention because the petitioner lacked standing to be in front of the Court having filed the petition for the writ inaccurately. The lower courts were not afraid to rule on the merits of the case and we can see based on the language of the Court in its attempts to maintain some order over habeas proceedings that judicial integrity and institutional roles played a part of the highest Court that were not at issue for the lower court decisions.

Incidentally, after the case was reheard at both the district and circuit court levels,[27] on November 25, 2005, Padilla was charged with "three counts—conspiracy to murder U.S. nationals, conspiracy to provide material support to terrorists and providing material support to terrorists."[28] The charges did not include conspiracy to conduct terrorist acts in the United States as he was originally accused of planning. Padilla was convicted by a civilian court jury in Miami, Florida on August 16, 2007 after having pled not guilty to all charges.

The second case dealing with American citizens involves Yaser Esam Hamdi. Hamdi was captured by the Northern Alliance in Afghanistan and delivered to the American Armed Forces. Hamdi was supposedly captured on the battlefield in Afghanistan sporting a Kalisnikov assault riffle, fighting for the Taliban. Hamdi's family maintained he was in Afghanistan as a humanitarian relief worker and his capture was a mistake. Hamdi, born in Louisiana, was raised in Saudi Arabia. Once the knowledge of his citizenship was discovered, he was transferred to a U.S. Navy brig in Virginia, and then transferred to the same military prison in South Carolina where Padilla was detained. Hamdi requested access to counsel and was granted this request by a district court, receiving time with a public defender without any military personnel in the room.[29] Hamdi's father filed a petition for the writ of habeas corpus, his entitlement as a U.S. citizen. Hamdi's father maintained that his right as an American was not to be held without charges being filed, without access to a tribunal, or without counsel (Yoo, 2006; 579). These arguments were made pursuant to the *Habeas Corpus Statute,* 18 U.S.C. s 4001(a), which maintains that "[n]o citizen shall be imprisoned or otherwise detained by the United States except pursuant to an Act of Congress" (Yoo, 2006; 580).

Hamdi was not denied his right as a citizen to seek habeas relief. Instead, the government argued that Hamdi was lawfully captured as an enemy combatant under the law of war. Government lawyers argued the due process afforded to an enemy combatant like Hamdi should be based on the Mobbs affidavit, where the word of the government is taken for truth on the matter. The Mobbs affidavit stated that "Hamdi was affiliated with a Taliban military unit and that he was captured with a rifle when his unit surrendered to the

Northern Alliance forces; in the light of his association with the Taliban he had been classified as an 'enemy combatant'" (Moeckli, 2005; 81).

The Bush Administration argued that the federal-courts system was no place for second guessing military actions, reminiscent of arguments made by the Court during World War II. In a brief to the Fourth Circuit, the Justice Department stated that "[a]t the very most, given the separation of constitutional powers in this unique area, a court could only require the military to point to some evidence supporting its determination. Either way, no evidentiary hearing is required to dispose of a habeas petition in this military context" (Government Brief, 2002, 12).[30] The government's brief points out that it is customary for the courts to defer to the other branches of government when asked to intervene in "sensitive constitutional areas and, in particular, when asked to review military decisions in a time of war as the branches of government should in no way impede the intelligence gathering on part of the military to further the war efforts (Brief, 19–20). While taking note of the classic argument that the national government is charged with providing for the common defense, the Court sought a balance between the government's restraints on liberty in favor of security versus the argument put forth by Hamdi's lawyers that he was entitled to all the rights afforded an American citizen.

The Supreme Court reversed the appeals decision and remanded the case to the district court for further proceedings. The Court of Appeals, in *Hamdi v. Rumsfeld,* 337 F. 3d 335; 2003, had wanted more deference shown to the Executive, by flat out denying the request to a hearing on the issue. The court argued it has been a long-time custom of war to hold your enemies in detention. The lower court further acknowledges the limited role of the Judiciary as being "ill equipped to serve as final and ultimate arbiters of the degree to which litigation should be permitted to burden foreign military operations" (Wilkinson's *Hamdi* concurrence). In these two regards the Supreme Court was in complete agreement. Four justices, signing on to the plurality court opinion, accepted the Bush administration's claim that it could detain Americans as enemy combatants because Congress authorized it to do so. In total, while five justices acknowledged that suspected terrorists could be held as enemy combatants, eight out of nine justices, however, found a violation of due process, holding that detainees are entitled to a procedure to challenge the legality of their status, even if that due process was less than citizens charged with crimes in the federal-courts system would receive.[31]

Not addressing whether the Executive possessed its own authority under Article II of the Constitution, the Court held that classification of American citizens as enemy combatants was legally authorized by Congress under the AUMF. The congressional authorization that allowed the government to use all necessary and appropriate force against the perpetrators of the 9/11 attacks was determined to extend to an authorization for detaining American citizens as enemy combatants. The Court states that "[t]here can be no doubt that individuals who fought against the United States in Afghanistan as part of the Taliban, an organization known to have supported the al Qaeda terrorist network responsible for those attacks, are individuals Congress sought to target in passing" the AUMF (O'Connor's *Hamdi* opinion).

The Court relied on *ex parte Quirin* as precedent. Justice Sandra Day O'Connor held that citizens, as well as non-citizens, had the same potential to return to the field against American troops if released from detention. However, U.S. citizens detained as enemy combatants also are entitled to challenge the status given to them by the government. The Court balanced the rights given to the detainees by Congress, under 28 U.S.C. s. 2241, and the need for government authority in the area of national security. A citizen detained who sought to challenge his classification as an enemy combatant "must receive notice of the factual basis for his classification, and a fair opportunity to rebut the Government's factual assertions before a neutral decisionmaker." However, the burden the Executive faces during armed hostilities could also be alleviated by allowing the government to present evidence that would be inadmissible during civilian criminal trials, such as hearsay. Lowering standards for admitting evidence into trials was a part of the balancing act between protecting individual liberties and the government's authority.

The outcome of the *Hamdi* decision was leave less than admirable. Because Hamdi received no due process at all, it was easy for the Court to find that this was unsatisfactory due process for detainees and to call for more safeguards, remanding the case back to the lower courts for the process to recommence. O'Connor left the door open for the government to come back with a compromise that would allow for the government to lessen its burden by lessening the standards on admitting evidence, at the same time allowing for a process that would give detainees an opportunity to challenge their legal status. With this decision, O'Connor, like justices before her, noted the "core strategic matters of warmaking belong in the hands of those who are best positioned and most politically accountable for making them." At the same time, a system of independent review would not threaten military operations and the government's position calling for a limited role for the federal courts was rejected.[32]

Justices Antonin Scalia, Clarence Thomas, David Souter, and John Paul Stevens all took part in shared dissenting opinions. Scalia, writing for Stevens, pointed out that "[w]here the Government accuses a citizen of waging war against it, our constitutional tradition has been to prosecute him in federal court for treason or some other crime." Scalia concludes that "Hamdi is entitled to a habeas decree requiring his release unless (1) criminal proceedings are promptly brought, or (2) Congress has suspended the writ of habeas corpus (Scalia's *Hamdi* dissent). The Scalia and Stevens dissent rests on substantive principles of due process due to the lack of congressional initiative on the issue. Thomas dissents arguing that the AUMF grants the president the ability to hold detainees without access to the writ of habeas corpus. Both dissents are based on the interpretation of congressional acts or lack of congressional action.[33]

Challenges to the government's policy not to allow foreign nationals held at Guantanamo Bay access to the federal courts were made in *Rasul v. Bush.* The Executive argued that the federal courts do not have jurisdiction to hear the case as the men in question were being held outside U.S. territory. The district and court of appeals agree with the position of the Executive and dismissed the claims of the petitioners. In *al Odah v. United States,* 321 F. 3d 1134; 2003, the Circuit Court emphasized that the courts not being open to the detainees ensured that they could not challenge whether parts of the Constitution or any laws of Congress had been violated by the government. As a result, a writ of habeas corpus could not be given based on the *Habeas Corpus Act* of Congress by any court in the country. However, the Supreme Court disagreed based on their belief that the courts did have jurisdiction to hear such cases as well as the language of the Act itself. It is important to note that the Court decided no constitutional questions in *Rasul,* but looked only at the availability of habeas corpus as authorized by the *Habeas Corpus* statute. Section 28 U.S.C. § 2241 states the federal courts have jurisdiction to hear cases concerning habeas corpus petitions of detainees held as violators of American laws. This jurisdiction also extended to aliens held in a territory over which the United States exercised plenary and exclusive jurisdiction, but not "ultimate sovereignty." The Court held that the right to petition for the writ extended to foreign nationals because nowhere did it explicitly deny the writ to them in the Constitution or in any section of the congressional statute.

Justice Stevens based his opinion on the legislative interpretation of the *Habeas Corpus Statute* holding that first, "[i]n 1867, Congress extended the protections of the writ to 'all cases where any person may be restrained of his or her liberty in violation of the constitution, or of any treaty or law of the United States.'" Second, and inferring from the first point, that "[c]onsidering that the statute draws no distinction between Americans and aliens held in federal custody, there is little reason to think that Congress intended the geographical coverage of the statute to vary depending on the detainee's citizenship." Since the United States was determined to have territorial jurisdiction over Guantanamo Bay, all detainees maintained statutory authorization to challenge the legality of their detention, regardless of citizenship.

Justice Kennedy concurred in the judgment but reached the conclusion that the federal courts retained jurisdiction over the detainees based on the precedent in *Eisentrager.* During WWII, the Court held that allowing enemy aliens access to the courts "would have had a clear harmful effect on the Nation's military affairs, the matter was appropriately left to the Executive Branch" by congressional authorization. Kennedy notes that the federal courts have acknowledged, as I have also detailed, that there is an area of policy making "where judicial power may not enter" that engages the "joint role of the President and the Congress, in the conduct of military affairs." Concluding, Kennedy continues that while this realm of power exists where the Judiciary lacks of role, the circumstances in *Rasul* do not fit in it as Guantanamo Bay is essentially under American control, far removed from hostilities.

With the ruling, the Court held for the first time that foreign detainees are entitled access to the federal-courts system under the federal habeas corpus statute to challenge the grounds for their detention. Scalia states that the opinion "extends the habeas statute . . . to aliens held beyond the sovereign territory of the United States and beyond the territorial jurisdiction of its courts. . . . [T]he Court evades explaining why *stare decisis* can be disregarded, and why *Eisentrager* was wrong." Scalia further notes that Congress could have passed a law amending the habeas statute to grant such authority to detainees. According to Scalia, because a petitioner was required to challenge their physical confinement in the same district where they were being held, and since Guantanamo Bay does not fall under a specific district, a "monstrous scheme in time of war" was created.

In rejected Scalia's suggestion that *Eisentrager* was overruled by Rasul, the Court decided that the logic of *Eisentrager* did not apply. The detainees in question at Guantanamo Bay were not nationals of countries at war with the United States. Furthermore, the detainees deny having committed any terrorist attacks. The Germans in the *Eisentrager* case were found guilty of war crimes. The Guantanamo Bay detainees were not charged with a crime at all. Finally, while the detainees in *Eisentrager* were captured and held in China, Guantanamo Bay remains effectively under American control.[34]

The issue of habeas corpus presented itself again with challenges to the legality of trying suspected terrorists by military commissions. Bush's order establishing military commissions gave exclusive jurisdiction over detainees to the Executive's created court. Section 7(b) of the order states that detainees "shall not be privileged to seek any remedy or maintain any proceedings, directly or indirectly, or to have any such remedy or proceeding sought on the individual's behalf, in (i) any court of the United States, or any State thereof,

(ii) any court of any foreign nation, or (iii) any international tribunal."[35] The Court had to decide whether the president possessed authority to set up military commissions by his own inherent or implied power or whether he needed congressional authorization. The Administration argued there was evidence to support the president's claim to inherent power found in *ex parte Quirin.* There, the Court held that "the [President] . . . exercise[d] . . . authority conferred upon him by Congress . . . An important incident to the conduct of war is the adoption of measures by the military command not only to repel and defeat the enemy, but to seize and subject to disciplinary measures those enemies who in their attempt to thwart or impede our military effort have violated the law of war" (Stone's *Quirin* opinion).

Critics of the military commissions set up by Executive Order in November 2001, point out that Article I of the Constitution confers upon Congress, not the Executive, the power to "define and punish . . . offenses against the Law of Nations." Part of defining and punishing offenses in times of war is determining the venue for trying detainees. President Bush, however, claimed he had congressional authorization to set up the military commissions under the AUMF. If the AUMF was not enough evidence to support the Executive's claim to set up the commissions, sections 821 and 836 of Title 10, of the United States Code provides that the jurisdiction of courts-martial are not exclusive and "do not deprive military commissions . . . of concurrent jurisdiction with respect to offenders or offenses that by statute or by the law of war may be tried by military commission" (Government Brief, 3). Nothing in the text of the United States Code restricts the jurisdiction of military commissions to times of war (Government Brief, 17). While it was suggested that the AUMF was authorization enough from Congress, it does not explicitly authorize the Executive's order and this latter position is the position that the Supreme Court took in the Spring of 2006 when it decided *Hamdan v. Rumsfeld,* 548 U.S. 557, 2006.

Hamdan's lawyers made the argument that the president lacked both statutory and constitutional grounds to establish military commissions. If Congress took away the Court's jurisdiction to hear habeas corpus claims from detainees, by passing the *Detainee Treatment Act* of 2005, then Congress suspended the writ of habeas corpus unconstitutionally because there was no state of invasion or armed rebellion that was required before the writ could be suspended.

The Supreme Court held that the Bush administration's military commissions lacked constitutional authority, were inconsistent with congressional statutes and with the Geneva Convention's common Article 3. Furthermore, the Court "necessarily concluded that the President could not disregard valid substantive limitations that Congress placed upon his authority during wartime" (Vladeck, 2007; 3). Stevens held that it was unnecessary to address the claim of presidential inherent power because "[o]rdinary principles of statutory construction suffice to rebut the Government's theory." Stevens' opinion focused on the separation of powers framework the Court traditionally employed in adjudicating war-powers cases where the Executive spearheads efforts to limit individual liberties, in military detention cases.

Stevens maintains that since the Civil War, there has been no occasion where the Court had to make a determination whether the president had the authority and conditions of military necessity to create military commissions without the sanction of Congress. Even during World War II, the Supreme Court found that under the Articles of War, the president did have authorization to set up the commissions in question. In rejecting the president's claim that the AUMF granted authority for the commissions, the *Hamdan* Court held that "the AUMF activated the President's war powers. . . . [T]hose powers include the authority to convene military commissions in appropriate circumstances" However, "there is nothing in the text or legislative history of the AUMF even hinting that Congress intended to expand or alter the authorization set forth in Article 21 of the UCMJ." As such, the president's commissions were in fact contrary to an existing Act of Congress, falling into Jackson's third prong of the *Youngstown* framework.

The Supreme Court did not accept the argument that *ex parte Quirin* was controlling precedent. In an intuitive argument made several years ago, it was suggested that *Youngstown* would be controlling (Tobias, 2003; 1371). According to Tobias, the case law shows that the Constitution stipulates it is Congress and not the Executive that has authorization to prescribe federal court jurisdiction. Article I states, "Congress shall have power . . . [to] constitute Tribunals inferior to the supreme Court." Furthermore, Article III holds that "[t]he judicial Power of the United States, shall be vested in one supreme Court, and in such inferior Courts as the Congress may from time to time ordain and establish" (Tobias 2003; 1382).

According to Tobias, the Bush administration initially asked Congress for authorization of the military commissions, but the request was denied, just as Truman asked Congress to sanction his seizure of the steel mills during the Korean War, but his letters ignored. The Administration then decided to "arrogat[e] to itself the power sought" (Tobias, 2003; 1383). Because Congress did not authorize the commissions and because authorization was asked for but not received, Tobias states that Bush acted on his own authority. As a result, *Youngstown* rather than *Quirin* was controlling because the president created legislation without authorization delegated to him from Congress and in fact against the legislative will of Congress (Tobias, 1390).

Stevens partly agrees with Tobias. While *Youngstown* is not the controlling precedent for the case, neither is *Quirin*. Stevens explains that *Quirin* met standards set forth in the law of war. In *Hamdan,* no charges for a crime violating of the law of war were laid. The crime of conspiracy, Stevens continued, does not even appear in the Geneva or Hague Conventions.[36]

More than once in the *Hamdan* opinion does Stevens mention the need for congressional action to authorize the Administration's commissions. Stevens points out that if the Executive wants to deny Hamdan evidence collected against him, it needs Congress to pass a law denying him that information. The Court further held that the commissions were not specifically authorized by any congressional statute and in fact directly violated the UCMJ, Article 36(b) (10 U.S.C.S. § 836(b)), "which required that the procedural rules that the President promulgated for military commissions and courts-martial be 'uniform insofar as practicable.'"

With the ruling of the Court, this reaffirmed "a straightforward conception of the proper separation of war powers that is almost as old as the Republic itself, dating back to Chief Justice Marshall's opinion in *Little v. Barreme,* one of the so-called 'Quasi-War' cases (Vladeck, 3)," where the Court held that orders of the Executive would be held unlawful if they ran contrary to a congressional statute, a concept Jackson recognized and emphasized in his *Youngstown* framework. Jack Balkin suggests that the *Hamdan* decision was a "democracy forcing" ruling, arguing that it "has limited the President by forcing him to go back to Congress to ask for more authority than he already has, and if Congress gives it to him, then the Court will not stand in his way (Balkin, 2006).[37] Balkin's argument coincides with the theory of judicial decision making that I have put forth, as exemplified by Jackson's *Youngstown* framework where the most leniency is given to the Executive when it works with the force of Congress behind it.

Congress took up the offer by the Court to remedy the Administration's legal problems. Less than 4 months after the *Hamdan* decision, Congress passed the *Military Commissions Act* of 2006 (MCA),[38] establishing authorization for the president to create commissions to try detainees. The MCA "granted vast delegation of power to the president to determine the rules of procedure; delegated to the president the power to determine by executive order what interrogation techniques would be used on detainees" (Pious, 2007; 78) and section 7(a) of the Act also "stripped the federal courts of their statutory jurisdiction to hear habeas corpus petitions or any other actions filed by aliens who are detained as enemy combatants or who are even awaiting a determination of whether or not they are enemy combatants" (Robertson, 2008; 2-3).

Since Congress passed the *Military Commissions Act,* Judge Robertson of the D.C. District Court dismissed Hamdan's claims due to a lack of jurisdiction because the act took jurisdiction to hear habeas petitions away from the federal courts (*Hamdan v. Rumsfeld,* 464 F. Supp. 2d 9, (D.D.C. 2006)). This ruling was reversed by the Supreme Court when it decided foreign detainees being held at Guantanamo Bay had a constitutional right to petition for the writ of habeas corpus in Boumediene v. Bush. The Court held that the MCA violates the suspension clause of the Constitution which states that "the privilege of the Writ of Habeas Corpus shall not be suspended, unless when in Cases of Rebellion or Invasion the public Safety may require it."

The decision is the most recent example of a Supreme Court decision that contradicts the thesis the Court will defer to the Executive when Congress has authorized the president's actions. The Court decided the case on a basis of a rights claim, not on the separation of powers framework. The Executive was acting at the zenith of its constitutional authority under Jackson's framework because it was Congress that had denied federal courts the jurisdiction to hear the habeas claims brought by alien detainees when the actions were pending at the time of the MCA's enactment, thus placing the Executive within the first prong of Jackson's framework. In *Boumediene v. Bush, 476 F 3d 981;* 2007, the D.C. Court of Appeals accepted that section 7 of the *Military Commissions Act* took jurisdiction away from the courts to hear habeas petitions from the Guantanamo detainees. However, the Supreme Court would reverse their decision, pointing out that Congress can only suspend the writ in times of invasion and armed rebellion. Neither situation having taken place, section 7 of the MCA was contrary to the Constitution and therefore void. A limit was placed on what the federal government as a whole could do.

While a right was protected against the encroachment of the government, Kennedy's decision also makes it clear that if Congress is going to suspend the writ, it has to be replaced with an adequate substitution. Like the *Hamdi* decision, procedural fairness in the suspension of rights was sought by the Court. Justice Kennedy argues that the "Constitution's essential design, ensuring that, except during periods of formal suspension, the Judiciary will have a time-tested device, the writ, to maintain the 'delicate balance of governance.' . . . Separation-of-powers principles, and the history that influenced their design, inform the Clause's reach and purpose." It should therefore be noted that Kennedy emphasizes it is because the DTA's procedures for reviewing the status of combatants in the Combatant Status Review Tribunals are an inadequate substitute for the writ of habeas corpus that makes the MCA's suspension of the writ unconstitutional. Though the Court places a limit on how far the federal government as a whole can act, it does so weary of the separation of powers balance it seeks to maintain.

Table 3.3. Judicial Deference to Congress during the War on Terrorism

	Court upheld executive action	*Court struck down executive action*
Congressional authorization	*Boumediene v. Bush,* 2007 *Hamdan v. Rumsfeld,* 2006 *Hamdi v. Rumsfeld,* 2004* *Hamdi v. Rumsfeld,* 2003 *al Odah v. U.S.,* 2003	*Boumediene v. Bush,* 2008
No Congressional *Boumediene v. Bush,* 2008		*Hamdan v. Rumsfeld,* 2006 *Hamdi v. Rumsfeld,* 2004** *Rasul et. al. v. Bush,* 2004 *Padilla v. Rumsfeld,* 2003

*As pertaining to holding American citizens as enemy combatants
**As pertaining to an American citizen challenging their status as an enemy combatant

Table 3.3 indicates that one of the war on terrorism cases present a break with past cases where individual liberties are limited by the Executive. The exercise of power by the Executive was struck down during the Civil War and upheld during World War II based on the Court's interpretation of statutory authorization. The more recent cases are also decided based on the court in question's interpretation of congressional authorization, with the lower courts more willing to not only discuss cases on the merits and tackle the constitutional issues, but also more likely to defer to the Executive, which brings to the forefront the possibility of rights being limited despite rights-based language being used by the courts. Table 3 indicates one instance where the Court found that the Congress authorized the Executive's action but that the federal government as a whole lacked the power to act. Moreover, there are no circumstances where the courts declared the Executive's actions constitutional without either implicit or explicit congressional authorization and in fact the Court goes to great lengths to not discuss or determine such possibilities.

CONCLUSION

This chapter shows that the federal courts mostly decide cases dealing with the Executive's war powers to conduct military commissions and to withhold the writ of habeas corpus consistently over time from the Civil War to the present "war on terrorism." When the courts determine that Congress authorized the actions of the Executive in regard to military detentions prior to the issues reaching the federal courts, the Executive's actions were upheld if the federal government as a whole could act.

The cases that have resulted from the current "war on terrorism" related conflicts show a constitutional dialogue between the three branches of government which is reminiscent of the framers vision of each branch of government playing a role in foreign affairs. The federal courts have looked for congressional authorization of executive actions. When seeing no authorization, the courts have suggested to the government to ask Congress for authorization. This was the case in *Hamdi* when the Court held that some procedural safeguards needed to be put in place for detainees to seek review of their status as an enemy combatant. This was the case in *Hamdan* when Congress reacted to the Court by passing the *Military Commissions Act,* giving the Executive the proper authority for its military commissions. And finally, this was the case in *Boumediene* when the Court held that the MCA included an unconstitutional suspension of the writ of habeas corpus as it the review process set up in the DTA as a result of the *Hamdi* decision was inadequate at providing safeguards enough to act as a substitute for the writ.

The dialogue between the Court, Congress, and the Executive during the war on terrorism cases is found more historically throughout the warrantless electronic surveillance cases, where the federal courts would need to determine the scope of the Fourth Amendment in relation to the right to privacy and unreasonable search and seizure in connection with war powers policies.

ENDNOTES

1. http://www.usconstitution.net/glossary.html (July 3, 2007).

2. To reiterate, Jackson argues that "[w]hen the President acts pursuant to an express or implied authorization of Congress, his authority is at its maximum" because such actions have the full sanction of the national government. The courts are most lenient towards the Executive in such cases. Actions of the Executive will only be struck down if the federal government as a whole lacks the authority to act in such a regard. The second prong of Jackson's framework is when the "President acts in absence of either a congressional grant or denial of authority, he can only rely upon his own independent powers, but there is a zone of twilight in which he and Congress may have concurrent authority." If there is a lack of action on the part of Congress, this also may "invite" the Executive to act. In the third prong, or category, of Jackson's framework the Court is to "scrutinize with caution" the actions of the Executive. In such cases, the Executive acts in contrast to the explicit or implicit wishes of Congress (Jackson's *Youngstown* concurrence).

3. http://bl.uk/treasures/magnacarta/translation.html (July 9, 2007).

4. This was in contrast to Blackstone's view that the colonies fell into the category of infidel territory, despite having been "found" and inhabited (Duker, 96–97), rather than conquered or occupied.

5. It would not be long until an issue concerning the writ of habeas corpus would reach the Supreme Court. Congress tried to suspend the writ for a period of three months to ensure that the conspirators of Aaron Burr would not be released from state prison. These efforts passed the Senate but failed in the House. Two conspirators, Erick Bollman and Samuel Swartwout, were charged with treason and subsequently applied to the Supreme Court for a writ of habeas corpus. In *ex parte Bollman*, 8 U.S. 75, 1807, Chief Justice John Marshall held that the Constitution allows for the Supreme Court to issue writs, such as habeas corpus, to the circuit courts unless Congress suspends the writ or takes away the court's jurisdiction to issue them. It would not be until the Civil War that an American president would suspend the writ of habeas corpus.

6. For example, Fisher points out that under the rule of Richard I, in 1190, the King ordered that anyone who committed murder on a ship would be bound to the man he killed and thrown into the sea (2005; 1).

7. Hardaway explains: Although other minor changes were made [prior to this time], the 1874 Articles of War were "technically a formal revision of the Code.' ...These articles were recognized as a clarification, modernization, and reaffirmation of the 1806 Articles of War. On September 7, 1890, Congress reduced the discretionary powers of the courts martial providing instead that punishment, 'shall not, in times of peace, be in excess of a limit which the President may prescribe." The President responded with an Executive Order on February 16, 1891, which contained a table listing maximum punishments for the various crimes under the code. . . . Congress again revised the Articles of War in 1916. . . . Some of the more obsolete articles were eliminated." (Hardaway, 2005; 183).

8. Kennedy points out that General George Washington established a tribunal called the Board of General Officers to try British Major John Andre who was accused of spying during the Revolutionary War in 1780.

9. Military Commissions were again used in 1862, when the American military had a run-in with the Dakota in Minnesota. Fighting ensued for five weeks and 77 American soldiers were killed (Fisher, 2003; 487). The Army set up a military commission to try violators of the law of war. No issue presented itself in front of the federal courts.

10. Justice Kennedy states that military commissions were needed at this time because courts martial did not enjoy a broad jurisdiction as they do today. At the time, as Winthrop argued and Kennedy quotes; "[t]he occasion for the military commission arises principally from the fact that the jurisdiction of the courts-martial proper, in our law, is restricted by statute almost exclusively to members of the military force and to certain specific offenses defined in a written code" (Kennedy concurrence, Winthrop p. 831). Courts-martial were so limited that even "[t]he early versions of the Articles of War addressed civilian crimes committed by the military personnel only indirectly, providing that these criminals be held until they could be turned over to the civilian authorities" (Hardaway, 2005; 182). This changed on March 3, 1863, when Congress passed the Civil War Draft Law, giving courts martial jurisdiction over civilian crimes of violence.

11. Pious cites Lincoln's July 4, 1861 speech as evidence for this claim. In a special address to Congress, the president explained the war measures that he had taken in the South while Congress was not in session: "These measures, whether strictly legal or not, were ventured upon, under what appeared to be popular demand and a public necessity trusting . . . that Congress would readily ratify them. It is believed that nothing has been done beyond the constitutional competency of Congress" (Pious, 2007; 72).

12. Such a statement was made by John Yoo and Glenn Sulmasy and can be found in an article for the Pennsylvania Law Review, *PENNumbra*, January 30, 2007 entitled "The Military Commissions Act: A bi-partisan Congress." http://www.penumbra.com/debates/dabate.php?did=4 (September 26, 2007).

13. In fact, the only instance of military detentions I found in the Supreme Court before the Civil War was *Bevans v. United States* (16 U.S. 336; 1818). In this case, a murder was committed on board a warship but was determined to be within the jurisdiction of Boston, Massachusetts. That said, there were two civil suits in the lower courts, dealing with damages awarded for false imprisonment during the War of 1812 (*Smith v. Shaw*, 12 Johns 257 (N.Y. 1815) and *McConnell v. Hampton*, 12 Johns, 234 (N.Y. 1815).

14. The writ had been filed improperly. The Court told the petitioner the right of the writ may exist, but the Court cannot decide the issue because the rules set up for proper application to obtain the writ were not followed. This happened once during the Civil War and we see it again during the "War on Terrorism." In *ex parte Vallandigham*, 68 U.S. 243; 1864. This decision largely rested with the actions of Congress as the appellate powers of the Court are both limited and regulated by the legislative branch of government. Where a writ was improperly filed and where the writ was denied due to a lack of jurisdiction, the reasoning of the Court was not because the president had the authority to curtail the individual liberties of the petitioner, but that the petitioner had erred in procedure.

15. See *In re Dunn*, 8 Fed. Cas. 93 (No. 4,171) (S.D. N.Y. 1863) and *In re Fagan*, 8 Fed. Cas. 947, 949 (No. 4,604)(D. Mass. 1863).

16. Despite the ruling, military commissions still functioned in the South under martial law where "[f]rom the end of April 1865 to January 1, 1869, 1, 435 trials by military commission took place, and others occurred in Texas and Mississippi in 1869 and 1870" (Fisher, 2003; 488 see also Neely, 1991; 176-77).

17. Justices James Wayne, Noah Swayne, and Samuel Miller joined Chase in his dissent.

18. By 1842 Congress had extended the writ to be available to "prisoners, being subjects or citizens of foreign states, in custody under National or State authority for acts done or omitted by or under color of foreign authority, and alleged to be valid under the law of nations." In February, 1867, Congress passed the Act that McCardle used to make his appeal to the Supreme Court challenging his detention. The Act extended the "original jurisdiction by habeas corpus of the District and Circuit Courts, and of the several judges of these courts, to all cases of restraint of liberty in violation of the Constitution, treaties, or laws of the United States" (Chase's *Yerger* opinion).

19. Between the Civil War and WWII, cases concerning trial by military commission did not come before the federal courts. However, a number of cases were presented before the Court dealing with military detentions that were upheld by the Court based on congressional authorizations of various sorts. The legality of the draft became an issue when young men refused to join the army when conscripted. The Court held that since Congress passed the Act to allow for conscription and because the Constitution says it is in the power of Congress to provide for an army, the *Selected Services Act* was therefore Constitutional (*Selective Draft Law Cases*, 245 U.S. 366; 1918, *Cox v. Wood*, 247 U.S. 3; 1918, *Jones v. Perkins*, 245 U.S. 390; 1918). Furthermore, in the case of a prisoner charged under a courts martial for the murder of another prisoner, the accused was not entitled to habeas corpus. As a member of the military, he was subject to military law and the court in question had been legally constituted by Congress (*Kahn v. Anderson*, 255 U.S. 1; 1921). Likewise, Congress delegated the authority to the president to empower "the commanding officer of any district or of any force or body of troops' to appoint general courts-martial (*Givens v. Zerbst*, 255 U.S. 11; 1921). These WWI cases show further examples of how essential congressional authorization was seen to be by the federal courts. Because the Constitution grants so many war powers to Congress in Article 1 section 8, but grants to the Executive the ability to be commander-in-chief of the Armed Forces once in battle, it was and is rational for Congress to delegate its authority to the Executive to better control the situation once the nation is in a perceived state of emergency. The Court applies this logic also in its rationales for its World War II decisions.

20. According to Fisher, "the Roosevelt Administration was so torn by its handling of the case that it adopted an entirely different procedure in 1945 to deal with two other German spies" (Fisher, 2003; 484). In 1944, the Nazis sent over two more saboteurs to the shores of Maine on November 29th. The goal of the spies was to purchase a short-wave radio and to send intelligence via the radio back to German officials. The FBI detained the men toward the end of December that same year (Fisher, 494). On January 12, 1945, the president issued a military order setting up a military commission to try the alleged spies but did not name the members of the commission or lawyers for the defense or prosecution, leaving this task to the army generals. Furthermore, review of the trial record would not go to Roosevelt, as it had during the first case of the Nazi saboteurs. Instead, the case would be reviewed by the judge advocate general's office (Fisher, 2003; 495). Despite claims that the change of procedure for the second military commission of German spies was an indication that the Roosevelt Administration had seen the error of its ways, the Bush Administration used the World War II precedent of *ex parte Quirin* as justification for the military commissions that the government established via an Executive Order in November 2001, as discussed in the following section.

21. Furthermore, lawyers for Yamashita also argued he was protected under the Third Geneva Convention. Under Article 63, prisoners facing charges are to be tried using the same procedures as would be used on members of the detaining power's army. The Court held that this Article referred to crimes committed as a Prisoner of

War and Yamashita was being tried for war crimes committed during armed hostilities while he was commanding Japanese forces.

22. Two other cases, *Homma v. Patterson*, 327 U.S. 759; 1946 and *Homma v. Styer*, 66 U.S. 515; 1946 saw the Court refuse cert based on their decision in *In re Yamashita*. Murphy dissented on the basis that lives were being taken without due process.

23. Hughes, Charles Evans "War Powers Under the Constitution", 42 *American Bar Association* N. Rep. 232, 238; 1912.

24. Murphy's *Duncan* concurrence addresses the constitutional claims. Murphy states that "the swift trial and punishment which the military desires is precisely what the Bill of Rights outlaws . . . It is our duty, as well as that of the military, to make sure that such rights are respected whenever possible."

25. It is important to distinguish detainees as unlawful combatants in contrast to lawful ones because lawful combatants cannot be charged with taking part in an armed conflict unless they are in violation of international law. Furthermore, being classified as an unlawful combatant means the fighter is not characterized as a member of a country's official army. When a fighter is not a part of an army, the individual is only entitled to prisoner of war benefits if certain conditions are fulfilled, which are detailed in Article 4(a)(2) of the Third Geneva Convention. The fighter needs to be "(a) . . . commanded by a person responsible for his subordinates; (b) That of having a fixed distinctive sign recognizable at a distance; (c) That of carrying arms openly; (d) That of conducting their operations in accordance with the laws and customs of war" (The Third Geneva Convention is available online at http://www.unhchr.ch/html/menu3/b/91.htm (August 23, 2007). According to the Bush Administration, al Qaeda members fighting in Afghanistan failed to satisfy these conditions. While the legal status of detainees remained uncertain, how one became classified as an enemy combatant also remained uncertain. Then Solicitor General Theodore Olson argued that no established guidelines could be followed for determining the classification of prisoners. Olson explained that "[t]here will be judgments and instincts and evaluations and implementations that have to be made by the executive that are probably going to be different from day to day, depending on the circumstances (Olsen's comment was in an interview he gave to Charles Lane of the Washington Post. The story appeared in *The Post* on December 1, 2002, http://www.washingtonpost.com/ac2/wp-dyn?pagename=article&contentId=A58308-2002Nov30¬Found=true (July 6, 2007). The Bush Administration wanted to avoid making a choice between declaring detainees as prisoners of war or as criminals, thus requiring the government to charge or release those in custody.

26. The District Court in held that Rumsfeld was the proper respondent, having jurisdiction over Padilla and ruled on the merits of the case. The court found in favor of the Bush Administration's claims that the president has the authority to detain American citizens captured on American soil as enemy combatants. The authority was said to come from the *Authorization for the Use of Military Force* (AUMF), passed by Congress on September 18, 2001. The AUMF allows the president to:

> use all necessary and appropriate force against those nations, organizations, or persons he determines planned, authorized, committed, or aided the terrorist attacks that occurred on September 11, 2001, or harbored such organizations or persons, in order to prevent any

future acts of international terrorism against the United States by such nations, organizations or persons. http://thomas.loc.gov/cgi-bin/query/z?c107:S.J.RES.23.ENR (August 23, 2007).

The District Court also considered the president's role as commander-in-chief to act accordingly during ongoing armed conflicts as authorization to detain Padilla. The Court of Appeals for the Second Circuit reversed the District Court decision (*Padilla v. Rumsfeld*, 352 F. 3d 695; 2003), using the separation of powers framework, on the basis that the Non-Detention Act of Congress required clear authorization from the legislative branch of government before American citizens could be detained by the military and that the AUMF was not clear enough authorization.

27. The case was reheard by the District Court and a decision in favor of Padilla was delivered. At the Circuit Court level, on September 9, 2005, the 4th U.S. Circuit Court of Appeals held that the Bush Administration had the authority to detain Padilla without pressing charges as Congress authorized such detentions with the AUMF.

28. http://www.cnn.com/2005/LAW/11/22/padilla.case/index.html. Last accessed July 6, 2007.

29. Jackman and Eggen, "Combatants lack rights, US argues. *Washington Post*, June 20, 2002 http://why-war.com/news/2002/06/20/combatan.html (July 6, 2007).

30. The government's brief is available online at: http://www.usdoj.gov/osg/briefs/2003/3mer/2mer/2003-6996.mer.aa.pdf (July 6, 2007).

31. Justice Thomas in his *Hamdi* dissent agreed entirely with the position of the government and would have required no additional protections of due process for detainees.

32. The Department of Defense set up a Combatant Status Review Tribunal after the *Rasul* decision to give foreign citizens an avenue to contest their designation as an 'enemy combatant.' The detainees did not have access to lawyers for these proceedings but rather received the assistance of assigned military officers as their representatives. The government used the passage in *Hamdi* that speaks to evidence that may be admissible on behalf of the government as their argument for satisfying the requirements of due process.

33. After close to three years of solitary confinement, *Hamdi* was released and deported to Saudi Arabia on October 11, 2004. Hamdi agreed to renounce his American citizenship as well as not to sue the government over his detainment in exchange for his release. The government released Hamdi stating that "considerations of United States national security did not require his continued detention (Moeckli, 2005; 93).

34. After *Rasul*, on December 30, 2005, President Bush signed into law the *Detainee Treatment Act*, an amendment to the *Department of Defense Appropriations Act*, which stripped federal courts jurisdiction to hear challenges to the legality of the detentions of detainees at Guantanamo Bay.

35. http://www.whitehouse.gov/news/releases/2001/11/20011113-27.html (August 23, 2007).

36. While the *Hamdan* decision does take into consideration the applicability of the Geneva Conventions to the detainees in Guantanamo Bay, the Court still rebuked the commissions based primarily on their lack of statutory authorization

from Congress. In its dismissal of the 1929 Geneva Convention, in a footnote, the *Eisentrager* Court held that:

> We are not holding that these prisoners have no right which the military authorities are bound to respect. The United States, by the Geneva Convention of July 27, 1929, 47 Stat. 2021, concluded with forty-six other countries, including the German Reich, an agreement upon the treatment to be accorded captives. These prisoners claim to be and are entitled to its protection. It is, however, the obvious scheme of the Agreement that responsibility for observance and enforcement of these rights is upon political and military authorities. Rights of alien enemies are vindicated under it only through protests and intervention of protecting powers as the rights of our citizens against foreign governments are vindicated only by presidential intervention (*Eisentrager*, as cited by Stevens in *Hamdan*).

The Government argued that since Hamdan was captured as an al Qaeda belligerent and since al Qaeda is a non-state actor and not a "High contracting party" to the Geneva Conventions, the Conventions do not apply to the circumstance in question. The Court decided not to address this issue because Common Article 3 of the Geneva Conventions applies to all fighters whether or not they are lawful. Common Article 3 appears in all four Conventions and provides that when conflict breaks out "in the territory of one of the High Contracting Parties, each Party to the conflict shall be bound to apply, as a minimum, certain provisions protecting, persons taking no active part in the hostilities, including members of armed forces who have laid down their arms and those placed *hors de combat* by . . . detention" (Stevens' *Hamdan* opinion, quoting the Common Article 3, emphasis in original). One of the provisions in question requires those detainees to be sentenced in a court of law that is "regularly constituted," which is a requirement that military commissions cannot fulfill since they are rarely constituted.

37. Jack Balkin, "*Hamdan* as a Democracy-Forcing Decision", *Balkinization*, June 29, 2006. http://balkin.blogspot.com/2006/06/hamdan-as-democracy-forcing-decision.html (July 9, 2007).

38. The *Military Commissions Act* of 2006 amended the *Habeas Corpus Act*, s 2241(e) to read:

(1) No court, justice, or judge shall have jurisdiction to hear or consider an application for a writ of habeas corpus filed by or on behalf of an alien detained by the United States who has been an enemy combatant or is awaiting such determination.

(2) Except as provided in [section 1005(e)(2) and (e)(3) of the *DTA*], no court, justice, or judge shall have jurisdiction to hear or consider any other aspect of the United States or its agents relating to any aspect of the detention, transfer, treatment, trial, or conditions of confinement of an alien who is or was determined by the United States to have been properly detained as an enemy combatant or is awaiting such determination.

The *Military Commissions Act* applies to all cases pending on or after the date the Act was enacted, thus overruling *Rasul* which held that detainees had a statutory right to the writ of habeas corpus and *Hamdan* which stated that the *Detainee Treatment Act* of 2005 (written in response to *Rasul*) did not take away from the courts' jurisdiction to hear pending habeas cases.

Chapter 4

Warrantless Electronic Surveillance

Intelligence gathering has been an important strategic component to maintaining the national security of the United States since the colonies fought for independence. The U.S. Army Basic Field Manuel (Vol. X, 1938) cites Chief Justice John Marshall saying that "[a] general must be governed by his intelligence and must regulate his measures by his information. It is his duty to obtain correct information." During the Revolutionary War, General George Washington stole British mail and received reports from agents about British military strength and strategy (Jeffreys-Jones, 2002; 13). In 1790, Congress authorized a fund to conduct secret intelligence operations to be spent at President Washington's discretion (Jeffreys-Jones, 11–23).

The Bush administration was not the first to get involved with warrantless electronic surveillance. As far back as President Lincoln, warrantless electronic surveillance was used to obtain intelligence concerning potential threats to the nation, with his decision to wiretap telegraph wires during the Civil War (O'Toole, 1988; 498). Electronic surveillance was used during the Spanish-American War (Bidwell, 1986; 62), and the practice continued under President Wilson during World War I (Exec. Order No. 2604, April 28, 1917). During World War II, President Roosevelt's Executive Order No. 8985 called for the electronic surveillance of any person suspected of spying against the United States, including American citizens (Dash, 1971; 23). The practice continued during the Vietnam War, and was continued by the Bush administration in its fight against terrorism. Even President Obama has pushed for the renewal of provisions from the Patriot Act, due to expire at the end of 2009, which makes it easier for the government to spy on American citizens.[1]

The power of gathering foreign intelligence is not an enumerated power of Congress articulated in Article I of the Constitution, nor is it listed among the

Executive's powers in Article II. Yet, despite its omission, it is unlikely that the framers intended for the individual states to handle foreign intelligence collection, denying authority to the federal government altogether (Bazan and Elsea, 2006; 3). As such, and like many areas of constitutional dispute, the federal courts have to decide controversies that arise as a result of warrantless electronic surveillance through constitutional and legislative interpretation which fall into the zone of twilight of the war powers, as highlighted in Justice Jackson's concurring opinion in *Youngstown Sheet & Tube v. Sawyer,* 343 U.S. 579; 1952. In these situations, the president "can only rely upon his own independent powers, but there is a zone of twilight in which he and Congress may have concurrent authority." Also, if there is a lack of action on the part of Congress, this may "invite" the Executive to act. The courts have typically allowed the president to act in the absence of congressional legislation, within the second prong of Jackson's framework. This is only the case, however, until Congress has passed legislation, at which point the courts look for first prong cooperation amongst the branches.

In contrast to the military detention cases where the Constitution details which branch of government can institute judicial tribunals and where the courts repeatedly look for congressional authorization to suspend the writ of habeas corpus, it is less clear which branch can act in what circumstances concerning warrantless wiretapping. However, in both issue areas, the courts use similar rationales in their reasoning. Like the military detention cases, the federal courts place an emphasis on the two elected branches of government to participate in some sort of a dialogue with one another, sharing authority in the domain of the war powers. To recap, Jackson argues that "[w]hen the President acts pursuant to an express or implied authorization of Congress, his authority is at its maximum." This is the case because such actions have the full sanction of the national government behind them. If the president is not working with Congress and does not find itself in the shared powers of the second prong's zone of twilight, then the president may be working alone in prong-III territory, contrary to the will of Congress. In the third prong of Jackson's framework the courts are to "scrutinize with caution" the actions of the Executive. In such cases, the Executive acts in contrast to the explicit or implicit wishes of Congress and must retain constitutional authority from the text of the Constitution itself for its actions to be legal.

Warrantless electronic surveillance raises several constitutional issues that predominantly pertain to the Fourth Amendment.[2] Because the Supreme Court has yet to make a definitive ruling on the matter, it remains unclear whether the Executive possesses inherent authority to use warrantless electronic surveillance in regard to foreign affairs. When there is a perceived risk to national security, the president argues that warrantless electronic surveillance is necessary. For

Congress and the lower federal courts, this issue was cleared up with the passage of the *Foreign Intelligence Surveillance Act* (FISA) in 1978. FISA requires the Executive obtain a warrant to collect foreign intelligence information of a foreign power or an agent of a foreign power when one party is in the United States. While the history of electronic surveillance is long and rich, it is worth noting how congressional action changes the powers of the Executive through interpretation of legislation by the federal courts. Incidentally, warrantless electronic surveillance is also a good example of Jackson's vision of the war powers being played out in one issue—area over time.

This chapter shows that Fourth Amendment rights are protected with the federal courts balancing act between the needs of security and the protection of liberty by using a separation of powers framework when adjudicating such cases, rather than using rights-based language. When the war powers are in play or when the Executive cites national security concerns for its use of warrantless electronic surveillance, the federal courts place emphasis on the prior role of Congress in regulating the issue. The courts defer to the decisions of Congress if they indeed have acted, allowing the Executive to act when Congress has not. What this means is that the federal courts will interpret congressionally enacted statutes before interpreting the appropriate clauses of the text of the Constitution when deciding the proper authority of the Executive. This emphasis on congressional approval of executive actions by the federal courts shows a consistency in regard to how justices decide warrantless wiretapping cases.

The chapter proceeds as follows. First, I briefly outline the evolution of the Fourth Amendment in front of the federal courts. I then examine how the issue of warrantless electronic surveillance evolved in front of the courts and in Congress. Finally, I will offer an explanation as to why issues pertaining to the recent National Security Agency Terrorist Surveillance Program will be decided based on statutory authorization and whether or not the program is contrary to existing legislation. It should be noted that a brief detailing of the history of warrantless electronic surveillance in front of the Judiciary, in Congress and implemented by the Executive, shows how the elected branches of government are expected to work together when making national security policy.

INTERPRETING THE FOURTH AMENDMENT

The inclusion of the Fourth Amendment in the Bill of Rights "was a direct response to the British authorities use of 'general warrants' to conduct broad searches of the rebellious colonists" (Darmer, 2004; 76). Proponents of the

Bill of Rights regarded privacy of the home as an important right to protect. The Fourth Amendment provides:

> The right of the people to be secure in their persons, houses, papers, and effects, against unreasonable searches and seizures, shall not be violated, and no Warrants shall issue, but upon probable cause, supported by Oath or affirmation, and particularly describing the place to be searched, and the persons or things to be seized.

The Fourth Amendment's right to privacy was recognized as early as 1886 in *Boyd v. United States,* 116 U.S. 616. The Supreme Court held that "[i]t is not the breaking of (a man's) doors, and the rummaging of his drawers, that constitutes the essence of the offence; but it is the invasion of his indefeasible right of personal security, personal liberty and private property." The federal courts have long maintained that a part of that liberty and privacy is not having one's property subject to a search without a warrant based on probable cause, as outlined in the text of the Amendment.

It was in 1914 that the exclusionary rule was developed. In *Weeks v. United States,* 232 U.S. 383, the Court held that when a man's home was unreasonably searched without a warrant, anything taken as evidence would be inadmissible in a court of law. Justice William Day held that "If letters and private documents can thus be seized and held and used in evidence against a citizen accused of an offense, the protection of the 4th Amendment, declaring his right to be secure against such searches and seizures, is of no value, and, so far as those thus placed are concerned, might as well be stricken from the Constitution." Six years later, in 1920, the Court, referring to *Weeks,* held that it was unlawful for authorities to go to a company and seize documents while the owners were being held in custody (*Silverthorne Lumber Comp. v. United States,* 251 U.S. 385). To rule in any other fashion, Justice Oliver Wendell Holmes stated, "reduces the Fourth Amendment to a form of words." A year later, Justice John Clark ruled similarly in *Gouled v. United States,* 255 U.S. 298; 1921. It was determined that an unreasonable search and seizure "does not necessarily involve the employment of force or coercion, but is committed when a representative of any branch or subdivision of the government, by stealth, through social acquaintance, or in the guise of a business call, gains entrance to the house or office of a person suspected of crime." This was the case regardless of whether the owner was present. The Court also held in 1921 that it was a violation of the Fourth Amendment for the police to tell the spouse of a suspect that they were present to search the house with no warrant. In *Amos v. United States,* 255 U.S. 313, Justice Clark, again writing for the Court, held that "[w]e need not consider whether it is possible for a wife, in the absence of her husband, thus to waive his constitutional rights, for it is perfectly clear that under the implied coercion here presented, no such waiver was intended or effected."

The actions of the officers in *Amos* demonstrate the importance of the protections offered by the Fourth Amendment. Justice Jackson explains in *Johnson v. United States,* 333 U.S. 10; 1948, that the Amendment was not to deny justice, but rather was to deny "zealous officers" the possibility of circumventing individual liberties in favor of collecting evidence. In this case, the Court decided that the Fourth Amendment was extended to sealed letters and could only be opened with a warrant. In 1948 the Court also decided *McDonald et. al. v. United States,* 355 U.S. 451. The evidence obtained against individuals charged with conducting an illegal lottery was obtained without a warrant. Authorities entered the room of the accused through the landlady's door. The government contented that the Fourth Amendment violation was in relation to the landlady's rights and not those of the accused. Similarly to Jackson's previously-held argument, the Court maintained it was "not dealing with formalities. The presence of a search warrant serves a high function. Absent some grave emergency, the Fourth Amendment has interposed a magistrate between the citizen and the police. This was done not to shield criminals nor to make the home a safe haven for illegal activities. It was done so that an objective mind might weigh the need to invade that privacy in order to enforce the law (Douglas' *McDonald* opinion).

The scope of the Fourth Amendment evolved to include conversations, however it was not until 1963 that the Court in *Wong Sun v. United States,* 371 U.S. 471; 1963, held that evidence obtained through overhearing a conversation was illegally obtained under the protections offered by the Fourth Amendment. The Court held that: "the exclusionary rule has traditionally barred from trial physical, tangible materials obtained either during or as a direct result of an unlawful invasion. . . . The Fourth Amendment may protect against the overhearing of verbal statements as well as against the more traditional seizure of 'papers and effects.'" While the Court will conclude that the Fourth Amendment protects people and not places (*Katz v. United States,* 389 U.S. 347; 1967), its protection is not absolute. Exemptions from the Fourth Amendment eluded to in the *McDonald* decision include using informants for surveillance purposes (*Hoffa v. United States,* 385 U.S. 293; 1966). Nor can a person assume a reasonable expectation of privacy when in public and can therefore be subjected to a physical search (*Fifth Avenue Peace Parade Committee v. Gray,* F. 2d 326; 1973). In *United States v. Miller,* 425 U.S. 435; 1976, the Court finds that the government is not in violation of the Fourth Amendment when it inspects a defendant's bank records. Because the records are property of the bank, a client cannot reasonably expect privacy in regard to business transactions. The same principle is extended to bank records in cases pertaining to national security (*Jabara v. Kelley et. al.*, 476 F. Supp. 561; 1979).

The above examples are situations where the Fourth Amendment is flat-out inapplicable. The federal courts have also recognized a small number of exceptions to the warrant requirement under the Fourth Amendment where under normal circumstances a warrant would be required. Each exception maintains a "common theoretical foundation—in each there is the element of a significant probability that the subject of the warrantless search is likely to do undesirable or unacceptable action if the search were delayed until a warrant could be obtained" (Kenny, 1972; 898).[3] Cases of national security, concerning domestic and foreign threats alike, at one time fell under this exception. The government argued if it was necessary to go to a judge for "prior authorization to conduct a national security wiretap, there [would be] a danger of a leak concerning either the existence of the wiretap or the information presented to the judge in order to secure the warrant" (Kenny, 899). Lives of informants and undercover agents could be jeopardized as a result (Kenny, 899). In *United States v. United States District Court,* 407 U.S. 297; 1972 (*Keith*), the Supreme Court argues that "individual freedoms will best be preserved through a separation of powers and division of functions among the different branches and levels of government." This decision stays true to the argument that congressional-executive relations and partnerships are key to deciphering how the federal courts decide war powers cases where individual liberties are being limited by the Executive. When national security cases are cited as cause for surveillance, the federal courts look to see if Congress has legislated on the issue, instead of basing decisions on the constitutional guarantee protecting individuals against unreasonable warrantless searches and seizures.

EXECUTIVE WARRANTLESS WIRETAPPING IN FRONT OF THE COURTS AND IN CONGRESS

Electronic wiretapping went unregulated by the government from the Civil War to World War I. President Wilson ordered the Federal Bureau of Investigation (FBI) to wiretap and keep files on American citizens suspected of aiding the enemy. The federal government controlled the telecommunications system and feared that wiretapping would be used against the state in ways detrimental to national security. As a result, Congress banned all wiretapping near the end of the war. Resulting in the first federal legislation concerned with wiretapping, Congress passed that "whoever . . . shall, without authority and without the knowledge and consent of the other users . . . tap any telegraph or telephone line" is guilty of committing a federal offense.[4]

After World War I, the absolute prohibition of wiretapping expired when the government no longer controlled the telephone system. The practice of wiretapping was revived and used in Attorney General Mitchell Palmer's raids against communism. Word got out that Wilson wiretapped law-abiding American citizens and Attorney General Harlon Fiske Stone banned wiretapping in 1924, arguing "a secret police may become a menace to free government and free institutions because it carries with it the possibility of abuses of power which are not always quickly understood" (Donnelly, 1954; 800).

In 1928, the issue of warrantless electronic surveillance found itself in front of the Supreme Court for the first time in *Olmstead v. United States,* 277 U.S. 438. Reaffirming the lower court decision (*Olmstead v. United States,* 19F.2d 842; 1927), in a 5-4 decision, the Court maintained no constitutional violation resulted from evidence being received by warrantless wiretapping being introduced into court against a criminal defendant. Violations of the Fourth Amendment had to be tangible with an actual physical invasion. Chief Justice William Howard Taft held: "that one who installs in his house a telephone instrument with connecting wires intends to project his voice to those quite outside, and that the wires beyond his house and messages while passing over them are not within the protection of the Fourth Amendment." The inapplicability of the Fourth Amendment is key to the decision. However, it is Taft's justification that is most interesting of all. Taft held even a liberal interpretation of the Fourth Amendment did not justify equating telephone conversations as property in the same sense as "persons, houses, papers, and effects." Taft did add, however, that if Congress disagreed with his assessment, "the policy of protecting the secrecy of telephone messages by making them . . . inadmissible as evidence in federal criminal trials, may be adopted" by the legislature. Taft believed the Court could not "without the sanction of Congressional enactment, subscribe to the suggestion that the courts have a discretion to exclude evidence, the admission of which is not unconstitutional because unethically secured."

In a now famous dissent, Justice Holmes stated that wiretapping was "dirty business" and that the "Government ought not to use evidence obtained . . . by a criminal act." Yet Holmes was unwilling to consider the constitutional question of the applicability of the Fourth Amendment. Justice Louis Brandeis, however, did not shy away from the issue stating in his dissent that "[w]hen the Fourth and Fifth Amendments were adopted, 'the form that evil had theretofore taken' had been necessarily simple. Force and violence were then the only means known to man by which a Government could directly effect self-incrimination. . . . Subtler and more far-reaching means of invading privacy have become available to the Government." Brandeis' points out that the Constitution evolves and must be expounded as Chief Justice Marshall reasoned more than a century earlier in *McCulloch v. Maryland,* 17 U.S. 316; 1819.

Brandeis highlighted how the Court repeatedly sustained new powers of Congress over a variety of issues and cited the *Weeks* case as an example showing that part of expounding the Constitution was placing limits on the government. Brandeis notes that new inventions made the Fourth Amendment applicable to new situations. This, however, was something the Court was not ready to recognize. Though Holmes and Brandeis would not wait for Congress to act to prohibit warrantless electronic surveillance, the federal courts' future path of analysis followed Taft's suggestion of creating a dependence on congressional legislation before taking away from the Executive the ability to act. This mode of analysis is exemplified in Justice Jackson's second prong of the *Youngstown* framework, where non-action on the part of Congress may invite the president to act when the Constitution is silent on an issue, instead of using rights-based language Brandeis calls for in his dissent.[5]

After the *Olmstead* decision, Congress attempted to pass several bills designed to prohibit wiretapping, taking up the Court's offer to legislate on the issue. These efforts failed, and Attorney General William Mitchell reversed the 1924 ban, and announced that wiretapping would be approved when it was requested by the director of the bureau that sought it (Donnelly, 1954; 800). Congress finally was able to pass the *Federal Communications Act* in 1934. Section 605 made it illegal for any "person not being authorized by the sender [to] intercept any communication and divulge or publish the existence, contents, substance . . . of such intercepted communication to any person." The interpretation of section 605 would become a matter of debate for executive officials and the federal courts for years to come. Despite the law, the Attorney General Mitchell's Office still maintained that warrantless electronic surveillance by federal agents was legal in criminal cases of "extreme importance" (Donnelly, 800).

The government's position was that intercepting messages was not outlawed in the language of the *Federal Communications Act.* While divulging, in other words releasing, the contents of intercepted messages by unauthorized people was prohibited, this did not include federal agents who were working in the best interest of the State. The government's analysis of section 605 maintained that since the language of the Act stated "divulge and publish," both must occur before there was an infraction of the statute. Since the federal government is an entity as it acts as one, there could be no divulgence of information when information received from a wiretap was passed from one agent to superiors in the government (Donnelly, 801).[6]

Three years after the *Federal Communications Act* was passed, the proper interpretation of section 605 came before the Supreme Court in *Nardone v. United States,* 302 U.S. 379; 1937. Justice Owen Roberts, writing for the Court, held that "Congress may have thought it less important that some offenders should go unwhipped of justice than that officers should resort to methods deemed inconsistent with the ethical standards and destructive of personal liberty," reversing the lower court opinion which interpreted the *Federal Communications Act* to be "silent as to the admissibility of messages intercepted contrary to its provisions" and as a result would have allowed the evidence in court using *Olmstead* as precedent (*United States v. Nardone,* 90 F. 2d 630; 1937). The decision of both the lower and Supreme Court did not depend on the language of the Fourth Amendment. In fact, the Supreme Court, at this point, does not extend the Fourth Amendment to protect conversations. What the Court does decide is that Congress made it illegal to wiretap individuals and this included for criminal investigations. The law of Congress conferred on citizens a statutory right of privacy, equated with the constitutional right of privacy conferred by the Fourth Amendment.

Two years later, the Supreme Court extended the application of section 605 to ban not only the evidence received from the wiretap itself, but also evidence obtained from the leads received from wiretapping suspects (*Nardone v. United States,* 308 U.S. 338; 1939), again overruling the lower court decision that made its ruling based on an interpretation of the *Federal Communications Act* allowing into court whatever was not explicitly denied in the Act (*United States v. Nardone,* 106 F. 2d 41; 1939). The rationale of the Supreme Court in reversing was that if the scope of section 605 was reduced to the exact words heard through the illegal interceptions, "allowing these interceptions every derivative use that they may serve . . . would largely stultify the policy which compelled our decision in *Nardone v. United States*" (Frankfurter's *Nardone II* opinion). At the same time, the Court upheld further restrictions on the use of wiretapping for criminal investigations, deciding that intrastate as well as interstate wiretapping of telecommunications was banned by the language of section 605 (*Weiss v. United States,* 308 U.S. 321; 1939). At the same time, the Court would limit the interpretation of section 605, holding it to be inapplicable to wiretapped conversations where one party agreed to the surveillance (*United States v. Polakoff,* 112 F.2d 888; 2d Cir. 1940). The federal courts reaffirmed this principle on numerous occasions over the next two decades culminating with *Rathburn v. United States,* 355 U.S. 107; 1957, at the Supreme-Court level. Messages were not intercepted when one party willfully handed over the taped conversations.[7]

The federal courts' prohibition on warrantless electronic surveillance was based on statute. By time the United States was preparing to enter World War

II, members of Congress attempted to pass legislation that was in line with the position of the Executive, which if successful may have changed the future federal courts decisions. Emanuel Celler, a Democratic member of Congress from New York, introduced a bill in 1940 to amend section 605 of the 1934 Act. Celler's bill would permit wiretapping approved by the attorney general in cases "involving interference or attempts to interfere with the national defense by sabotage, espionage, conspiracy, violation of the neutrality laws or 'in any other manner'" (Theoharis and Meyer, 757). The bill did not pass Congress, though Celler received the support of then Attorney General Robert Jackson. In a letter to Celler, Jackson stated that:

> In a limited class of cases, such as kidnapping, extortion, and racketeering, where the telephone is the usual means of conveying threats and information, it is the opinion of the present Attorney General as it was of Attorney General Mitchell that wiretapping should be authorized under some appropriate safeguard. Under the existing state of the law and decisions, this cannot be done unless the Congress sees fit to modify the existing statutes (Theoharis and Meyer, 758).

Jackson's vision as attorney general was consistent with his vision of congressional-executive relations in *Youngstown,* calling for Congress to act in giving the Executive the power it lacked on its own to better protect the State.

As attorney general, Jackson's position was that wiretapping suspects would not continue without congressional action sanctioning the practice. President Roosevelt intervened and ordered Jackson's position to be reversed, allowing federal officials to wiretap so long as no divulgence of information took place. Roosevelt's directive of May 21, 1940 was despite the *Nardone* decisions. The argument, for the first time, was being made by the Executive that wiretapping was essential to the national security of the country.[8]

Attempts continued to secure congressional authorization for conducting warrantless electronic surveillance under certain limited circumstances without a warrant. Jackson, in support of another bill submitted by Celler, wrote to the House Judiciary Committee on March 19, 1941. Ultimately unsuccessful, Jackson justified the proposed legislation because "to use evidence obtained by wiretapping for the protection of society against criminals often requires that it be divulged in open court. It is this divulging in law enforcement that court decisions hold to violate the statute . . ."[9] A month earlier Jackson defended wiretapping in certain circumstances as those President Roosevelt pinpointed as essential for the defense of the nation. In a 1941 statement, and in echoing the president, Jackson stated that "[the] monitoring of telephone communications is essential in connection with investigations of foreign spy rings. It is equally necessary for the purpose of solving such crimes as kidnapping and extortion. In the interest of national defense . . . the interception of communications should in limited degree be permitted to Federal law enforcement officers."[10]

Shortly after the attack on Pearl Harbor, December 7, 1941, President Roosevelt set up an office for conducting warrantless surveillance, in accordance with the *War Powers Act* of 1941. This office allowed the government access to "communications by mail, cable, radio, or other means of transmission passing between the United States and any foreign country" (Gonzales, 2006; 16).

With the United States now officially involved in the war, Celler again attempted to get Congress to legalize warrantless wiretapping under certain conditions. The 1942 effort differed from the 1940 campaign, with the more recent bill providing for section 605 of the *Communications Act* to be waived in the "interest of prosecution of the war" (Theoharis & Meyer, 760). Again, Celler was unsuccessful. A House Resolution in 1942 passed the House but died in the Senate. The proposed Resolution would have allowed the FBI and intelligence sections of the Armed Forces to authorize warrantless wiretaps in investigations that involved "suspected sabotage, treason, seditious conspiracy, espionage and violations of the neutrality laws." These attempts to pass legislation to authorize warrantless surveillance were ultimately unsuccessful, but they were indicative of the mood of parts of Congress to want to work with the Executive in advancing the nation's war efforts.

It is reasonable to conclude that opposition to wiretapping was at least weakened "under the stress" of the Second World War (Donnelly, 807). During that time, two cases went through the federal courts that lent support to the Executive's interpretation of the 1934 statute. Limiting the interpretation of section 605, in *Goldstein v. United States,* 316 U.S. 114; 1941, the Court, in affirming the lower court decision, held that third-party individuals had no legal standing to object to evidence submitted in court if it was obtained indirectly by electronic surveillance. Justice Roberts held that "even though the use made of the communications . . . to induce the parties to them to testify was . . . a violation of the statute, this would not render the testimony so procured inadmissible against a person not a party to the message" (Roberts' *Goldstein* opinion). The lower court was more direct in regard to the separation of powers recognizing that "an interest" of the petitioner was in fact invaded but not an interest the *law* recognized (emphasis added) (*United States v. Goldstein,* 120 F. 2d 485; 1941).

The Supreme Court also defined what interception meant according to section 605 of the Act. When a conspirator attempted to violate the *Bankruptcy Act,* both the lower and Supreme Court made rulings based on interpreting section 605 of the Act. The lower court held that "no communication by wire or radio was intercepted to make applicable the provision of section 605 of the *Communications Act,*" in *United States v. Goldman,* 118 F. 2d 310; 1941. In affirming that ruling, Justice Roberts, again writing for the Court, held, in *Goldman v. United States,* 316 U.S. 129; 1942, that "[w]ords spoken in a room in the presence of another into a telephone receiver do not constitute a communication by wire within the meaning of the section . . . [Interception] indicates the taking or seizure by the way or before arrival at the destined place." In both cases, it was held that government agents were not in violation of section 605. Fourth Amendment considerations did not apply, citing *Olmstead* as precedent. Two Justices in the *Goldman* case, Frankfurter and Stone, were inclined to overturn *Olmstead,* but only if the other members of the Court were willing to do so.

After the war, the scope of the Executive's authority continued to reach the federal courts. Judith Coplon, a former employee of the Justice Department was indicted on two counts of attempting to defraud the government and for attempting to deliver information to a foreign agent. The FBI intercepted Coplon's telephone conversations. When the evidence was challenged, a hearing was held to ensure no evidence admitted resulted from evidence gained from the wiretapped phone conversations. Some of the conversations were withheld from Coplon due to national security considerations. In *United States v. Coplon,* 185 F. 2d. 629; 1950, District Judge Ryan pointed out that section 605 was "still the law; it has not been repealed or modified, it contains no exemptions . . . The fact these interceptions were carried on under written authorization of the Attorney General imparts no sanctity to them; they remain unlawful and prohibited," under the Act of Congress.

In response to the *Coplon* decision, then Attorney General Tom Clark wrote to President Truman, quoting FDR's presidential directive of 1940. Clark wanted the government to maintain the policy of using wiretaps, stating FDR's directive "was followed by Attorneys General Jackson and Biddle, and is being followed currently in this Department . . . It seems to me imperative to use [wire taping] in cases vitally affecting the domestic security, or where human life is in jeopardy" (as quoted in Rogers; 1954, 795). Clark even lobbied for legislation that would support the government's position, submitting an internal security bill to Congress. Clark argued, "[i]t seems incongruous that existing law should protect our enemies and hamper our protectors." The next attorney general, Howard McGrath also submitted legislation for consideration. In lobbying for his bill, McGrath argued that the Justice Department was being hampered "in fulfilling its statutory duty of prosecuting those who violate the Federal laws relating to national defense and security because of the failure of Congress to enact legislation of this type" (Rogers, 796). In the meantime, McGrath refused to use wiretaps without the proper statutory backing required (McNabb, 2006; 2). This position was again reversed by Herbert Brownell, who became attorney general in 1953. Brownell argued that if it was in the national interest to do so, the FBI was entitled to use wiretapping devices with or without the legislative support of Congress.

Brownell's position resulted in section 605's continued defiance by the federal government. While the Justice Department resorted to warrantless wiretapping before World War II for national security purposes, it was not until after the war when government officials openly admitted their actions were conducted in the name of national security. In 1951, 1953, 1954, 1958, and 1959, a number of bills were introduced in Congress that, if passed both houses would have legalized warrantless electronic surveillance for matters of national security (Rogers, 763).

By the early 1960s, congressional hearings disclosed that warrantless electronic surveillance was used by the federal government regularly in dozens of cases, domestic in nature, and not pertaining to national security concerns. Because the government interpreted the *Nardone* cases to refer only to divulging information for criminal prosecutions, national security wiretaps for gathering intelligence information continued. In fact, between 1940 and 1960, the Justice Department conducted 6,769 wiretaps (Eggert, 1983; 621). After this exposure, President Johnson, in 1965, ordered all federal agencies to cease wiretapping, except in cases dealing with national security concerns. Another bill concerning electronic surveillance was introduced in 1967, but failed to pass Congress. The intention of the proposed piece of legislation was to prohibit intercepting or divulging any wire communication or the use of any electronic surveillance device sold in interstate commerce, with an exception again for national security cases. *Berger v. New York,* 388 U.S. 41; 1967, was decided as this failed bill attempt was being considered in both houses of Congress. The petitioner was charged with bribing a public official. Evidence of the crime was secured through wiretapping. A court order was received for the wiretap for a period of 60 days. The 60 days was the maximum under the New York state law. The warrant was obtained on the word of the attorney general that the search was reasonable. The Court held that the law did not allow for electronic surveillance without any belief or evidence that a crime was being or was about to be committed and therefore violated the Fourth Amendment because there was a lack of probable cause. Now a member of the Supreme Court, Tom Clark argued that probable cause only "exists where the facts and circumstances within the affiant's knowledge, and of which he has reasonably trustworthy information, are sufficient unto themselves to warrant a man of reasonable caution to believe that an offense has been or is being committed." An order authorizing the use of electronic devices required the same procedures to be followed as the use of conventional warrants.

Justice Byron White's dissenting opinion noted the proposed intention of Congress to leave the president's ability to protect the nation from attack out of the restrictions on wiretapping that the proposed Act being debated in Congress created. If the law passed, the Executive could "authorize wiretapping or eavesdropping 'to protect the Nation against actual or potential attack or other hostile acts of a foreign power or any other serious threat to the security of the United States, or to protect national security information against foreign intelligence activities'" (White's *Berger* dissent).

Between 1934 and 1968, only one legislative proposal on wiretapping passed Congress, but a litany of cases made their way through the federal courts. In each decision since its passage in 1934, the courts consistently decided cases based on the statutory regulations put in place by Congress. However, the Supreme Court briefly would extend the meaning of the Fourth to protect conversations if overheard as a result of eavesdropping (*Silverman v. United States,* 365 U.S. 505; 1961). Two years later in *Lopez v. United States,* 373 U.S. 427; 1963, the Court returned to its position of not extending the Fourth Amendment to new situations. Justice John Harlan argued that the Court "sustained instances of 'electronic eavesdropping' against constitutional challenge, when devices ha[d] been used to enable government agents to overhear conversations which would have been beyond the reach of the human ear." The Court reasoned that "the electronic device [was] not planted by an unlawful physical invasion of a constitutionally protected area." The government agent involved in the conversation wore an electronic recording device only to ensure the collection of the best evidence possible.

Near the end of the decade, the Court would decide a case that would forever alter the meaning of the Fourth Amendment, but would not end the debate over warrantless electronic surveillance in regard to national security. In reversing the lower court decision (*Katz v. United States,* 369 F. 2d 130; 1966) which held that the precedents *of Goldman* and *Olmstead* did not allow the court to extend the benefits of the Fourth Amendment, the Supreme Court, also ruling on the constitutional question itself, held for the first time that electronic surveillance was subject to the requirements of the Fourth Amendment. Writing for the Court, Justice Potter Stewart concluded that "[t]he Government's activities in electronically listening to and recording the petitioner's words violated the privacy upon which he justifiably relied while using the telephone booth and thus constituted a 'search and seizure' within the meaning of the Fourth Amendment." Warrantless electronic surveillance was within the meaning of the Fourth Amendment. Relying on *Berger,* Stewart held that when you pay the toll and shut the door of a phone booth, the person making the phone call expects privacy. To suggest a more narrow reading of the Constitution "is to ignore the vital role that the public telephone has come to play in private communications."

The *Katz* decision concluded that the Fourth Amendment was meant to protect "people," not just "places." However, the division between times of peace and times of emergency found itself within the rationale of the Court decision. Justice Stewart's footnote #23 states that "[w]hether safeguards other than prior authorization by a magistrate would satisfy the Fourth Amendment in a situation involving national security is a question not presented by this case." This created a loophole that would allow the government to argue the Fourth Amendment's warrant requirement to conduct electronic surveillance was not required in national security cases.

It was not until after the 1967 Supreme Court decision in *Katz v. United States,* 389 U.S. 347; that Congress was again able to legislate on the issue. A year after the *Katz* decision, Congress passed the *Omnibus Crime Control and Safe Streets Act* of 1968. Title III of the Act sets out procedures that were to be followed for obtaining judicial warrants to wiretap criminal investigations. The Act also notes the legislation was not meant to limit the constitutional power that the president may hold to conduct warrantless surveillance in defense of the nation in section 2511(3).[11] The courts did not treat section 2511(3) as a delegation of power to the Executive, but rather as an affirmation that the president may already have the ability to conduct warrantless electronic surveillance for national security purposes (Kenny, 1972; 889).[12]

Just two years after *Katz* was decided, and one year after Title III was passed, the Supreme Court held in *Alderman et. al. v. United States,* 394 U.S. 165; 1969, that "suppression of the product of a Fourth Amendment violation can be successfully urged only by those whose rights were violated by the search itself, not by those who are aggrieved solely by the introduction of damaging evidence. Coconspirators and codefendants have been accorded no special standing."

The petitioners were convicted of "conspiracy to transmit murderous threats in interstate commerce" (White's *Alderman* opinion). The Court rejected the petitioners' argument that they had a constitutional right for evidence against them to be excluded from court because it was illegally seized from another individual, unless Congress passed legislation banning such evidence from being admissible in criminal proceedings. It was up to Congress to extend the rights of the Fourth Amendment to include evidence obtained from a wiretap being used against persons who were not in any way connected to the wiretap in question. The Court did add, however, that if the surveillance was

Table 4.1. Reliance on Congressional Action for Warrantless Wiretapping of Criminal Investigations

	Court upheld executive action	Court struck down executive action
Congressional authorization	*Olmstead v. U.S.,* 1926 *Olmstead v. U. S.,* 1928 *U.S. v. Nardone I,* 1937 *U.S. v. Nardone II,* 1939 *U.S. v. Polakoff,* 1940 *U.S. v. Goldman,* 1941 *Goldstein v. U.S.,* 1941 *Goldman v. U.S.,* 1942 *U.S. v. Lewis,* 1950 *Billeci v. U.S.,* 1950 *U.S. v. Sullivan,* 1953 *U.S. v. Pierce,* 1954 *Flanders v. U.S.,* 1955 *U.S. v. Bookie,* 1956 *Rathburn v. U.S.,* 1957	*Katz v. U.S.,* 1967
No Congressional authorization/ contrary to the wishes of Congress		*Nardone v. U.S.,* 1937 *Nardone v. U.S.,* 1939 *Weiss v. U. S.,* 1939 *Berger v. New York,* 1948 *U. S. v. Coplon,* 1950 *Silverman v. U.S.,* 1961

unlawful, transcripts would be turned over to the individual to determine if evidence from the surveillance was determinative of the conviction.

Table 4.1 indicates that the federal courts have not found the Executive to have congressional authorization to conduct warrantless electronic surveillance. For the purposes of criminal investigations, there are a number of circumstances where section 605 of the *Federal Communications Act* of 1934 does not apply or does not address the issue in question. When these circumstances arose, since the Fourth Amendment was not controlling until 1967, the federal courts allowed executive actions to stand. They were not considered sanctioned by the Congress, but were not prohibited either.

In 1967, the federal courts answered the constitutional question on the merits in the *Katz* decision at the lower and Supreme Court levels. The Court of Appeals held that the Fourth Amendment was not applicable, while the Supreme Court reversed, extending the benefits of the Fourth Amendment's protections to circumstances surrounding warrantless electronic surveillance for the first time. Neither court based their decision on the statutory framework set up by Congress as had previously been done. After the *Katz* decision in 1967, it might be expected for all cases concerning warrantless electronic wiretapping to be adjudicated based on whether warrantless wiretapping is in violation of the Fourth Amendment. However, this did not occur when national security was the argued reason for the surveillance.

WARRANTLESS WIRETAPPING AFTER *KATZ* FOOTNOTE #23

The Nixon Administration maintained it held authority to issue warrantless wiretaps because the "government interest in preserving national security against domestic dangers justified an exception to the warrant requirement" (Quint, 1981; 18). The federal courts disagreed. In *United States v. Smith,* 321 F. Supp 424; 1971, phone calls were monitored without a warrant for national security purposes resulting in the conviction of unlawful possession of firearms. *Alderman* required that surveillance records be turned over to see if the conviction was based on evidence illegally obtained. The court, in quoting the First Amendment case of *Brandenburg v. Ohio,* 395 U.S. 444; 1969, held that unlike the area of foreign affairs, "in the area of domestic political activity the government can act only in limited ways." A warrant was required in the case of domestic security threats because there was no reason why government officials could not present evidence to an impartial judicial officer to obtain a legal warrant for the surveillance. Furthermore, "limitations which are artificial in the international sphere, are reasonable and proper when solely domestic subversion is involved" (Judge Furgerson's *Smith* opinion).

The same year as *Smith* was decided, the case of three defendants charged with conspiracy to bomb the CIA office in Michigan was heard before the district court. Judge Keith held that when it came to domestic warrantless surveillance in the name of national security "[a]n idea which seems to permeate much of the Government's argument is that a dissident domestic organization is akin to an unfriendly foreign power and must be dealt with in the same fashion. There is great danger in an argument of this nature for it strikes at the very constitutional privileges and immunities that are inherent in United States citizenship (Keith's opinion in *United States v. Sinclair,* 321 F. Supp. 1074; 1971). While the defendants were not agents of a foreign power, the Government argued the wiretaps were legal because they were used to "protect the nation from attempts of domestic organizations to attack and subvert the existing structure of the Government" (Pohlman, 2007; 19). However, the court reasoned that Fourth Amendment protections were all the more essential when the targets of government surveillance were those who disagreed politically with the governing Administration.

When the case was granted *certiorari* by the Supreme Court, the Court held that when it came to domestic security cases, there was no Fourth Amendment exemption to the judicial warrant requirement, but the Court framed the issue as a matter of the president circumventing the authority of Congress. Though the two branches of government shared power in this regard, Justice Lewis Powell argues in *United States v. United States District Court* (*Keith* case) that "[s]uccessive Presidents for more than one-quarter of a century have authorized such surveillance in varying degrees, without guidance from the Congress or a definitive decision from this Court. . . . Its resolution is a matter of national concern, requiring sensitivity both to the Government's right to protect itself from unlawful subversion and attack and to the citizen's right to be secure in his privacy against unreasonable Government intrusion."

The Court was adamant that Congress prohibited such activity and a warrant was therefore required. In fact, Powell explained that Title III was a "comprehensive attempt by Congress to promote more effective control of crime while protecting the privacy of individual thought and expression" (Powell's *Keith* opinion). Powell says that Congress did not delegate to the president any additional powers in Title III, it "simply left Presidential powers where it found them." It was up to the courts to decide the limits of presidential war powers in relation to those of Congress and in relation to the limits placed on the government as a whole by the Constitution. In offering evidence for this position, Powell quotes Senator Hart who stated that nothing in § 2511(3) defines or limits the power of the president in matters concerning national security, it "merely says that *if* the President has such power, then its exercise is in no way affected by Title III (emphasis added).[13] While the district court ruling was upheld, the Court adds the case did not require any comment on "the scope of the President's surveillance power with respect to the activities of foreign powers, within or without the country."

With the passage of Title III in 1968, Congress left wiretapping for national security purposes in the second prong of Justice Jackson's *Youngstown* separation of powers framework, neither granting nor denying authority to the Executive. Powell further suggests the procedures set up in Title III were not necessarily the standards required to be followed in domestic security cases. It was up to Congress to decide what "different policy and practical considerations from the surveillance of 'ordinary crime'" domestic national security cases required. When domestic security was at issue, "different standards may be compatible with the Fourth Amendment (Powell's *Keith* opinion). The issue of domestic warrantless electronic surveillance was thus settled with the *Keith* case. The role of the courts in coming to such a conclusion was legitimate as there was nothing to suggest the courts would be "insensitive to or uncomprehending of the issues involved in *domestic* security cases." Congress gave this role to the federal courts in sections 2561 (1) a & c of the Act.

After the *Keith* case, warrantless electronic surveillance for gathering foreign intelligence continued. Two observations are key. By and large cases before the federal courts have been decided during times of relative peace, but the powers in question are said to be in the context of war powers or for the importance of national security. Despite the peacetime decisions, when national security is claimed to be key, the separation of powers framework is looked to as guidance for determining the proper scope of executive authority to conduct warrantless electronic surveillance. That being the case, the federal courts have not shied away from making decisions on the legality of warrantless wiretapping for national security purposes on domestic groups. The Court cites that no extraordinary circumstances exist for the Executive to behave in a way that requires an exemption to the Fourth Amendment, as may be the case in regard to foreign intelligence gathering. Second, the Supreme Court has been extremely reluctant to make a ruling on warrantless electronic surveillance to obtain foreign intelligence and as a result the cases are at the District and Court of Appeals levels. Incidentally, Justice White's concurrence in *Keith* argues the case should have been decided on statutory grounds alone. White criticized the district and circuit courts for proceeding too quickly to the constitutional issues. These lower courts did not avert "to the time honored rule that courts should not abjure constitutional issues except where necessary to the decision of the case before them" (White's *Keith* concurrence).

Prior to and after *Keith,* the courts upheld executive authority to conduct warrantless electronic surveillance for the collection of foreign intelligence. This deference to the Executive was a result of the lack of legislation on the subject matter. In *United States v. Clay,* 430 F. 2d 165, 171 (5th Cir. 1970), after refusing to be inducted into the Armed Services, five conversations of Cassius Clay's were overheard by the FBI, though he was not the original target of the surveillance. The government admitted that four out of five conversations were illegal and transcripts were given to the petitioner. The fifth conversation, it was argued, was related to gathering foreign intelligence, was therefore legal, and would not be turned over to Clay.[14] Ainsworth states that "further judicial inquiry would be improper and should not occur. It would be intolerable that courts, without the relevant information, should review and perhaps nullify actions of the Executive taken on information properly held secret (Ainsworth citing *Chicago & Southern Airlines v. Waterman SS Corp.,* 333 U.S. 103; 1948). The same sentiments were expressed in *United States v. Enten et al.* 388 F. Supp. 97; 1971, when Judge Sirica held that "it is the Executive and not the Judiciary which alone possesses both the expertise and the factual background to assess the reasonableness of such a surveillance."

In *United States v. Brown,* 484 F.2d 418; 5th Cir.; 1973, a conviction of a firearm violation was upheld after a warrantless wiretap was authorized by the attorney general, citing national security for foreign intelligence purposes. Writing for the Fifth Circuit Court of Appeals, Judge Bell held that:

> As United States District Court teaches, in the area of domestic security, the President may not authorize electronic surveillance without some form of prior judicial approval. However, because of the President's constitutional duty to act for the United States in the field of foreign relations, and his inherent power to protect national security in the context of foreign affairs, we reaffirm . . . that the President may constitutionally authorize warrantless wiretaps for the purpose of gathering foreign intelligence (Judge Bell's *Brown* opinion).

Bell argues that inherent power in the domain of national security is "adverted to, although not conferred, by Congress in Title III of 1968."

Judge Adams comes to the same result as Judge Bell in *United States v. Butenko,* 494 F. 2d 593; 3rd Cir.; 1974. The court held that warrantless wiretapping of a suspected spy was "lawful, violating neither section 605 of the *Communications Act* nor the Fourth Amendment, if its primary purpose was to gather foreign intelligence information." Judge Adams shows that the legislative history of the Act includes "the absence of any indication that the legislators considered the possible effect of § 605 in the foreign affairs field." As such, the courts could "not lightly ascribe to Congress an intent that section 605 should reach electronic surveillance conducted by the President in furtherance of his foreign affairs responsibilities. This would seem to be far too important a subject to justify resort to unsupported assumptions" (Adams' *Butenko* opinion). The court also held that "[f]oreign security wiretaps are a recognized exception to the general warrant requirement and disclosure of wiretaps not involving illegal surveillance is within the trial court's discretion" (*United States v. Buck,* 548 F. 2d 871; 9th Cir.; 1977). In this case, an individual convicted of giving false information to acquire ammunition did not receive all the transcripts of illegally wiretapped conversations, as required by the *Alderman* decision. The withheld transcript was based on national security considerations made by the government. After an in-camera session, the court determined that the wiretap was related to national security and was therefore lawful.

The same year Congress passed the *Foreign Intelligence Surveillance Act* (FISA), the district court for the Eastern District of Virginia held that there is no Fourth Amendment requirement for the government to apply for a warrant to have a wiretap for foreign intelligence gathering purposes

(*United States v. Humphrey,* 456 F. Supp 51 (E.D. Va. 1978). Only when intelligence was gathered for criminal proceedings could the court grant the defendants' motion for the suppression of evidence. Otherwise, the court reasoned that because a foreign government had financial resources and technological advancements far surpassing those of the average individual or domestic group, warrantless electronic surveillance of foreign powers and their agents was reasonable. Judge Bryan, in expressing concerns over the role and legitimacy of the Judiciary in this regard, by pointed out that a "judicial officer can't evaluate the threat posed" by foreign powers. Furthermore, in *United States v. Truong Dinh Hung,* 629 F. 2d 908; 1982, the Fourth Circuit Court of Appeals held that placing a warrant requirement on the president's effort to collect foreign intelligence "unduly frustrate[s]" his duties as commander-in-chief to protect the nation. The court notes the Executive's expertise in the matter of foreign affairs as well as its "stealth, speed, and secrecy" makes it the right branch of government to handle such issues.

When a national security threat posed by a domestic group results in warrantless electronic wiretaps, the *Keith* decision won out and the federal courts held that it did not matter that the president authorized the wiretaps. A warrant is always required when a domestic organization, not an agent of a foreign power, is the subject of surveillance because Congress passed legislation requiring such (*Zweibon v. Mitchell,* 516 F. 2d 594; D.C. Cir.; 1975). In *Zweibon,* 16 individuals were convicted of blowing up buildings which were connected to the Soviet government. Soviet dissidents living in the United States were bombing the buildings in protest against restrictive policies on Soviet Jewish immigration. The Soviet Union blamed the American government for the attacks. In the absence of congressional action, the court was not prepared to limit the Executive. While the court in *Zweibon* wanted to limit the Executive in relation to foreign threats, in an explanation of the court's position, Judge Wright states in a footnote that:

> Congress was at pains not 'to limit or disturb such power as the president may have under the Constitution.' . . . Since, on the record before us, the surveillance of JDL headquarters was installed for national security reasons, it at least arguably falls within the language of the proviso; thus we must first analyze whether a national security surveillance instituted under these circumstances is subject to prior judicial scrutiny . . . the legislative history and language of that section reflect a congressional intent that in any case in which no warrant is constitutionally mandated, Congress did not intend to impose a statutory warrant requirement. Indeed, although the premise is questionable . . . Congress apparently believed it would be unconstitutional to restrict any inherent Executive power to engage in warrantless surveillance.

The *Zweibon* court also addressed why it was ready to decide a case pertaining to national security. Title III did not legislate with regard to warrant requirements pertaining to national security concerns. The Act did provide both procedures and remedies that were to be applicable to national security wiretaps where a "warrant is otherwise required by the Constitution." The court explains that Congress has delegated authority to the courts to judge domestic national security cases. Judge Wright states that "Congress apparently concurs in the belief that judges are competent to analyze the substance of matters allegedly pertaining to the national security. However, with that said, the Court in *EPA v. Mink*, 410 U.S. 73; 1973, interpreted 5 U.S.C. § 552(b)(1), which exempted from the forced disclosure mandate of the Act those matters "specifically required by Executive order to be kept secret in the interest of the national defense or foreign policy," to not be subject to judicial review.

The court also recognizes that the Judiciary is likely to defer to the Executive's "determination concerning the need to install a wiretap, particularly where a judicial error might substantially harm the national interest" (Judge Wright's *Zweibon* opinion). The lack of clear rules prior to the passage of the FISA pertaining to wiretapping to collect foreign intelligence may explain the deference of the courts to the Executive in this regard.

The warrant requirement for U.S. citizens considered threats to national security was reaffirmed in *Halperin v. Kissinger et al.*, 606 F.2d 1192; (D.C.Cir.1979). Following the rulings in *Zweibon* and *Keith,* there was no Fourth Amendment exemption for the Executive to conduct warrantless electronic surveillance on Americans. While the Nixon Administration was concerned with leaks of information coming from the inside, its own employees were wiretapped with no judicial authorization. The claim was that the wiretaps were needed to protect national security information.[15] The court contends that records kept were minimal and stored in a White House safe. While the court held it had to "carefully consider any impact that our decision might have on the nation's abilities to defend itself and its vital interests," it was decided that "whatever special powers the Executive may hold in national security situations must be limited to instances of immediate and grave peril to the nation," unless powers were granted or delegated to the Executive through congressional statute.

Table 4.2 shows that the federal courts have consistently looked to congressional legislation to determine how far the Executive can act in conducting warrantless electronic surveillance. Since passing Title III in 1968, and not speaking to the powers of the Executive in collecting foreign intelligence, the federal courts followed the lead of Congress. When the Executive placed warrantless wiretaps on American citizens considered to be parts

Table 4.2. Federal Courts' Reliance on Congress to Limit Warrantless Wiretapping Pre-FISA

	Court upheld executive action	*Court struck down executive action*
Congressional authorization	*U.S. v. Clay* *U.S. v. Enten,* 1971 *U.S. v. Brown,* 1973 *U.S. v. Hoffman,* 1971 *U.S. v. Fox,* 1972 *U.S. v. Butenko,* 1974 *U.S. v. Buck,* 1977 *U.S. v. Humphrey,* 1978 *U. S. v. T. Dinh Hung,* 1982	
No Congressional authorization/ contrary to the wishes of Congress		*U.S. v. Smith,* 1971 *U.S. v. Sinclair,* 1971 *U.S. v. U.S. District,* 1972 *Zweibon v. Mitchell,* 1975 *Halperin v. Kissinger,* 1979

of dissident groups, the courts consistently ruled that the Executive would required a warrant in line with the intentions of Title III, as well as the Fourth Amendment. In Jackson's second prong of the *Youngstown* framework, congressional inaction or indifference was one situation where the courts may defer to the Executive's initiatives. Because Congress acted on the domestic front, it is easy to determine their likely position on the Executive's ability to conduct electronic surveillance of a domestic nature without a warrant.

THE *FOREIGN INTELLIGENCE SURVEILLANCE ACT*

In 1975, the Church Committee (the Senate Select Committee to Study Governmental Operations with Respect to Intelligence Activities), declared that federal agencies such as the FBI and the CIA abused their powers by conducting warrantless national security surveillance (Pohlman, 2007; 20). The Church Committee revealed "decades of mail openings, decades of illegal interceptions of international telegrams, a history of illegal burglaries, misuse of the NSA for non-foreign intelligence purposes, spying to gather political intelligence and embarrassing personal information on political opponents and dossiers on political dissenters" (Fein, 2007; 27). As a result of the committee's report and in response to domestic warrantless wiretapping by not only the Nixon Administration but forty years of unchecked spying powers (Fein, 2007; 26), Congress enacted FISA.

The Nixon Administration argued it maintained an inherent power to wiretap domestic groups it believed pose a threat to national security. The Supreme Court held differently in the *Keith* Case, but the ruling concerned domestic groups, leaving the question of foreign intelligence up to the political branches of government to resolve. Presidents contend that FISA is an unconstitutional encroachment on the Executive's inherent powers to protect the nation (Fein, 2007; 28).[16] Fein casts FISA in a different light, however, arguing that "the statute does not aggrandize Congress at the expense of the White House, but simply subjects foreign intelligence surveillances and physical searches to independent judicial scrutiny" (Fein, 2007; 28).

FISA requires the attorney general to submit an application for a warrant to conduct electronic surveillance to gather foreign intelligence from a court created specifically to hear the government's applications.[17] American citizens are not subject to FISA surveillance "unless the executive branch could link them to certain types of crimes: espionage, sabotage, terrorism, fraud, or conspiracy" (Pohlman, 2007; 21). Furthermore, if the target of surveillance is a U.S. citizen, the government is required to show evidence apart from speech or association that showed the target "had committed, was committing, or was about to commit a specific criminal offense" (Pohlman, 22). The attorney general must show probable cause that an American target is "implicated in international terrorism or is otherwise acting as an agent of a foreign power" (Fein, 2007; 27). If probable cause is shown, a FISA warrant is issued to the government for a period of up to ninety days. Only information concerning foreign intelligence can be collected through wiretapping.[18] In addition to these restrictions on foreign intelligence gathering, the government must also specify what methods will be used to obtain the information.

In 1968, Title III recognized a large grant of "constitutional power of the President to take such measures as he deems necessary to protect the Nation against actual or potential attack . . . , [and] to obtain foreign intelligence information deemed essential to the security of the United States" (Bazan and Elsea, 2006; 13). It is suggested that this power was repealed when FISA was signed into law.[19] The Act closed the possibility that the president retained inherent power to conduct warrantless electronic surveillance with 18 U.S.C. § 2511(2)(f) which states that "procedures in . . . the *Foreign Intelligence Surveillance Act* of 1978 shall be the exclusive means by which electronic surveillance, as defined in [FISA] . . . may be conducted" (as quoted in Kris, 2006; 2).

The Senate Judiciary Committee's explanation for the purpose of the FISA states the congressional stance on inherent executive authority was an "understanding . . . that even if the President has an 'inherent' constitutional power to authorize warrantless surveillance for foreign intelligence purposes,

Congress has the power to regulate the exercise of this authority by legislating a reasonable warrant procedure governing foreign intelligence surveillance."[20] Congress recognizes the Supreme Court could find that the president has inherent authority to conduct warrantless electronic surveillance to gather foreign intelligence.

Whereas Title III sets out procedures for electronic surveillance on the domestic front, FISA did the same in regard to foreign intelligence gathering initiatives. The 1972 *Keith* case "simply left presidential powers where it found them," and further notes that Congress could establish standards that were different from Title III and still consistent with the Fourth Amendment. FISA "would substitute a clear legislative authorization pursuant to statutory, not constitutional standards. Thus, it is appropriate to repeal this section [of Title III], which otherwise would suggest that perhaps the statutory standard was not the exclusionary authorization for the surveillances included therein" (Kris, 2006; 2).[21]

By enacting FISA, Congress was not trying to place the Executive in a position that would inhibit it from protecting the State. In *ACLU v. Barr et al.*, 293 U.S. App. D.C. 101; 1991, Judge Randolph held that "[b]y enacting FISA, Congress sought to resolve doubts about the constitutionality of warrantless, foreign security surveillance and yet protect the interests of the United States in obtaining vital intelligence about foreign powers." The court also determined that FISA's requirement that the courts decide whether the surveillance was lawful, equates to "an acceptable means of adjudicating the constitutional rights of persons who have been subjected to FISA surveillance."[22] Since the enactment of FISA, the federal courts have concluded that the Act "did not intrude upon the President's undisputed right to conduct foreign affairs, but protected citizens and resident aliens within this country, as 'United States persons'" (*United States v. Falvey,* 540 F. Supp. 1306 (E.D.N.Y. 1982), as explained in *ACLU v. NSA,* 438 F. Supp. 2d 754; 2006).[23] In following Jackson's *Youngstown* framework, FISA created a framework[24] in which the Executive Branch conducts legitimate electronic surveillance to gather foreign intelligence purposes as delineated by the statute, according to congressionally enacted rules.[25]

Table 4.3 indicates that all challenges to the constitutionality of FISA have been met with the courts affirming the right of Congress to pass laws necessary and proper for carrying out the functions of the federal government. Since evidence obtained through the use of FISA warrants is regarded as Congress and the Executive working together, each of these cases falls within prong 1 of Jackson's Youngstown framework and the courts have responded accordingly, granting the most leniency in regard to the Executive's claims to carry out electronic surveillance.

Table 4.3. Challenges to FISA in Front of the Lower Courts

	Court upheld executive action	*Court struck down executive action*
Congressional authorization	*U.S. v. Nicholson,* 1997 *U. S. v. Johnson,* 1992 *ACLU v. Barr,* 1991 *In re Grand Jury...,* 1988 *U. S. v. Pelton,* 1987 *U.S. v. Cavanagh,* 1987 *U.S. v. Belfield,* 1982 *U.S. v. Ott,* 1987 *In the Matter... Kevork,* 1986 *U.S. v. Megahey,* 1982 *U.S. v. Falvey,* 1982	
No Congressional authorization/ contrary to the wishes of Congress		

After 9/11, FISA was amended with the *USA PATRIOT Act* so the government no longer was required to show that the primary purpose of the search was to gather foreign intelligence information before being granted a warrant. As amended, FISA requires that a "significant purpose" of the investigation be to collect foreign intelligence information, thus expanding the types of investigations that are now permitted under the Act (Bazan and Elsea, 19). FISA requirements were further amended when, on March 6, 2002, then Attorney General John Ashcroft issued a memorandum on the minimization of procedures. The memorandum stated that FISA powers could "be used primarily for a law enforcement purpose, so long as a significant foreign intelligence purpose remains" (as quoted in Darmer, 95). This change in terminology made securing a FISA warrant possible for a broader array of activities.

The provisions also called for closer consultations between law enforcement and intelligence personnel.[26] Prosecutors could now use FISA powers in criminal investigations where the purpose of the surveillance to collect evidence rather than prevent future action. FISA was also amended to allow foreign intelligence and counterintelligence agents to meet with law enforcement officers to coordinate investigative efforts. Previously, FISA was used only in a preventive nature.[27] These changes were controversial and the Foreign Intelligence Surveillance Court unanimously rejected several key provisions of the attorney general's memorandum in May, 2002. In *In re All Matters Submitted to the FISC,* 218 F. Supp. 2d. 611; 2002, Judge Lamberth held that Congress provided guidance for the federal courts in regard to dealing with information gathered on American citizens as a result of a FISA search. The FISA's § 1801(h)(3) and § 1821(4)(c) allows that "the court would give these procedures most careful consideration. If it is not of the opinion that they will be effective, the procedures should be modified" (Lamberth's *All Matters* opinion). The court's decision was predominantly based on the congressionally enacted minimalization procedures set out in the original FISA, not the Fourth Amendment. The attorney general's memorandum violated a "provision of FISA that governed the retention and dissemination of FISA information" (Pohlman, 2007; 17).

The Bush Administration challenged the FISA Court's ruling to the Foreign Intelligence Surveillance Court of Review, something which was never done before (Darmer, 95–96). The government suggests in its brief that "FISA surveillance was permissible in certain types of criminal cases even if prosecution was the *sole* purpose of the surveillance" (Pohlman, 31). Prosecutions in cases concerning foreign intelligence information, which ranged from terrorist activities to sabotage, geared towards the protection of national security could, therefore, rely on FISA surveillance to collect evidence. The government contends that the information must be used for purposes of protecting the nation, but notes that"[p]rosecution is often a most effective means of protecting national security" (Government Court Brief).[28]

The government's brief suggests that even if the court of review did not accept its first argument, it would accept the second argument that "the *USA PATRIOT Act* permitted a FISA order if there was a 'significant purpose' of collecting 'foreign intelligence information.' Even if the primary purpose of the FISA order was to prosecute the target, the order was valid if the government had a significant purpose of obtaining foreign intelligence information" (Pohlman, 32). During oral arguments, then Solicitor General Theodore Olsen stated that the change in terminology was to make it easier for the Justice Department to obtain a FISA warrant and that "it's difficult for the judiciary to evaluate and second guess what a high level executive branch person attempting to fight terrorism is attempting to do" (Pohlman, 44).

On September 10, 2002, the Senate Judiciary Committee held a public hearing concerning the May 17th FISC decision. Senator Orrin G. Hatch (R-UT), the ranking Republican member of the committee, reaffirmed the Administration's position discussed during oral arguments of the FISC Court of Review the previous day. In interpreting the legislative intent of the Act, Hatch stated that the *USA PATRIOT Act* permitted "greater use of FISA for criminal purposes." At the same time, the Act allowed for increased intelligence information sharing and coordination between intelligence and law enforcement officers (Pohlman, 46). Incidentally, Hatch also said that it was for the federal courts to decide where the line would be drawn between criminal investigations and intelligence gathering (see Pohlman, 46).

In its first ever opinion, the court of review sided with the Executive in November, 2002. In *In re Sealed Case,* Case No. 02-001; 2002, the court held in a three judge unanimous decision, that FISA did not exclude the use of foreign intelligence for criminal prosecution of national security crimes. Further, Congress did not intend for it to do so. The court cited a House Committee report that explained "foreign intelligence information can include evidence of certain crimes." A Senate report added that "intelligence and criminal law enforcement tend to merge in this area." Congress, therefore, knew that FISA could very well be used for criminal investigations, but that it could only be done so if the "primary purpose" of the electronic surveillance was to gather foreign intelligence information. The court of review quotes Senator Patrick Leahy (D-VT) on the bill stating that it "breaks down the traditional barriers between law enforcement and foreign intelligence. This is not done just to combat international terrorism, but for any criminal investigation that overlaps a broad definition of foreign intelligence" (*Per Curiam Sealed* opinion). The court of review points out that the role of the court is to police the *statutory* separation of powers in this regard.[29]

THE NSA TERRORIST SURVEILLANCE PROGRAM[30]

On December 17, 2005, in a radio address to the nation, President Bush admitted that following 9/11, he "authorized the National Security Agency, consistent with U.S. law and the Constitution, to intercept the international communications of people with known links to al Qaeda and related terrorist organizations."[31] The Bush Administration made two key arguments about the legitimacy of the domestic spying program. First, the Executive can intercept messages as part of the president's "inherent constitutional authority as Commander in Chief and sole organ for the Nation in foreign affairs" (Gonzales, 2006; 30). Second, the Administration suggests that when FISA was passed it did not "limit its own future authority by barring subsequent Congresses from authorizing the Executive Branch to engage in surveillance in ways not specifically enumerated in FISA" (Gonzales, 22). The government continued that Congress granted the Executive statutory authorization to conduct the warrantless wiretapping when it passed the *Authorization for the Use of Military Force (AUMF).* The AUMF allowed the president to use "all necessary and appropriate force" against the perpetrators of the terrorist attacks. Wiretapping international communications is considered one way of using appropriate force to stop future attacks from occurring.

The Congressional Research Service found that the AUMF "does not constitute a declaration of war" (Bazan and Elsea, 26). Even if the AUMF could be regarded as equivalent to a declaration of war, the warrantless surveillance could still only be authorized for 15 days and not indefinitely as has been the case since 2002. However, Gonzales, in a letter to former Senate Majority Leader, Hon. Bill Frist, argued otherwise, suggesting that the NSA activities are necessary to ensure the government of "an early warning system to detect and prevent another catastrophic terrorist attack on American soil" (Gonzales, 5).[32]

Gonzales points out that the language used in the AUMF was repeated over a year later in the *Authorization for Use of Military Force Against Iraq,*[33] suggesting that the broad grant of presidential authority was not simply a "product of excitement in the immediate aftermath of September 11" (Gonzales, 11). Gonzales misses the point. Hamdi's detention is upheld because the AUMF, as an Act of Congress, satisfies the requirements of the *Non-Detention Act* of 1971 which states that no citizen will be detained by the United States unless pursuant to an Act of Congress. It is the congressional authorization required in the *Non-Detention Act* that allows the Court to determine that the AUMF satisfies those statutory requirements, enabling the deference to the Executive in *Hamdi.*

Until the passage of FISA, federal-court rulings continuously set aside the issue of warrantless foreign intelligence gathering, waiting for the Supreme Court to make a ruling on the subject. On the domestic front, it has long been decided that the president needs a warrant when parties are American, regardless of the importance of the matter to national security. With lower federal-court rulings holding FISA to be Constitutional and not encroaching on any inherent powers of the Executive, we could expect a similar and definitive answer from the Supreme Court. This issue is an area where there has been a lot of interplay between the three branches of government and exemplifies Jackson's typology. As such, because of the historical importance the federal courts have placed on congressional action concerning warrantless electronic surveillance, if the current debate does make its way to the Supreme Court and *certiorari* is granted, FISA will likely be upheld, but this does not mean that the Bush Administration's alleged spy program would be declared unconstitutional as contrary to the FISA requirements.

Incidentally, there have been a number of other cases to go through the federal-courts system concerning the NSA domestic spying program since its existence was made public in late 2005. There is a class-action suit, but it is a civil case and as a result does not address the constitutional questions.[34] In *Hepting v. AT&T Corp. et al.*, 439 F. Supp. 2d 974, 2006, Judge Walker wrote for the district court that this case differed from the 2006 *El-Masri v. Tenet,* 437 F. Supp. 2d 530; 2006, case where a man was wrongly accused of being a member of al Qaeda, was tortured, and sued for damages. In that case, the court held evidence could not be released concerning the circumstances of the events in question due to the state secrets privilege. In the *Hepting* case, the NSA was working with the records of potentially millions of Americans' phone calls. The court argued that the TSP having been reported about in the mainstream media in May 2006 meant it was not secret and the case can proceed to discovery. This ruling was delivered despite the government's claim of statutory authorization under the U.S. Code, *War National Defense,* 50 U.S.C. § 403-1(i)(1) which allows for the Director of National Intelligence to protect its sources. The court rejects this claim as being too soon to make.

In *Terkel et al. v. AT&T,* 441 F. Supp. 2d 899; 2006, Kennelly, in contrast to *Hepting,* held there was no proof of record turnover so the government motion to dismiss was granted. The case was different from *Hepting,* which concerned content monitoring. *Terkel* concerned using the information monitored, or in other words record disclosure monitoring. The case was decided on statutory grounds pointing to section 6 of the *National Security Agency Act* as well as the 2004 *Intelligence Reform and Terrorism Prevention Act* which state that the government is not required to disclose any information concerning what the NSA does to protect national security.

A three-panel judge heard the *Hepting v. AT&T* case at the Nine Circuit Court of Appeals in San Francisco on August 15, 2007. No judgment has been released, but in the summer of 2008, Congress passed the *FISA Amendments Act,* a law that does not give retroactive immunity to telecommunications companies for violations of FISA, but does put the process behind closed doors and allows the federal courts to dismiss suits if the White House provides evidence that the records were collected for national security purposes.[35] The law also allowed the Bush Administration to continue its domestic wiretapping program so long as it does so under FISA requirements. As a result, the court reversed to make a ruling and remanded the case back to the district court, where arguments were held in front of the court in December 2008.

Reversing a district court decision, on July 6, 2007, the 6th U.S. Circuit Court of Appeals dismissed the case in *ACLU v. NSA,* 438 F. Supp. 2d 754, 782 (E.D. Mich. 2006), due to a lack of standing on the part of the plaintiffs because it was impossible for them to demonstrate they were direct targets of warrantless electronic surveillance. Judge Batchelder stated that the "problem with asserting only a breach-of-privacy claim is that, because the plaintiffs cannot show . . . they have been or will be subjected to surveillance personally, they clearly cannot establish standing under the Fourth Amendment or FISA." The court continues by suggesting that the First Amendment claims cannot be addressed because the plaintiffs cannot prove their conversations were recorded. The rest of the case falls on the statutory requirements under FISA.

The court held that "it is reasonable to assume that the FISA Court would authorize the interception of this type of communication, *see* 50 U.S.C. section 1805, and keeping this likelihood in mind, the issuance of FISA warrants would not relieve any of the plaintiffs' fears of being overheard" (Judge Batchelder's *ACLU* opinion). The court also rejects that the president created a separation of powers problem by authorizing the TSP, violating congressional statutes. After dismissing claims that the president violated Title III, the court rejected that the NSA program violated FISA and Title III's exclusivity requirements. Batchelder explained his rationale for siding with the government:

> Specifically, the plaintiffs contend that the NSA cannot lawfully conduct any wiretapping (under the TSP or otherwise) in a manner that is outside *both* the Title III and the FISA frameworks; the NSA's conduct *must* fall within the governance of one statute or the other. Based on this reading, the plaintiffs believe that they need not demonstrate the specific applicability of either statute — that is, they need not demonstrate *either* that the NSA is engaging in "electronic surveillance," in order to place it under FISA, *or* that the NSA is engaging in domestic surveillance, in order to place it under Title III.[36]

Jackson's *Youngstown* framework points out that the powers of the president "are not fixed but fluctuate, depending upon their disjunction with those of Congress." If FISA, as amended, can be read to grant the president the authority to institute the NSA domestic wiretapping program, President Bush would have found himself in Justice Jackson's first prong of the *Youngstown* framework, receiving the most leniency from the federal courts, unless the courts decide that the federal government as a whole is without authority to conduct such surveillance programs.

The constitutionality of the TSP and the *Protect America Act* was questioned as a result of an appeal by two men convicted of "helping an undercover informant posing as a weapons dealer who was plotting to buy a shoulder-launched missile that would be used to kill the Pakistani ambassador in New York City."[37] The appeal was filed in the U.S. Court of Appeals for the 2nd Circuit in Manhattan. An FBI sting directed at Yassin Aref was set up because of information found on a laptop in conjunction with a raid in Iraq in 2003. A notebook containing the name and phone number of Aref, the leader of an Albany mosque, was found.[38] Evidence received from the FBI's fake terrorist plot was used to convict Aref and his friend, Mohammed Hossain, giving them each 15 years in prison. It was leaked that evidence to support Aref's guilt was obtained as a result of the NSA's warrrantless surveillance. Under the TSP, 14 phone conversations by Aref to a Syrian number linked to al Qaeda were recorded.[39] In a pretrial proceeding, Judge McAvoy blocked the prosecutors from telling the jury why Aref was targeted by the FBI in the first place. The Court of Appeals upheld the conviction on July 2, 2008 and the Supreme Court denied hearing the case.

CONCLUSION

In June 2004, the McCormick Tribune Foundation and the American Bar Association Standing Committee on Law and National Security held a conference, examining issues of counterterrorism technology and privacy of individuals. Many core principles—or suggestions—for the government to pursue were put forth, three of which dealt with electronic surveillance. The conference participants concluded that first, "the legislative and executive branches share the fundamental constitutional responsibility to protect the privacy and safety of all U.S. citizens and resident aliens—and should act in partnership." Second, the recommendations ask Congress to provide statutory authority for the Executive to have "appropriate, lawful access to and use of information stored in government and commercial databases for national security and law enforcement purposes." And finally, "[t]he executive branch should have clear and robust statutory authority to access and use all relevant information stored in government and commercial databases in support of its constitutional responsibilities and subject to its constitutional limitations" (McMahon, 2005; 11).

The recommendations from the foundation's report suggest that a partnership between the elected branches of government in preventing future attacks against the country is required for a most effective effort. While the recommendation of extending executive power through statute may not seem to be the best course of action for ensuring the privacy of individuals is maintained, the acknowledgement that the Executive needs congressional authority in a post-9/11 world to conduct warrantless electronic surveillance seems clear. This, I have shown, has not always been the case. However, it has been the case that the federal courts have called upon Congress to act where legislation did not exist regulating warrantless wiretapping when such cases arose.

Before the passage of FISA, each court of appeals that was asked to rule on the president's authority in authorizing warrantless wiretapping in regard to foreign powers upheld that supposed authority. At the lower court level, it was determined that presidential authority to conduct warrantless surveillance in regard to foreign affairs lay somewhere in the second prong of Jackson's *Youngstown* framework. Statutes, court decisions and actions of the Executive all point towards warrantless surveillance being a showcase of the twilight zone of executive/congressional authority that Jackson pointed to in his *Youngstown* concurrence. Congress did not legislate on the issue and its reluctance to do so was seen by the courts as leaving the powers of the president where they were until the Supreme Court gave a definitive answer on the issue.

Judge Wright in *Halperin et al. v. Kissinger et al.,* 196 U.S. App. D.C. 285; 1979), recognized this balancing act:

> Standards for evaluating the legality of this electronic surveillance derive from the Constitution and from Title III of the *Omnibus Crime Control and Safe Streets Act* of 1968. The Government has conceded that the Fourth Amendment's ban on Unreasonable searches and seizures applied to national security wiretaps in 1969, but disputes the application of the Amendment's judicial warrant requirement . . . we must acknowledge that the Fourth Amendment's warrant requirement may not always apply, while a reasonableness standard may vary in different situations. In Contrast, Title III bans most electronic surveillance and specifies procedures for wiretapping and eavesdropping in particular situations; but the statute expressly does not limit the President's constitutional power to wiretap in national security situations. Although the mandate of the statute is more precise, the reach of the constitutional provision may be seen as greater (Wright's *Halperin* opinion).

Furthermore, echoing Jackson's three-pronged approach in *Youngstown,* the Congressional Research Service puts forth the notion that:

> where the Congress has exercised its constitutional authority in the areas of foreign affairs and thereby has withdrawn electronic surveillance, as defined by FISA, from the 'zone of twilight,' between Executive and Legislative constitutional authorities, it might be argued that the President's asserted inherent authority to engage in warrantless electronic surveillance was thereby limited (Bazan and Elsea, 32).

The federal courts have decided cases along the institutional lines that I suggest they do when they allow for the curtailment of individual liberties by the Executive. It was, therefore, quite appropriate for Congress to draft legislation dealing with these issues as it is in Congress' power "under Article I to shape executive prerogative by making 'all laws . . . necessary and proper for carrying into execution . . . all . . . Powers vested by . . . [the] Constitution . . . in . . . any . . . officer of the United States'" (Eggert, 1983; 635).

ENDNOTES

1. http://www.reuters.com/article/politicsnews/idustre58g7592000909 17 (September 23, 2009).

2. Other issues arise under the First, Fifth, and Sixth Amendments. In regard to the First Amendment, the fear is that electronic surveillance creates a prior restraint

on speech as individuals, upon becoming aware of the surveillance, will be less inclined to speak freely. This claim, is often cast aside as the courts rule that having rights "chilled," or being afraid to freely exercise one's rights, is not the same thing as proving a right has been violated (see *United States v. Ahmad*, 347 F. Supp. 912; 1972; *Laird v. Tatum*, 408 U.S. 1; 1972, *Fifth Avenue Peace Parade Committee v. Gray*, 480 F. 2d 326; 1973, *Zweibon et al. v. Mitchell*, 516 F.2d 594; 1975, *ACLU v. Barr*, 952 F.2d 457; 1991, *Hepting v. AT&T Corporation*, 2006). The objection to wiretapping based on the Fifth Amendment concerns self-incriminating evidence used against defendants obtained through electronic surveillance. Here it should also be mentioned that there are Sixth Amendment violations when electronic surveillance records legal counsel-client conversations.

3. Exceptions to the Fourth Amendment's warrant requirement also include: searches subsequent to "an arrest; a stop and frisk of a suspicious individual; or a search conducted either in hot pursuit to prevent destruction of evidence or in a foreign country" (Pohlman, 2007; 18). These requirements have come out of several court cases. See *Chimel v. California*, 395 U.S. 752; 1969, *Terry v. Ohio*, 392 U.S. 1; 1968, *United States v. Santana*, 427 U.S. 38; 1976, and *United States v. Verdugo-Urquidez*, 494 U.S. 259; 1990. Furthermore, in *United States v. Martinez-Fuerte*, 428 U.S. 543; 1976, the Court upheld permanent immigration check points due to the volume of illegal immigrants in the country. That circumstances arise where a warrantless search and seizure for law enforcement purposes is reasonable was outlined again in the 2001 case *Illinois v. McArthur*, 531 U.S. 326. Justice Breyer held that because the police had probable cause to think the defendant not only had illegal drugs in his home but would destroy them before a warrant could be obtained, it was reasonable for the police to search the home without a warrant and was therefore not in violation of the Fourth Amendment (Brennan's *McArthur* opinion).

4. *The Act of October 29*, ch. 197, § 1 40 Stat. 1017-1018; 1918.

5. That said, Brandeis did make the argument that the laws of the state of Washington prohibited wiretapping and therefore independently of the constitutional questions, the judgment should have been reversed: "The 18th Amendment has not in terms empowered Congress to authorize anyone to violate the criminal laws of a state" (Brandeis' *Olmstead* dissent).

6. It should be noted that after reviewing the original text of the Act, the FCA stated divulge or publish, not divulge and publish as government officials relied upon.

7. Before *Rathburn*, a number of lower-court cases came to this same conclusion. See *United States v. White*, 228 F.2d 832; 1956, *Flanders v. United States*, 222 F.2d 163; 1955, *United States v. Sullivan*, 116 F. Supp. 480; 1953, *United States v. Lewis*, 87 F. Supp. 970; 1950, *Billeci v. United States*, 87 U.S. App. D.C. 274; 1950, *United States v. Bookie*, 229 F.2d 130; 1956, and *United States v. Pierce*, 124 F. Supp. 264; 1954.

8. The text of FDR's directive is as follows:

> I have agreed with the broad purpose of the Supreme Court decision relating to wiretapping in investigations. The Court is undoubtedly sound both in regard to the use of evidence secured over tapped wires in the prosecution of citizens in criminal cases; and

it is also right in its opinion that under ordinary and normal circumstances wire-tapping by Government agents should not be carried out for the excellent reason that it is almost bound to lead to abuse of civil rights.

However, I am convinced that the Supreme Court never intended any dictum in the particular case which it decided to apply to grave matters involving the defense of the nation. It is, of course, well known that certain other nations have been engaged in the organization of propaganda of so-called "fifth columns" in other countries and in preparation for sabotage, as well as in active sabotage.

It is too late to do anything about it after sabotage, assassinations and "fifth column" activities are completed. You are, therefore, authorized and directed in such cases as you may approve, after investigations of the need in each case, to authorize the necessary investigating agents that they are at liberty to secure information by listening devices direct to the conversation or other communications of persons suspected of subversive activities against the Government of the United States, including suspected spies. You are requested furthermore to limit these investigations so conducted to a minimum and to limit them insofar as possible to aliens.

The directive is available online. www.spector.org/dsp_article.asp?art_id=9790-50k (September 9, 2006).

9. 87 Cong. Rec. 5764

10. Report to the Senate Committee on the Judiciary on a Wiretap Bill, February 10, 1941, Hearings before the Committee on the Judiciary on H.R. 2266 and H.R. 3099, 77th Congress., 1st Sess. 16-20, 1941.

11. Section 2511(3) states that "[n]othing contained in this chapter or in section 605 of the *Communications Act* of 1934 … shall limit the constitutional power of the President to take such measures as he deems necessary to protect the Nation against actual or potential attack or other hostile acts of a foreign power, to obtain foreign intelligence information deemed essential to the security of the United States, or to protect national security information against foreign intelligence activities." This section of the Criminal Code is available online. http://www.usdoj.gov/criminal/cybercrime/18usc2511.htm (August 24, 2007).

12. Cases to make such a declaration include *United States v. Butenko*, 318 F. Supp. 66, 73 D.N.J. 1970; *United States v. Clay*, 430 F. 2d 165, 171 (5th Cir. 1970); *United States v. Brown,* 317 F. Supp. 531, 535-36 (E.D. La. 1970).

13. 114 Cong. Rec. 14751.

14. The federal courts made similar rulings in relation to placing phone conversations pertaining to foreign intelligence gathering outside the requirements of the *Alderman* rule. It should be remembered that in *Alderman*, the Court required transcripts of recordings to be turned over in a hearing if there was a conviction of an accused who had been subject to an illegal surveillance. The point of the hearing was to determine if that conviction was the result of evidence obtained by the illegal wiretap. See *United States v. Hoffman*, 334 F. Supp. 504; (D.D.C. 1971) and *United States v. Fox* 455 F.2d 131; (5th Cir. 1972).

15. The courts have also been asked to decide cases concerning the Fourth Amendment where the government claims state secrets privilege. In *Laird v. Tatum,* 408 U.S. 1; 1972, the Department of the Army created a program for the surveillance of domestic

groups. The Supreme Court held that "to pass judgment on whether the army should have such a program" would see the federal courts monitor the "wisdom" and the "soundness" of the Executive's actions. The Court held it was for Congress to act in this oversight role "absent actual present or immediate threatened injury resulting from unlawful government action." In *Halkin et al. v. Helms*,194 F.2d 598, 1979, the court of appeals denied an en banc hearing of a previous decision which upheld the government's contention that information requested to be released to the petitioner, concerning warrantless electronic surveillance, for national security reasons. Judge Bazelon would have allowed the hearing. Bazelon stated that the "'utmost deference' which the panel has given governments ex parte, in camera assertions is not justified in precedent."

16. Fein points out that while Article II of the Constitution may in fact grant authority to the president to collect foreign intelligence, "FISA, nevertheless, is a 'necessary and proper' law regarding the execution of that authority" (Fein, 2007; 25). In *McCulloch v. Maryland*, 17 U.S. 316; 1819, Chief Justice Marshall stated that the Congress is empowered in Article I, section 8 of the Constitution to "make all laws which shall be necessary and proper for carrying into Execution the foregoing powers...vested by this Constitution in the Government of the United States or in any Department or Officer thereof "(Marshall's *McCulloch* opinion).

17. The Foreign Intelligence Surveillance Court, FISC, originally consisted of seven Article III judges, and was later amended to 11 judges by the *USA PATRIOT Act.*

18. Under 50 U.S.C. section 1805 (a)(3)0, (a)(5) FISA defines "foreign intelligence information" as: (1)information that relates to, and if concerning a United States person is necessary to, the ability of the United States to protect against:

(A) actual or potential attack or other grave hostile acts of a foreign power or an agent of a foreign power;
(B) sabotage or international terrorism by a foreign power or an agent of a foreign power; or
(C) clandestine intelligence activities by an intelligence service or network of a foreign power or by an agent of a foreign power; or

(2) information with respect to a foreign power or foreign territory that relates to, and if concerning a United States person is necessary to

(A) the national defense or the security of the United States; or
(B) the conduct of the foreign affairs of the United States.

19. Harvey Mansfield, a political philosopher, writes:

> In the current dispute over executive surveillance of possible terrorists, those arguing that the executive should be subject to checks and balances are wrong to say or imply that the president may be checked in the sense of stopped. The president can be held accountable and made responsible, but if he could be stopped, the Constitution would lack any sure means of emergency action. Emergency action of this kind may be illegal but it is not unconstitutional; or, since the Constitution is the law, it is not illegal under the Constitution (Mansfield, 2006).

This view is not widely shared and ignores the case law that suggests that the president may have inherent power to conduct warrantless surveillance to gather foreign intelligence, but it is for Congress to limit any powers the president might argue to possess on his own that are not clearly stated in the Constitution.

20. S. Rep. No. 95-604(I) at 16 1978 U.S.C.C.A.N. at 3917, as quoted in the CRS Report on warrantless electronic surveillance to gather foreign intelligence, 29.

21. See H.R. Rep. No. 95-1283, Part I, at 101–102.

22. In making this determination, the court cites *United States v. Belfield*, 223 App D.C. 417 (D.C. Cir. 1982), and *United States v. Ott* 827 F. 2d 473 (9th Cir. 1987).

23. However, "FISA regulates but a tiny crumb of foreign intelligence collection" (See H.R. 5825, concerning the proposed bill, the *Electronic Surveillance Modernization Act* of 2006). The NSA testified in front of a congressional hearing that targets are usually aliens abroad. Ninety-nine percent of foreign intelligence gathering takes place outside the constraints of FISA (Fein, 2007; 27).

24. FISA does, however, allow for the authorization of electronic surveillance without a warrant in times of war when such a situation is so declared by Congress. In 50 U.S.C. § 1811, Congress provides for the attorney general to authorize the surveillance without a court order for a period of no more than 15 days following a declaration of war. After the 15 calendar days the president needs either a judicial warrant or an Act of Congress passed to amend FISA.

25. As detailed in footnote 7 in United States v. Nicholson, 955 F. Supp 550; 1997, the Constitutionality of FISA has been questioned on a number of occasions and has survived all such challenges. See United States v. Pelton, 835 F.2d 1067 (4th Cir. 1987), cert. denied, 486 U.S. 1010, 100 L. Ed. 2d 204, 108 S. Ct. 1741 (1988), and n. 5, below; see also United States v. Cavanagh, 807 F.2d 787, 790-92 (9th Cir. 1987); Belfield, 692 F.2d at 148 (D.C. Circuit rejected argument that FISA violates Fifth and Sixth Amendments); Spanjol, 720 F. Supp. at 58; United States v. Ott, 637 F. Supp. 62 (E.D. Cal. 1986), aff'd, 827 F.2d 473 (9th Cir. 1987); In the Matter of Kevork, F.2d 566; 9th Cir.1986; *United States v. Falvey*, 540 F. Supp. 1306; E.D.N.Y. 1982.

26. Specifically, the memorandum stated: "Consultations may include the exchange of advice and recommendations on all issues necessary to the ability of the United States to investigate or protect against foreign attack, sabotage, terrorism, and clandestine intelligence activities, including protection against the foregoing through criminal investigation and prosecution...Relevant issues include, but are not limited to, the strategy and goals for investigation; the law enforcement and intelligence methods to be used in conducting the investigation; the interaction between intelligence and law enforcement components as part of the investigation; and the initiation, cooperation, continuation, or expansion of FISA searches or surveillance. Such consultations are necessary to the ability of the United States to coordinate efforts to investigate and protect against foreign threats to national security." See "Intelligence Sharing Procedures for Foreign Intelligence and Foreign Counterintelligence Investigations Conducted by the FBI," March 6, 2002. http://www.fas.org/irp/agency/doj/fisa/ag030602.html (August 7, 2007).

27. Differences between FISA and regular criminal investigations where wiretapping is used by government officials are as follows:

- FISA surveillance is permitted after showing only a diluted form of suspicion not equivalent to the traditional criminal standard of probable cause.

- FISA authorizes intrusive investigative techniques, such as clandestine physical searches, that are normally impermissible in criminal investigations.
- Surveillance and physical searches can continue over more extensive periods of time, with less judicial supervision.
- Normally, the person targeted is never notified that he was the subjected of surveillance.

Furthermore, if that person is prosecuted, attorneys normally cannot review the surveillance documents for purposes of their client's defense, as they could if surveillance was conducted under conventional law enforcement standards (Darmer, 2004; 93–94).

28. Available online http://www.fas.org/irp/agency/doj/fisa/082102appeal.html (August 7, 2007).

29. Not all, however, was made simple for the government. The court of review held that by requiring that a significant purpose of the surveillance be used for foreign intelligence gathering, the *USA PATRIOT Act* and the attorney general's memorandum in fact had "muddied the landscape." If the sole purpose of gathering the intelligence was for criminal prosecution, FISA could not be used and a purpose "distinct from criminal prosecution" was required (Pohlman, 62). Before the new policies, gathering evidence for criminal investigations could have been assumed to have been authorized by FISA. The result was that the amendments which were supposed to broaden the government's surveillance activities had in fact narrowed them (Pohlman, 62).

30. It should be noted that on January 17, 2007, then Attorney General Alberto Gonzales sent a letter to the Senate stating that the Terrorist Surveillance Program (TSP) would not be reauthorized by the president and that "[a]ny electronic surveillance that was occurring as part of the Terrorist Surveillance Program will now be conducted subject to the approval of the Foreign Intelligence Surveillance Court." For full text of the letter: http://jurist.law.pitt.edu/pdf/fiscletter.pdf (August 2, 2007).

31. http://www.whitehouse.gov/news/releases/2005/12/20051217.html (August 7, 2007).

32. Gonzales outlines why the AUMF authorizes the program and also argues that the program is consistent with the regulations under FISA. The rationale used by Gonzales was that the AUMF had to be broadly interpreted to allow for warrantless electronic surveillance just as the Supreme Court had done in interpreting the AUMF in *Hamdi v. Rumsfeld* (2004) to be statutory authorization enough for detaining American citizens as enemy combatants. The "detention of combatants who fought against the United States as part of an organization 'known to have supported' al Qaeda 'is so fundamental and accepted an incident to war as to be an exercise of the 'necessary and appropriate force' Congress has authorized the President to use" (Gonzales quoting *Hamdi*, 12). To take the argument one step further, it could be reasoned that "the AUMF authorizes what the laws of war permit" (Bradley and Goldsmith, 2005; 2092). Just as detaining enemy combatants has always been a part of warfare and characterized as a use of force, the same can be said in regard to the collection of intelligence. As evidence that wiretapping is a recognizable method of warfare under

the laws of war, Gonzales points to article 24 of the Hague Regulations of 1907 that states "the employment of measures necessary for obtaining information about the enemy and the country [is] considered permissible" (as quoted by Gonzales, 14). Gonzales also makes mention of a number of early 20th century texts on the rules of war which suggest that intelligence gathering is a legitimate act of warfare. For more information see L. Oppenheim, *International Law vol. II*, (7th ed.), 1952; 159, Joseph Baker and Henry G. Crocker, *The Laws of Land Warfare* 1919; 197, and J.M. Spaight, *War Rights on Land*, 1911; 205.

33. Pub. L. No. 107-2432, October 16, 2002.

34. "US court hears suit against AT&T's collaboration with domestic spying program." The story is available online. http://www.indybay.org/newsitems/2007/08/22/18442321.php (September 23, 2007).

35. The amendments to FISA come after the Protect American Act (PAA), signed into law on August 5, 2007 expired in early 2008. The PAA amended FISA so that obtaining records from telecommunications service providers is not to be included in the definition of conducting electronic surveillance. The provisions of the *FISA Amendment Act* enumerated above incorporated section of the PAA which were set to expire. In January 2009, the Foreign Intelligence Surveillance Court of Review released its second opinion, *In re: Directives* (2009), where it held that the FAA was Constitutional.

36. This opinion is in contrast to the August, 2006, Detroit district court opinion where Judge Taylor ruled the NSA program was illegal under FISA as well as unconstitutional under the First and Fourth Amendments of the United States Constitution. Taylor held that in policing the separation of powers, the court had to look to Justice Jackson's *Youngstown* concurrence for guidance. Taylor points out that the NSA warrantless domestic surveillance program was not instituted in the absence of congressional legislation where the president would find himself perhaps sharing joint or concurring powers with Congress. Because Congress had passed FISA and amended it after the terrorist attacks of 9/11, President Bush took measures incompatible with the wishes of Congress as his actions were "as FISA forbids. FISA is the expressed statutory policy of our Congress" (Taylor *ACLU* opinion). The case was decided on statutory lines, though the court states that congressional statutes aside, the NSA program was contrary to the Fourth Amendment, despite the opinion's lack of emphasis in explaining the rationale for this argument.

37. *Foxnews.com* "Feds Nab Two in Albany, N.Y., Mosque Raid." August, 2004. http://www.foxnews.com/printer_friendly_story/0,3566,128088,00.html (September 23, 2007).

38. Adam Liptak, "Appeal of conviction challenges legitimacy of wiretapping program, *New York Times*, August 26, 2007 http://www.sfgate.com/cgi-bin/article.cgi?file=/c/a/2007/08/26/MNACRPJQ9.DTL (September 23, 2007).

39. Albany Times Union. http://www.timesunion.com/aspstories/storyprint.asp?storyID=618763 (September 23, 2007).

Chapter 5

Economic Property Rights

One of the guiding principles of American political philosophy is an individual has the right to own property. Even during the Constitutional Convention, South Carolina's John Rutledge stated that "property was certainly the principal object of Society" (Farrand, 1937; Vol. 4, 534). Framers of the Constitution made repeated warnings against "factionalism and attempts to level the unequal distribution of property" (Ely, 1992; 1), in an attempt to prevent its democratic control. The result was a regime where "property once provided the conceptual balance of the legitimate scope of government" (Nedelsky, 1990; 3). In fact, for the first 150 years of American constitutional development, "the sanctity of private property" was considered "central to the new American social and political order" (Ely Jr., 1992; 1, quoting Adams, 1980; 217, n.103).[1]

The Bill of Rights protects private property. Starting with the Second Amendment, Americans are entitled to keep and bear arms. The owner's consent is required to quarter soldiers in the home, as prescribed by the Third Amendment, and the protection of property against unreasonable search and seizure is guaranteed in the Fourth. Finally, the Fifth Amendment contains two relevant clauses for the protection of private property. The Amendment states that "No person shall . . . be deprived of life, liberty, or property without due process of law; nor shall private property be taken for public use, without just compensation." What happens to these protections of property when Congress authorizes the Executive to take property away from its owner in times when the nation is involved in armed hostilities?

When a core right is interfered with by the Executive, just as is the case with limits to a trial in civilian courts, the right to petition for the writ of habeas corpus and the right to be protected from unreasonable search and seizure, the government is considered to be most intrusive. The right to own private property is so fundamental a right in our system of government that "if property could not be protected, not only prosperity, but liberty, justice, and the international strength of the nation would be destroyed" (Nedelsky, 1990; 6).[2] Economic emergency legislation to confiscate property cuts at the core of property ownership by allowing the government, through explicit terms set out in legislation, to take possession of private property. This chapter looks at the *Trading with the Enemy Act* (TWEA) of 1917 and its subsidiary, the *International Emergency Economic Powers Act* (IEEPA) of 1977. While the focus of these pieces of legislation directly concern foreign nationals, it should be noted that American citizens often get caught up in litigation concerning their scope.

I look at economic emergency laws specifically for two reasons. First, the emphasis on the protection of private property in the Bill of Rights is in line with the suggestion that the protection of property is so fundamental that justice and liberty in general are potentially at risk without it. The second rationale is to provide some contrast in relation to the military detention and warrantless surveillance cases. This contrast is provided in two ways. First, in military detention and warrantless surveillance cases, the federal courts look for legislation to back the claims of the government. While the president may act pursuant to an Act of Congress authorizing detentions and surveillance, the president does so in a way that differs from the authorization offered in emergency economic legislative powers. The TWEA and the IEEPA outline *how* the Executive is to go about confiscating property of those considered to be a threat to society during such trying times. Congress creates an entire policy that is implemented by the Executive, whereas the other cases the courts are left looking to see if the policies created by the Executive have legislative backing. In other words, in military detention and warrantless electronic surveillance cases, the courts look for authorization from Congress where power is delegated to the Executive to create policies that curtail individual liberties. In regard to the economic emergency powers, Congress uses its legislative powers to create policies which call upon the Executive to act in limiting individual liberties. I examine how the courts decide related cases during armed hostilities and explore if the cases automatically fall within the first prong of Jackson's *Youngstown* framework.

In another contrast between economic emergency legislation and military detention and warrantless surveillance cases, emergency economic legislation presents a situation where Congress grants jurisdiction for the federal courts to decide issues arising from challenges to the Executive's actions. This contrasts with the other cases where no clear role for the Judiciary exists. The interesting question then becomes when no jurisdictional issues act as a constraint on the courts, do the courts still decide cases within Jackson's framework? We see in the military detention cases the situation where the federal courts are likely to defer to the military officials so long as Congress is on board. In chapter 4, the courts readily deferred to Congress when legislation was in place and to the Executive when Congress failed to act in regard to warrantless electronic surveillance that concerned national security. In considering the adjudication of emergency economic laws where Congress has legislated guidelines on the confiscation of property, including granting the courts the jurisdiction to hear claims questioning the legitimacy of the property confiscation, the courts remain active in adjudicating cases arising under the two acts.

When examining emergency economic legislation, we would expect—having already determining that the courts defer to Congress when it delegates war powers to the Executive—that the courts would decide all cases within the first prong of the separation of powers framework presented in the *Youngstown* decision. Prong 1 determines that when "the President acts pursuant to an express or implied authorization of Congress, his authority is at its maximum" as the national government as a whole is acting. While it is difficult to imagine how emergency economic legislation could be found in Jackson's second prong, the federal courts rule that if a law does not explicitly exclude certain actions the Executive has historically undertaken, the Congress is sharing power with the Executive, something we see from time to time in the warrantless wiretapping cases with the federal courts varied interpretations of section 605 of the *Federal Communications Act*.

In the third prong of Jackson's framework, the Executive acts in contrast to the explicit or implicit wishes of Congress and must retain constitutional authority from the text of the Constitution itself for its actions to be legal. My research shows that despite Congress legislating on the issue of confiscating property with the TWEA and IEEPA, the federal courts do at times maintain these legislative statutes have been either misinterpreted or applied inappropriately. With the loss of congressional intention, these situations see the courts finding the president's actions in the third prong of Jackson's framework.

This chapter concerns emergency economic legislation, but there are other cases where property rights are curtailed by the Executive in times of war and other national emergencies. That said, litigation before the courts that arise as a result of situations such as prize cases, nationalization of industries,[3] economic price control legislation,[4] and the destruction of property[5] by the Armed Forces do merit further investigation.

This chapter proceeds as follows. First, I note the history of the delegation of legislative powers from the Congress to the Executive during times of armed hostilities in general and economic emergency legislation in particular. I then show how the federal courts adjudicate cases where the Executive is infringing on property rights with authority claimed under the TWEA and IEEPA.

ARMED HOSTILITIES AND EMERGENCY ECONOMIC LEGISLATION

The two explanations for the growth of executive power are the resourcefulness of the "strong" president and the historical circumstances that arise which allow for the strong president to grab power (Fisher, 1970; 251). While the Congress delegates its authority to the Executive for a number of reasons, including its "ability to fill in details, continuity in office, flexibility of timing, acting as a channel of communication with other nations, 'unity' . . . and 'speed'" (Fisher, 251), it is the "speed," or the necessity of taking action during armed hostilities that is of concern.

The term emergency does not present itself in the text of the Constitution, but as chapter 1 demonstrates, the framing generation debated which branch of government should exercise power when the nation faced imminent danger. The main debate surrounding the Constitution was the distribution of power between the national government and the states, not the distribution of power between the two branches of the national government. That said, when the issue of war emerged, the governor of Virginia, Edmund Randolph, was quick to point out congressional deficiencies in its ability to either prevent wars between states or to protect the nation from foreign attack (Farrand, Vol. 1; 25). Recognizing the "dangerous time gap" that presents itself between the actual outbreak of hostilities and the response by Congress, James Madison and Elbridge Gerry convinced the delegates to change the language from Congress having the right to make war to declare war, leaving the actual conduct of hostilities in the hands of the president as commander-in-chief.

The structure of the government requires cooperation amongst the three elected branches of government to protect the nation when its security is threatened, as my case studies on military detention and warrantless electronic surveillance have shown. Therefore, it should come as no wonder that a body of law numbering over 170 statutes has been created to deal with emergencies that delegate authority from Congress to the Executive. It was generally understood that while public administration was "largely an executive function" to "fill in the details" of the law," it was not "tantamount to presidential possession of a blank check" (Monaghan, 1993; 39). In fact, president, and later Chief Justice, William Howard Taft argued that "the

President can exercise no power which cannot be fairly and reasonably traced to some specific grant of power . . . either in the Federal Constitution or in an act of Congress passed in pursuance thereof" (Taft, 1925; 143).

The power of Congress to delegate authority to the other branches of government was questioned before the federal courts. In *Wayman v. Southard,* 23 U.S. (10 Wheat) 311; 1825, the Supreme Court was asked to decide whether or not the legislative powers of Congress included delegating legislative authority to the Judiciary with the *Judiciary Act* of 1789. The Act authorized the courts to make and establish rules concerning the conduct of their own business. Chief Justice Marshall held that "the maker of law may commit something to the discretion of the other departments, and the precise boundary of this power is subject to the delicate and difficult inquiry, into which a court will not enter unnecessarily." This position would be reaffirmed on a number of occasions. Despite the *Field v. Clark* (143 U.S. 649; 1891) decision where the Court held that legislative power could not be delegated from Congress to the Executive, one year later in *Field v. United States,* 143 U.S. 649; 1892, the Court held that Congress has the ability to delegate its powers to the Executive, within limits: "[t]he legislature cannot delegate its power to make a law, but it can make a law to delegate a power to determine some fact or state of things upon which the law makes, or intends to make, its own action depend."[6] It would take more than 30 years before the Court would again confirm that Congress cannot delegate the power to make laws but it can confer "authority or discretion as to its execution, to be exercised under and in pursuance of the law (Taft's *Hampton & Co v. United States,* 276 U.S. 394; 1928 opinion). With that said, however, Congress is not free to delegate whatever power it wants to the Executive.

Valid delegation requires legislative declaration of policy which must broadly outline actions to be taken by the Executive (Tanenhaus, 1956; 109). In *Schechter Poultry Corp. v United States* (295 U.S. 495; 1935), the Supreme Court held that Congress could not "delegate sweeping authority to the Executive to establish codes of fair competition governing all business subject to national regulation" (Tanenhaus, 109). Rejecting peacetime emergency delegation of authority to regulate commerce from Congress to the Executive, the Court held that "extraordinary conditions do not create or enlarge constitutional power . . . Such assertions of extraconstitutional authority were anticipated and precluded by the explicit terms of the Tenth Amendment. There are only two instances of the Court striking down actions of the Congress delegating power to the Executive, *Schechter Poultry Corp. v. United States,* 295 U.S. 495; 1935, and *Panama Refining Co. v. Ryan,* 293 U.S. 388; 1935" (Cohen et al., 1981; 850). To sum up, delegation of powers from Congress to the Executive was originally viewed as having boundaries between implementing law and the ability to create it.[7] However, the barrier against authorizing the Executive with the power to legislate has all but collapsed (Monaghan, 1993; 5).

The emergency statutes and extra powers delegated to the Executive can be brought into play in a number of ways under a number of circumstances. The important point to remember is that a state of war does not need to exist before legislation meant to aid the president in dealing with emergencies can be called into action. As early as 1792, residents of Pennsylvania, Virginia, and the Carolinas violently opposed a tax on whiskey. Congress passed legislation that would allow the president to call forth the militias to suppress insurrection, a power specifically given to Congress in the Constitution. A state of war did not exist, and certainly was not declared, but in August, 1794, President Washington issued the proclamation for the first time calling troops to protect the nation. This was the start of a pattern of policy implementation regarding war powers where Congress delegated its power to the Executive. The president gets authorization to act swiftly in situations where Congress is unable to do so.

During the Civil War, Lincoln's efforts to protect the Union included a blockade of Southern ports, an expansion of the Army and the Navy as well as a suspension of the writ of habeas corpus. Each action received retroactive congressional authorization as if these uses of the war powers were committed with previous authority and direction from the Congress. By time of the First World War, laws delegating power to the Executive in emergency situations included laws that were economic in nature.

There was "a major procedural development [that] occurred in the exercise of emergency powers" during World War I and World War II (Relyea, 2005; 7). The first executive proclamation of a national emergency was declared by President Wilson on February 5, 1917. Wilson's authority for the proclamation came under an Act authorizing the establishment of the United States Shipping Board. The national emergency was terminated in March 1921. Congress also authorized Wilson to do a number of things related to economic emergency powers during the war, including the power to "take possession of American vessels and to declare embargoes, fix prices and sell war material, operate the railroads and take control of communications systems, provide for war housing, license commerce, and manufacture and store and distribute the necessaries of life" (Fisher, 1970; 269). By the end of the war, however, Wilson relinquished his wartime authority, and also asked Congress to repeal all of the emergency statutes that were enacted for national security purposes. Congress obliged with the exception of the *Trading with the Enemy Act,* maintaining the shift of power from Congress to the president to regulate trade and financial transactions between Americans and foreign nationals.

Three separate categories of laws exist which are triggered depending on the type of emergency facing the nation. First, Congress can declare war. Second, a state of war can exist without a formal declaration. Emergency legislation is often triggered when such a state exists. I refer to these situations as times when the United States have been involved in armed hostilities. Finally, other emergency legislation is triggered when a state of national emergency is declared by the president.[8] Economic emergency legislation delegated to regulate the economy varies from a declaration of war by Congress to a national emergency. A declaration of war gives the Executive full control over regulating trade with foreign nations considered to be the enemy. Other economic powers transferred to the president upon a declaration of war include the ability to "order plants to convert to the production of armaments and to seize those that refuse to do so . . . to condemn land for military uses . . . to have the right of first refusal over natural resources . . . It also gives the President full power over agricultural exports" (Ackerman and Grimmett, 2003; 30). A congressional authorization for the use of force, however, does not in and of itself trigger these statutes.

There are statutes that come into effect if armed hostilities exist but Congress does not declare the situation a war. The *Trading with the Enemy Act* fell under this category until it was amended in 1977 with the passage of the *International Emergency Economic Powers Act,* thus ensuring the TWEA is invoked only during declared wars. Other powers triggered by the existence, but not necessarily the declaration of war, include the power to take control of the Tennessee Valley Authority for the production of explosives and other wartime materials, as well as giving the Executive the authority to, under the *Tariff Act* of 1930, authorize the importation of material needed for emergency relief work free of duty (Ackerman and Grimmett, 2003; 60). Congress has also authorized the Executive to sell arms to any nation that is at war with a nation at war with the United States.

Standby authorities available to the Executive in a time of national emergency do not come into effect automatically as they do when Congress declares war or when a state of war simply exists. Procedures for the statutes to be enacted are followed pursuant to requirements laid out in the National Emergencies Act of 1970. Prior to their use, the president is required to specify in the proclamation of emergency, or by Executive Order, which emergency statutory authorities the Executive will exercise. Examples include the authority to increase or terminate quotas for wheat production, as well as other goods such as cotton, rice, tobacco, and peanuts in efforts to meet demands due to a national emergency (Ackerman and Grimmett, 2003; 68), as well as freeze assets of foreign nations involved in creating the national emergency.

The IEEPA was passed as a statute that would be used in times of perceived peace as the Iran hostage situation shows, but my analysis regards how the federal courts deal with Executive limitations to rights during armed hostilities. If the Act is used to limit rights when the nation is involved in military conflicts abroad, it is appropriate to be included in my analysis. The IEEPA falls under an Act that comes into play only when a national emergency is declared and grants power to the Executive to regulate the financial dealings of foreign powers with the United States to "deal with any unusual and extraordinary threat, which has its source in whole or substantial part outside the United States, to the national security, foreign policy, or economy of the United States."[9]

Knowing that the delegation of authority from Congress to the Executive will rarely be struck down by the courts, is there any protection for property rights when the Executive invokes its power delegated by Congress in the TWEA and the IEEPA? The federal courts protect individual property rights when the actions in question are considered contrary to the intent of Congress. This shows that legislating emergency powers to the Executive does not automatically equal a blank check to the president as all actions taken in the name of such laws do not by design fall into the first prong of Jackson's framework where the president receives lenient scrutiny from the federal courts.

TRADING WITH THE ENEMY ACT

It is within congressional jurisdiction to regulate foreign-owned property in the territory of the United States. This authority is derived from Congress' power to regulate transactions that affect money and currency as well as the powers to regulate interstate and foreign commerce found in Article I of the Constitution. Traditionally, property of the enemy living within American borders could not be confiscated. Alexander Hamilton, in the Camillus Letters, No. 18 and 19, stated that "[n]o powers of language at my command can express the abhorrence I feel at the idea of violating the property of individuals, which, in an authorized intercourse, in times of peace, has been confided to the faith of our Government and laws, on account of controversies between nation and nation" (as quoted in Hays, 1923; 62). It was held in *Brown v. United States,* 8 Cranch 110; 1814 that "[w]hen war breaks out, the question, what shall be done with enemy property in our country, is a question rather of policy than of law. The rule which we apply to the property of our enemy will be applied by him to the property of our citizens." According to the Court, an act authorizing the confiscation of enemy property by the Executive would be required from Congress.

In the 1800s, it was only during the Civil War that government officials confiscated enemy property. Secretary of the Treasury, and future Chief Justice of the Supreme Court, Salmon P. Chase argued in favor of confiscating enemy property.[10] Confiscation legislation introduced in December 1861 allowed for the widespread confiscation of rebel property. The Act called for "the property of all persons out of reach of ordinary process of law who were found in arms against the United States or giving aid or comfort to the rebellion, was to be forfeited, the seizures to be carried out by such officers, military or civil, as the President should designate for the purpose" (Randall, 1912; 80).

After the Civil War, when the constitutionality of the *Confiscation Acts* reached the Supreme Court in *Union Insurance Company v. United States,* 73 U.S. 759; 1868, the Court found an Act of Congress passed "to confiscate property used for insurrectionary purposes" including "all descriptions of property, real or personal, on land or on water. All alike were made subjects of prize and capture, and, under the direction of the President, of seizure, confiscation, and condemnation" (Chase's *Union Insurance* opinion). Likewise, in *Miller v. United States,* 11 Wall. 268; 1870, the Court also held that confiscating the property of the enemy was a "lawful exercise of the war powers of the Government, and not an exercise of its sovereign or municipal power, and consequently not subject to restrictions imposed by the Fifth and Sixth Amendments" (Sommerich, 1945; 158). In Justice William Strong's Court opinion, Congress had the "full power to provide for the seizure and confiscation of any property which the enemy . . . could use for the purpose of maintaining the war against the government." Strong held that "the power to declare war involves the power to prosecute it by all means and in any manner in which war may be legitimately prosecuted. It therefore includes the right to seize and confiscate property of an enemy and dispose of it at the will of the captor" (Strong's *Miller* opinion).

The Court found a right expressed in the Constitution for Congress to provide for rules that included the confiscation of property, but the dissenting faction on the Court, held that the war powers were subject to limitations set out in the law of nations. Justice Stephen Johnson Field argued that "[t]here is a limit to the destruction which government, in the prosecution of war, may use, and there is a limit to the means of capture and confiscation, which government may authorize, imposed by the law of nations, and is no less binding upon Congress than if the limitation were written in the Constitution" (Field's *Miller* dissent).

It seemed as though government officials were initially in line with Field's *Miller* dissent at the outbreak of World War I. Two months before the United States entered the war, Secretary of State Robert Lansing stated that the

American Government would not "take advantage of a state of war to take possession of property to which international understandings and the recognized law of the land give it no just claim or title. It will scrupulously respect all private rights alike of its own citizens and of the subjects of foreign states" (Sommerich, 1945; 159). However, the *Trading with the Enemy Act* passed Congress eight months later; six months after the United States entered the War. The Act authorized the president to take possession of any money or property within the territory of the United States that belonged to an enemy. The Act also provided a means for owners to make claims on the property as having been taken erroneously (Sommerich, 159).

The *Trading with the Enemy Act* was supposed to be different than the confiscation of enemy property. In a hearing before the House Committee on the *Trading with the Enemy Act* in May 1917, Secretary of State Lansing stated the intentions of the Act were "a very decided protection to the property owner, because enemy property is subject to seizure by act of Congress. There is no question about the fact that under the general principle of international law property of enemy subjects would be liable to seizure . . . and this protects them from what might be considered unjust action by the Government because of its hardship on individuals (as quoted in Hays, 57). Before becoming Attorney General, Mitchell A. Palmer, the Alien Property Custodian in 1917, stated that "[t]he broad purpose of Congress, as expressed in the *Trading with the Enemy Act,* is first to preserve enemy-owned property situated in the United States from loss, and, secondly, to prevent every use of it which may be hostile or detrimental to the United States . . ." (as quoted in Hays, 60). The rhetoric concerned protection of property, but the rational basis for the *Trading with the Enemy Act* was "to prevent any transaction which might give aid, material or moral, to the enemy. This end would seem to justify, for instance, freezing regulations calculated to prevent the enemy from cashing in on foreign-owned American-held assets" (McNulty, 1945; 138).

The Act called for the president to determine if the property in question was enemy owned (Hays, 1923; 19). The president delegated this authority to the Alien Property Custodian. The position of custodian was first authorized, on October 12, 1917 and again on February 26, 1918, by Executive order. The custodian had the "power to determine after investigation whether property was enemy-owned etc., and to require the surrender or seizure of such as he should determine was so owned" (Lourie, 1943; 394).[11] Section 5 of the Act delegated authority to the Executive to appoint a Custodian, someone charged with being the caretaker or the guardian of the assets in question. The powers vested in the president could then become the powers of the custodian. Section 5(b) allows the president, or an individual appointed by the president, to freeze the property of the enemy and furthermore allows the Executive to "order that such foreign property shall be held, used, administered, liquidated, sold, or otherwise dealt with in the interest and for the benefit of the United States (Lourie, 1943; 396). This section of the Act applied during armed hostilities, but also during other periods of national emergency.

With only seven cases concerning the TWEA presented before the Supreme Court from the First World War, the Court by and large upheld the restrictions on individual liberties. However, the Court also refuses to shy away from saying when officials of the Executive overstep their boundaries by misinterpreting the intent of Congress.

Oftentimes, American citizens were caught in battling the legitimacy of the TWEA. The Supreme Court affirmed the lower court opinion (256 F. 565; 1919) in *Rumely v. McCarthy,* 250 U.S, 283; 1919, where an officer failed to report to the Alien Property Custodian stock he owned in a corporation on behalf of the government of Germany. Rumely argued he had the right not to incriminate himself, pursuant to the Fifth Amendment. The district court did not address the constitutional questions and dismissed the writ purely on the authority of the TWEA. The Supreme Court held that Fifth Amendment claims were premature as the "appellant's constitutional point merely raises a probability that a defense will be interposed, and that thus a controversy will arise, the determination of which is within the proper jurisdiction of the court in which the indictment was found" (Pitney's *Rumely* opinion). The case would be decided on jurisdictional issues, thus respecting Congress' wish to give broader authority to the Executive. Challenges to the legality of the Act itself under the Constitution would therefore not be addressed.

The Supreme Court again, in interpreting the TWEA, affirmed the lower court opinion[12], in *Central Union Trust Co. v. Garvan,* 254 U.S. 554; 1921. The property of German insurance companies was held by trustees in the United States. The property was seized by the Alien Property Custodian. Petitioners argued it was not an authorized seizure of property because they were not alien enemies. However, the Alien Property Custodian argued that it was in his power to decide what property was liable for seizure. The federal courts agreed, further directing the trustees' attention to section 9 of the TWEA which "provided for immediate claim and suit and required the property in such event to be retained in the custody of the Alien Property Custodian." Because it was provided for by statute, the delegation of authority from the president to the custodian was not seen as a violation of the Fifth Amendment. After all, due process of law was provided for in relation to the return of property under section 9 of the Act. Holmes held that "there can be no doubt that Congress has power to provide for an immediate seizure in war times of property supposed to belong to the enemy . . . if adequate provision is made for a return in case of mistake."[13]

That same year, the Court placed emphasis on the ability of Congress to meet the terms of the emergency at hand with legislation that would allow for the emergency to be adequately dealt with. Justice Van Devanter, relying on the *Central Union* decision, held "that Congress in time of war may authorize and provide for the seizure and sequestration through executive channels of property believed to be enemy-owned, if adequate provision be made for a return in case of mistake, is not debatable . . . There is no warrant for saying that the enemy ownership must be determined judicially before the property can be seized (Van Dervanter's *Stoehr* opinion). Furthermore, section 7(c) of the Act authorizes the president to determine enemy ownership of property before seizing property and the Court decided that "a personal determination by the President is not required; but he may act through the Custodian, and a determination by the latter is in effect the act of the President" (Van Devanter's *Stoehr* opinion). The delegation of power from Congress to the president and then to the Custodian was therefore upheld in *Stoehr v. Wallace,* 255 U.S. 239; 1921. The Court upheld the district court ruling in *Stoehr v. Wallace,* 269 F. 827; 1920, where Judge Learned Hand held that the text of the Act was clear that Congress delegated authority to the Executive to determine what property is considered to be enemy property. The case concerned 14,900 shares of Botany Worsted Mills corporation stock which was seized by the Alien Property Custodian as the property of a German corporation called Kammgarnspinnerei Stoehr & Co. Aktiengesellschaft. It was argued the shares were owned by a New York corporation. If this was the case, the confiscation of the shares was not consistent with due process guarantees found in the Fifth Amendment. A judicial proceeding where the owners of the shares would be able to defend their claims was sought. While the actions of the Executive are upheld based on a congressional delegation of power, the Supreme Court stated that the Fifth Amendment's due process clause was not violated because Congress provided for property owners the ability to "establish his right in a court of equity and compel a return of the property if wrongly sequestered."[14]

The Supreme Court did offer protection to neutrals mistaken for enemies, reversing a lower court decision that offered a more limiting construction of what was the intention of Congress regarding non enemy property confiscated by the Alien Property Custodian. In *Behn, Meyer & Company v. Miller,* 296 F. 1002; 1924, Judge Van Orsdel held that while recognizing the petitioner is in fact a non-enemy, a portion of its stock was enemy-owned, "and this is sufficient to prevent it from recovering [the stock] in its corporate capacity." The TWEA states that a corporation set up in a non-enemy country cannot recovery property unless it is owned by at least 50% by people who are not from states at war with the United States, so for Van Orsdel, the Congress had written the rules. However, the Supreme Court interpreted the Act differently. In *Behn, Meyer & Company Limited v. Miller,* 266 U.S. 457; 1925, a corporation that was not set up in and did not do business with any nation at war with the United States was entitled to "recover by suit the proceeds of its property, unlawfully seized by the Alien Property Custodian" (McReynolds' *Behn* opinion). The Court held that "section 7 (c) of the *Trading with the Enemy Act,* in authorizing seizure of property held 'on account of, or, on behalf of, or for the benefit of an enemy or ally of enemy,' was not intended to empower the President to seize the property of a non-enemy corporation merely because of enemy stockholding interests therein." Since the Court denied power was given to the Executive, the Court places *Behn* in the third prong of Jackson's framework where the Court is more critical of executive actions because it must possess power on its own constitutionally delegated authority to act. Put simply, the TWEA was misused by the Executive in *Behn* and the Court would again hold that the government overstepped its authority in *Russian Volunteer Fleet v. United States,* 282 U.S. 481, where the Court distinguished between aliens that are friend and foe. The Court held that an alien friend cannot have property confiscated without just compensation being paid.

Prior to the *First War Powers Act* (FWP Act), Congress, on May 7, 1940, passed a Joint Resolution ratifying the president's executive orders regulating enemy property. The *Trading with the Enemy Act* was amended during the Second World War to be used with the FWP Act in 1941. The Joint Resolution provided for "the regulation of the transfer, withdrawal or exportation of, or dealing 'in any evidences of . . . ownership of property in which any foreign state or a national or political subdivision thereof, as defined by the President, has any interest'" (Lourie, 1943; 208). This allowed the president the ability to decide whose citizens would have their assets frozen. Further, authority extended to all foreign property interests not only those from countries defined by the president. The president was authorized not only to "'freeze' foreign property, or interest in property, but to *vest* it" (Lourie, 1943; 212). To vest the assets of foreign nations was therefore to unconditionally take control of and to deny to third parties any control over said property.

Like President Wilson during World War I, Roosevelt appointed an Alien Property Custodian in March, 1942 with Executive Order 9095, amended by Executive Order 9192 from July 6, 1942, authorizing the Custodian to seize assets "payable or deliverable to, or claimed by, a designated enemy country or national thereof" (Jackson's *Brownell* dissent). As was the case during WWI, these Executive orders vesting power in the custodian derived their authority from the *Trading with the Enemy Act.* When challenges to the Act emerged, the Court again interpreted the specific clauses when deciding whether the Executive received authority from Congress to take the property in question. In *ex parte Don Ascandio Colonna,* 314 U.S. 510; 1944, the Italian Ambassador claimed a vessel and its cargo seized at the outbreak of the war were property of Italy and thus was entitled to sovereign immunity. The Court held that a state of war existed between the United States and Italy. Under section 7 of the TWEA, access to the federal courts was denied to any enemy of the State. The Court concluded that since Italy was an enemy of the United States, the right of the Ambassador to sue was suspended.

Other custodian-declared enemies sued for a return of confiscated property. A Swiss Corporation, German owned, sued because the owner had a usufruct property agreement with his son who no longer lived in Germany. The usufruct agreement meant that though the owner of the property was the father in Germany, the son could enjoy all the benefits of the assets without having the legal papers of ownership. In 1942, the Alien Property Custodian took possession of the stocks. The Supreme Court held in *Uebersee Finanz-Korporation, A. G. v. McGrath,* 343 U.S. 205; 1952, that "because of direct and indirect control and domination by an enemy national, petitioner was affected with an 'enemy taint' and cannot recover under s 9 (a)" of the TWEA, affirming the lower court decision which held similarly based on what was believed to be the "essence" of the TWEA—that being to deny financial benefit to the enemy (*Uebersee Finanz-Korporation, A. G. v. McGrath,* 191 F. 2d 327; 1951). However, in *Guessefeldt v. McGrath,* 342 U.S. 308; 1952, the Court held differently. The petitioner lived in the United States, went on a trip with his family to his native country and was detained in Germany by German forces and then again by Soviet Troops. Because he was forced to stay in Germany, unable to return for many years, he could hardly be considered an alien enemy under the terms of the TWEA and was afforded the protections that a friendly alien would receive. The Court considered the actions of the Executive to be overstretching its powers delegated to it by Congress in reversing the lower court decision (191 F. 2d 639; 1951) that held the property could not be returned because the petitioner was a German national and the terms of the law clearly stated he was an enemy of the nation by birth and subject to property confiscation.[15] Again, as was the case during WWI, we have a situation where the Supreme Court is willing to uphold the rights of those they believe the Executive has unfairly taken away their property, protecting constitutional rights, but using statutory interpretation to do it, when the lower courts are unwilling to do so.

The principle of protecting the property of friendly aliens was again upheld in *Kaufman et al. v. Societe Internationale pour participations industrielle et commerciales et al.,* 343 U.S. 156; 1952. Justice Hugo Black, writing for the Court again reversed the lower court's decision, which held that the petitioners need to have an interest in the corporation before they had the legal standing to intervene. Determining no interest to exist, the case was dismissed without ruling on the merits of the issue (188 F. 2d 1017; 1951). The Supreme Court, believing an interest to intervene was present, held that "when the Government seizes assets of a corporation organized under the laws of a neutral country, the rights of innocent stockholders to an interest in the assets proportionate to their stock holdings must be fully protected."

The Court's rationale is based not "on any technical concept of derivative rights appropriate to the law of corporations. It is based on the Act which enables one not an enemy as defined in § 2 to recover any interest, right or title which he has in the property vested" (Black's *Kaufman* opinion). However, five years earlier, the Custodian seized stock from a Swiss corporation that "organized under the laws of various States of this nation and of an interest in a contract between two such corporations" (Douglas' *Uebersee Finanz-Korporation* opinion). The petitioners claimed that the Corporation being set up in Switzerland was not liable to be taken as enemy property. Because it was discovered that Germany became astute in concealing its ownership of foreign companies, Congress broadened the powers of the Custodian between World War I and World War II to grant wider scope of vesting powers in the president.

In *Clark v. Uebersee Finanz-Korporation, A.G.,* 332 U.S. 480; 1947, the Court affirmed the Court of Appeals decision[16], holding that the Executive was allowed to vest the "property of all foreign interests . . . not to appropriate friendly or neutral assets but to reach enemy interests which masqueraded under those innocent fronts" (Douglas' *Uebersee* opinion). While the Court maintained the legitimacy of the amendments to the TWEA of Congress, it affirmed that a non-enemy could still reclaim property if confiscated erroneously. Justice Douglas notes that some process of review of the Custodian's actions must occur. Douglas reasoned that "[i]t is not easy for us to assume that Congress treated all non-enemy nations, including our recent allies, in such a harsh manner, leaving them only with such remedy as they might have under the Fifth Amendment" and that a legislated scheme was put in place by Congress to ensure that companies free of enemy taint would be able to steer clear of the TWEA's clutches. The Court, as mandated by statute, not addressing the constitutional claims, allowed for foreign nationals to reclaim property taken if they were non-enemies.

In *Markham v. Cabell,* 326 U.S. 404; 1945, the Supreme Court held that just because Congress amended the TWEA between wars did not mean it intended to take away any jurisdiction to use the courts in an attempt to regain property if wrongly taken. Section 9 states that "'unless it was owing to an owner by the claimant prior to October 6, 1917' nor 'unless notice of the claim has been filed, or application therefore has been made, prior to the date of the enactment of the *Settlement of War Claims Act* of 1928.'" If this section was applicable, the claim would be dismissed because of the date. The Court held that the legislation in question was not reenacted with the outbreak of WWII and that it instead automatically went into effect. The Court continues that section 9(e) extended rights of property recovery to any person who is a citizen of a country at war with the United States. The use of past tense indicated that the clause referred only to cases during World War I, having been added in 1920 at the end of the War. Finally, the Court continues that "these considerations indicate to us that it would be a distortion to read section 9(e) as if Congress in December 1941 decided that the statute of limitations applicable to World War I claims should likewise be applicable to World War II claims." Thus, the Court affirmed the lower court opinion that again decided the case by interpreting the intentions of Congress (*Markham v. Cabell,* 148 F. 2d 737; 1945).

In consideration of who can and who cannot sue to reclaim their property, *Cities Services Co. et. al. v. McGrath,* 342 U.S. 330; 1952, was similarly held as *Markham* when the Court unanimously decided that section 7 of the TWEA "authorizes the vesting of obligations evidenced by negotiable debentures payable to the bearer, the obligators of which are within the United States, even though the debentures themselves are not in the possession of the Custodian and are outside of the United States" (Clark's *Cities* opinion). The Court had affirmed the lower court opinion that, while deciding the case by a statutory construction of the TWEA, as all the cases before it, did mention the Fifth Amendment in pointing out that protects the property of those not at war with the United States. This is noted because it implies that the Fifth Amendment may be inapplicable during war for those at war with the United States, though no Supreme Court decision makes such a bold claim. If this is in fact the case, we have another example of the Court offering protections for individual liberties during armed conflict that the Court may be unwilling to extend when looking to the Bill of Rights directly for such protections.

The Court also protects the rights of individuals by ruling that treaties are to be interpreted as laws of the land and that the outbreak of the war did not necessarily suspend treaty provisions. In *Clark v. Allen et. al.,* 331 U.S. 503; 1947, the Court held that the TWEA and the pursuant Executive Orders "do not evince such hostility to ownership of property by alien enemies as to imply that its acquisition conflicts with the national policy" (Douglas' *Clark* opinion). Therefore, the intent of the TWEA could not be meant to deny German nationals of their inheritances. As such, when Alvina Wagner, a resident of California, passed away in 1942 and left her estate to relatives in Germany, the property could not be taken by the Property Custodian as enemy property.

As international laws were taken into consideration if they conflict with the intent of the TWEA, on occasion, state laws too were examined. When the administration of frozen property was a concern, the Supreme Court held that state court decisions were not contrary to the First *War Powers Act* of 1941 or the executive orders on the matter. The Court was firm that "since the New York court conditioned enforcement of the claims upon licensing by the Alien Property custodian, federal control over alien property remains undiminished" (*Lyon v. Singer,* 339 U.S. 841; 1950). When the transfer of assets belonging to German nationals was prohibited by Executive Order, pursuant to section 5(b) of the TWEA, some American holders of claims against German "banks levied attachments on the debtors' accounts." The Alien Property Custodian issued vesting orders to claim the property of the debtors. The Court held that section 5 (b)(1) of the TWEA "authorized the vesting of such foreign-owned property in the Custodian and was a liquidation measure for the protection of American creditors" (*Zittman v. McGrath,* 341 U.S. 471; 1951), and the Executive Order prevented any creditors from acquiring interest in property held by the custodian (*Orvis et. al. v. Brownell,* 345 U.S. 183; 1953). These cases all affirmed lower court decisions based on the TWEA.[17]

On the flip side, however, "because outstanding attachments had been levied, the New York bank refused to release the property to the Custodian. Writing for the Court, Jackson held that the state courts, having granted attachments, judgments did not "control or limit . . . federal control over alien property, when the creditors were obligated to secure a license before obtaining payment from funds" (*Zittman v. McGrath,* 341 U.S. 446; 1951). In fact, the Custodian is charged with "preserving and distributing blocked assets for the benefit of American creditors. . . . If, as the Custodian now contends, the freezing program puts all assets of an alien debtor beyond the reach of an attachment, it is not difficult to see that there can be no adjudications of the validity of the American claims and consequently the claims, not being settled, would not be satisfied by the Treasury. . . . We cannot believe that the President intended the program to reach such a self-generated stalemate" (Jackson's *Zittman* opinion). In this case, the Court acknowledged the power the Act gave the president but interprets the Executive Order where the president implements the power given to him in the TWEA as not to be so overreaching as the policy put in place by the Custodian suggests. The Court therefore holds that the power Congress gave to the president remains intact, but the interpretation of presidential directives on the part of the Custodian was mistaken to the intent of the federal government.[18]

Section 17 of the TWEA proscribed penalties. The Court allowed the Custodian to seek judgment in the district courts over probate matters of deciding heirship to the possession of property as mandated by statute. When such power was challenged, Justice Stone held that the act "plainly indicated that Congress had adopted the policy of permitting the Custodian to proceed in the district courts to enforce his rights under the Act, whether they depended on state or federal law" (Stone's opinion in *Markham v. Allen,* 326 U.S. 490; 1946). This section of the Act, allowing for taking of property by the Executive, would be upheld twice more in *McGrath v. Manufacturers Trust Co.,* 338 U.S. 241; 1949 and *Propper v. Clark,* 337 U.S. 472; 1949.[19] The Court also allowed the Alien Property Custodian to vest in himself stock being held by a friendly national on behalf of an enemy (*Silesian-American Corp. et. al. v. Clark,* 332 U.S. 469; 1947). Justice Reed restates the *United States v. Chemical Foundation,* 272 U.S. 1; 1926 decision where the Court held that upon statutory authorization, the Executive has authority to vest in itself the property of an enemy national. In only one of these cases did the Supreme Court overturn a lower court decision interpretation of the TWEA. *Markham v. Allen* overturned *Allen v. Markham,* 147 F.2d 136; 1945, because the court of appeal was unwilling to make a ruling on the matter since the issue was in probate court. *McGrath v. Manufacturers Trust Co.* affirmed *Clark v. Manufacturers Trust Co.,* 169 F.2d 932; 1948. *Propper v. Clark* affirmed *Clark v. Propper,* 169 F.2d 324; 1948, *Silesian-American Corp.* affirmed *Silesian-American Corp. v. Markham,* 156 F.2d 793; 1946 and *Chemical Foundation* affirmed *United States v. Chemical Foundation,* 5 F.2d 191; 1925.

Between the mid 1950s and the passage of the *International Economic Emergency Powers Act* in 1977, only one case dealing with the Executive curtailing individual liberties under the authority of the *Trading with the Enemy Act* made its way to the Supreme Court. Concerning World War II, in *Honda et. al. v. Clark,* 386 U.S. 484; 1967, the Court decided whether the government was stopped from asserting the 60 day limitation on making claims on property seized during the war. Section 34 (f) of the TWEA, added in 1946, provided for the payment "from the vested assets to American citizens or resident creditors of persons who property was vested" (Justice John Marshall Harlan's *Honda* opinion). The lawsuit was brought on behalf of 4,100 citizens who had yen certificates in the *Yokohama Specie Bank.* The Court held that "since the statutory scheme of § 34, which was modeled on the *Bankruptcy Act,* was intended to provide a fair and equitable distribution of vested enemy assets to America residents and citizens . . . petitioners' right to bring their suit was not foreclosed (Harlan's *Honda* opinion).

Table 5.1 shows that cases concerning the *Trading with the Enemy Act* are decided neatly along statutory lines, with each case falling under either

Table 5.1. *Trading with the Enemy Act* before the Federal Courts

	Court upheld executive action	*Court struck down executive action*
Congressional authorization	*Rumely v. McCarthy,* 1919	
	Central Un. v. Garvan, 1920	
	Stoehr v. Wallace, 1920	
	Central Un. v. Garvan, 1921	
	Stoehr v. Wallace, 1921	
	American v. Garvan, 1921	
	Behn... Co., v. Miller, 1924	
	U.S. v. Chemical Found, 1925	
	U.S. v. Chemical Found, 1926	
	Silesian Corp v. Clark, 1946	
	ex parte ... Colonna, 1944	
	Markham v. Allen, 1946	
	Uebersee v. Markham, 1946	
	Clark v. Manufacturers, 1946	
	Clark v. Uebersee, 1947	
	Clark v. Propper, 1948	
	McGrath v. Manuf..., 1949	
	Propper v. Clark, 1949	
	McGrath v. Chase Nat., 1950	
	Zittman v. McGrath I, 1951	
	Guessefeldt v. McGrath, 1951	
	Kaufman v. Societe..., 1951	
	Uebersee v. McGrath, 1951	
	Uebersee v. McGrath, 1952	
	Orvis et. al. v. McGrath, 1952	
	Orvis et. al. v. Brownell, 1953	
No Congressional authorization/ contrary to the wishes of Congress		*Russian Volunteer... v. U.S.,* 1931
		Markham v. Cabell, 1945
		Clark v. Allen, 1947
		Yokohama Specie Bank, 1949
		Lyon v. Singer, 1950
		Zittman v. McGrath II, 1951
		Cities... v. McGrath, 1951
		Cities... v. McGrath, 1952
		Guessefeldt v. McGrath, 1952
		Kaufman et. al. v. Societe..., 1952
		Honda v. Clark, 1967

the first or third prong of the Jackson framework. If the Court considered the Act to have authorized the Executive's actions, they are upheld. The cases where the actions of the Custodian are not upheld are in situations where the Court finds the property owner was withheld due process in claiming to get the property back, if so authorized. These decisions are based on the TWEA actually providing for the due process in question by appealing to the federal courts for remedies when property is taken contrary to the stipulations in the Act of Congress.

THE *INTERNATIONAL EMERGENCY ECONOMIC POWERS ACT*

In more recent years, the private property of aliens has been curtailed via executive orders pursuant to an Act of Congress that stemmed from the TWEA. Congress passed the *International Emergency Economic Powers Act* (IEEPA) in 1977. Until 1977, authority to regulate foreign economic transactions was granted by the *Trading with the Enemy Act.* The Act was exercised in times of both war and peace. Congress passed the IEEPA, changing the TWEA to only apply during times of declared war. The IEEPA would only be applicable during times of declared national emergency. Though duplicating many of the TWEA's powers in regulating international financial transactions, the IEEPA did "not include TWEA authorities relative to purely domestic transactions, the regulation of bullion, and seizure of records. It also does not contain TWEA's general authority to take title of foreign assets (Ackerman and Grimmett, 2003; 29).[20]

The Act was meant to limit executive authority, curtailing the peacetime powers of the president exercised as a result of section 5(b) of the TWEA.[21] Section 202(a) of the IEEPA grants to the president the proper ability that "may be exercised to deal with any unusual and extraordinary threat, which has its source in whole or substantial part outside the United States, to the national security, foreign policy, or economy of the United States, if the President declares a national emergency with respect to such threat" (*Dames & Moore* v. *Regan,* 453 U.S. 654; 1981). Cases concerning the IEEPA have reached the Supreme Court only twice. Neither case specifically concerned armed hostilities, but both are important to show how the Supreme Court viewed the power of the Executive to control assets of foreign powers.

On November 4, 1979, the American Embassy in Tehran was seized and hostages were taken. An agreement was fostered between Iran and the Carter Administration where the states were obliged to "[t]erminate all legal proceedings in United States courts involving claims of United States persons and institutions against Iran . . . to nullify all attachments and judgments obtained therein, to prohibit all further litigation based on such claims, and to bring about the termination of such claims through binding arbitration" (Rehnquist *Dames & Moore* opinion). Iran's assets in the United States were unfrozen as part of a deal to have American hostages released. Carter issued a series of executive orders following these guidelines. Upon taking office, President Reagan issued an Executive Order ratifying all of Carter's orders.

Carter cited inherent executive power as his authority to issue the orders. The IEEPA was used by President Reagan to "nullify the attachments and order the transfer of Iranian assets . . . [as the IEEPA] empowers the President to 'compel,' and 'nullify' or 'prohibit' any transfer with respect to, or transactions involving, and property subject to the jurisdiction of the United States, in which any foreign country has any interest" (Rehnquist's *Dames & Moore* opinion).

The Court argued that despite the IEEPA not offering explicit authorization of his actions, congressional acceptance of the actions existed, acting as a delegation of authority of sorts to the office of the Executive. In *Dames & Moore v. Regan,* 453 U.S. 654; 1981, the decision of the Court unanimously gave its consent for the implementation of the Algerian Declarations, stopping several court cases in progress where American citizens were suing for their property believed to be owed to them by companies in Iran. The president argued that statutory authorization existed under the IEEPA and the *Release of Citizens Imprisoned by Foreign Governments Act* of 1868.[22] The Court decided that the Act of 1868 did not apply because its intent was specific and limited in nature where those detained were done so in utter disregard of their citizenship with no intention of being returned, not because of their citizenship was the case in Iran (Cohen et al.; 848). The Court examined the statutory provisions in relation to the settlement of foreign claims in the IEEPA and found no explicit congressional authorization. However, the Court found other statutory authorization that allowed the president to unfreeze the assets as well as "a history of executive action in this field" (Covey, 1996; 1328). After all, there were "no fewer than eighty executive agreements to liquidate claims . . . between 1817 and 1917, and at least ten had been entered into since 1952" (Raven-Hansen and Banks, 1994; 851). Since Congress had ample opportunity to limit this practice of the Executive as well as its "enactment of collateral, but consistent, legislation, may be taken as acquiescence sufficient to establish customary law" (Raven-Hansen and Banks, 852). The decision allowed the Reagan Administration to officially end the hostage crisis "without being embarrassed by the judicial branch" (Covey, 1328).

While the statutes mentioned did not specifically grant authority for the president to unfreeze the assets, Rehnquist continued that "[w]e think both statutes highly relevant in the looser sense of indicating congressional acceptance of a broad scope for executive action in circumstances such as those presented in this case." Because Congress did not authorize the actions of the president, but allowed the actions to occur over a number of decades without having done anything about it, the Court decided that this was enough to acquiesce to the Executive's actions as suggested takes place in Jackson's *Youngstown* concurrence where Executive and Congress have concurrent powers and must work in the "zone of twilight" of foreign affairs. The Court actually uses a statute to place the Executive in the second prong of Jackson's framework, because it held that Congress' inability to restrict executive actions in the legislation in the face of decades of precedent. Since the IEEPA was supposed to limit the power of the president, Congress' omission of prohibiting the unfreezing foreign assets therefore allowed the Executive to continue its practice of doing so. Whereas Rehnquist quotes the first prong of Jackson's framework, he actually finds executive authority using a second prong analysis.[23]

The other case to specifically address the IEEPA at the Supreme Court level is *Regan v. Wald,* 468 U.S. 222; 1984. The Court held that the president does not need to declare a new national emergency to continue an embargo on Cuba. Moreover, the Court deemed that the grandfather clause of the TWEA allowed for current embargoes to stay in place in light of the new legislative requirements. Rehnquist states that "[s]ince the authority to regulate travel-related transactions was among those 'authorities conferred upon the President' by 5(b) of TWEA 'which were being exercised' with respect to Cuba on July 1, 1977, it seems to us to follow from a natural reading of the grandfather clause that the authority to regulate such transactions 'may continue to be exercised' with respect to Cuba after that date" (Rehnquist's *Wald* opinion). The Court concludes that due process was not infringed upon by the Government's effort to limit the flow of hard currency to Cuba and was able to restrict travel of Americans to the island.

The dissent in *Wald* is also based on statutory claims, not constitutional ones. Justice Blackmun points out that the entire purpose of the IEEPA was to limit executive authority in controlling foreign assets in times of peace. Acknowledging that the IEEPA left in tact the TWEA powers conferred on the Executive in times of war, Blackmun points out that the Act

> removed from the TWEA the authority for presidential action in a national emergency. As a substitute for those powers, Congress promulgated the IEEPA to confer upon the President in national-emergency situations. The substantive reach of the President's power under the IEEPA is slightly narrower than it had been under the TWEA, and Congress placed several procedural restrictions on the President's exercise of the national-emergency powers, including congressional consultation, review and termination (Blackmun's *Wald* dissent).

Despite the dissent on statutory claims, the Court does not consider the president's actions under the Act an overreach of delegated authority.

With only two cases reaching the Supreme Court concerning the Act, 37 cases have gone through the federal court of appeals. Most of these cases deal with national emergencies stemming from the Iranian hostage situation as well as issues concerning Libya and terrorist activity prior to 9/11. However, there are some key cases that have occurred during times when the nation was engaged in armed hostilities, specifically in Iraq during the first Gulf War, in relation to the former Yugoslavia and today during the armed hostilities in Afghanistan and Iraq. The courts have yet to limit the power of the Executive under the IEEPA.

When Iraq invaded Kuwait on August 2, 1990, President G. H. W. Bush declared a national emergency and issued an Executive Order denying to Americans the right to have dealings with the Iraqi government or its agents including the exportation of goods and technology. The Arch Trading Company violated the terms of the Executive Order. In *United States v. Arch Trading Company,* 987 F. 2d 1087; 1993, the Arch Trading Company argued that Congress unconstitutionally delegated authority to the president to create crimes. The court rejected the claim that "violation of an executive order cannot constitute an offense. . . . While it may be that executive orders cannot alone establish crimes, when such orders are duly authorized by an act of Congress and Congress specifies a criminal sanction for their violation, the consequence is different" (Judge Niemeyer's *Arch Trading* opinion). The same broadly interpreted authority can be found in the conclusions of *United States v. Al M. Harb,* 111 F.3d 130; 1997 and *United States v. Rafil Dhafir,* 461 F. 3d 211; 2006.

During the first Gulf War, the president also froze all assets to which Iraq had an interest. A part of this process was freezing $6.4 million sitting in an Iraqi bank that was payment for furnaces bought by the Iraqi Ministry of Industry and Minerals from an American company, Consarc. The government also froze the goods that Consarc sold. Consarc resold one of the furnaces to Mitsubishi and the government wanted the proceeds from the sale to be frozen, as well as the $1.1 million down payment the company received for the furnaces from Iraq. In *Consarc Corporation v. United States Treasury Department,* 315 U.S. App. D.C. 201; 1995, Judge Sentelle held that "[a]lthough Iraq may no longer have any interest in its down payment, it still has some interest in the goods for which the down payment was paid and some interest in the transaction." Like the *Dames & Moore* decision, the court reasoned that since the text of the statute did not restrict the Office of Foreign Assets Control (OFAC) from enforcing its regulation by using the money received from the down payment or the goods themselves, then the Executive's officials could proceed in this manner, again finding the Executive in the second prong of Jackson's framework by way of congressional acquiesce.

After the legislative line-item veto was struck down by the Supreme Court in *INS v. Chadha,* 462 U.S. 919; 1983,[24] the constitutionality of the IEEPA was challenged. In *United States v. Manuel Romero-Fernandez,* 983 F. 2d 195; 1993, the defendants were convicted of violating Executive Order 12724 and the IEEPA for "knowingly and willfully dealing and engaging in activity that promoted and intended to promote dealing in one million barrels of Iraqi crude oil for exportation from Iraq" (*per curiam Romero-Fernandez* opinion). The circuit court held that "section 208 of the IEEPA provided for severability, and the court noted that the inclusion of a severability clause created a presumption that the U.S. Congress did not intend the validity of the statute to depend on the validity of the constitutionally offensive provision" (*per curiam Romero-Fernandez* opinion). The legislative veto component to the Act could be taken out of the IEEPA without jeopardizing the spirit of the law. In other words, Congress lost this important check on presidential power but it did not affect the overall way the courts would view the powers delegated to the Executive under the Act in the first place. After all, the type of check on the powers of the Executive by way of the legislative veto was unconstitutional while the delegation of power under the IEEPA was not.

A number of cases also arose concerning the conflict in the former Yugoslavia. When a property owner's lease with the Socialist Federal Republic of Yugoslavia (SFRY) was terminated after the United States froze the State's assets once it ceased to exist. In *767 Third Avenue Associates et. al. v. United States,* 48 F.3d 1575; 1995, the property owners sued saying the government's actions constituted a property taking under the Fifth Amendment. The court rejected the claim that a taking occurred determining that the government did not physically occupy the premises. When the court heard claims to determine if the Yugoslavian government had a vested interest in all vessels owned by Yugoslavian companies, the court sided with the OFAC stating that this position was "reasonable in implementing economic sanctions." In *Milena Ship Management Company v. R. Richard Newcomb,* 995 F. 2d 620; 1993, the president issued two executive orders that imposed UN mandated economic sanctions against the Federal Republic of Yugoslavia, which was unrecognized internationally. The OFAC argued it could not release the vessel because such action would be contrary to *Security Council Resolution 757* and that the government of the FRY retains an interest in all companies because it receives proceeds from the sale of what are called social capital stock, shares in each company retained by the government rather than being sold as personal shares. Because the FRY retains interest in the company, the IEEPA allows for the Executive to block the vessel in question because Congress' Act allows the Executive to prevent "transactions involving any property in which any foreign country or a national thereof has any interest, by any person, or with respect to any property, subject to the jurisdiction of the United States."

After the terrorist attacks on September 11, 2001, President Bush formally declared a national emergency on September 14 and 23, 2001 in accordance with the *National Emergencies Act.* The national emergency invoked the IEEPA. On September 24, 2001, Bush issued Executive Order 13224, pursuant to the IEEPA, with the purpose of "Blocking Property and Prohibiting Transactions With Persons Who Commit, Threaten to Commit, or Support Terrorism."[25] Furthermore, upon the intervention in Iraq, Bush issued Executive Order 13303 in May 2003, declaring a national emergency "for purposes of protecting the development fund for Iraq and certain other property in which Iraq has an interest" (Relyea, 2005; 6). Authorization for this Executive Order was also the IEEPA.

To date, no cases have reached the Supreme Court level dealing with the IEEPA concerning 9/11. However, most recently, in February 2007, the Circuit Court of Appeals for the District of Columbia, held that organizations have no Fifth Amendment rights to fund incidents related to terrorism. Further, the government, under the IEEPA, is within its power to block terrorist assets. The OFAC determined that the Islamic American Relief Agency's parent company was a Specially Designated Global Terrorist liable to have its assets frozen pursuant to Executive Order and the IEEPA. The relief agency maintained it was a different entity from the Islamic African Relief Agency, arguing that as an American agency its constitutional rights of equal protection, free exercise of religion and free association were violated. Judge Sentelle rejected these claims holding that the "President may exercise his authority under the IEEPA to deal with any unusual and extraordinary threat, which has its source in whole or substantial part outside of the United States, to the national security, foreign policy, or economy of the United States, if the President declares a national emergency" (*Islamic American Relief Agency v. Gonzales,* 375 U.S. App. D.C. 93; 2007 opinion). Similar results were held in *Holy Land Foundation for Relief and Development v. Ashcroft,* 357 U.S. App. D. C. 35; 2003. Furthermore, in *Global Relief Foundation v. O'Neill,* 315 F.3d 748; 2002, the court again upheld the power of the government to freeze the funds of a relief agency designated by the government as funding terrorism, despite the agency being Illinois based, not foreign. The court held it was who benefits from the funds and not just who has legal interest that was the intent of Congress in passing the IEEPA, when legislating that assets of a company where a foreign government has an interest in the assets can be frozen.

In *United States v. Abdurahman M. Alamdoudi,* 452 F.3d 310; 2006, the court held that Congress allowed the government "to seize substitute property when the defendant has placed the assets initially sought—and to which the Government is legally entitled—beyond the court's reach." Finally, in *Smith v. Federal Reserve Bank of New York,* 346 F.3d 264; 2003, relatives of victims from the World Trade Center attacks brought a wrongful death suit against Afghanistan, the Taliban, al Qaeda, Osama bin Laden and Iraq. No defendants showed up in court and because a reasonable amount of evidence existed against the respondents, summary judgment was filed in favor of the plaintiffs. By time a monetary judgment against Iraq was issued, the funds were frozen by the government, arguing that such funds were necessary to "return to Iraq where they were needed for military and rebuilding efforts" (Judge Katzmann *Smith* opinion). The Court of Appeals listed several statutory reasons why the Executive could freeze foreign assets and ends with suggesting that Congress had no intention of withholding any of this power away from the president. The court cites that in 2001, Congress amended a list of presidential authorities in times of armed hostilities to grant the president additional authority (50 U.S.C. s 1702 (a)(1)(c). With the *USA PATRIOT Act,* Congress empowered the president to

> confiscate any property, subject to the jurisdiction of the United States, of any foreign person, foreign organization, or foreign country that he determines has-planned, authorized, aided, or engaged in . . . hostilities or attacks against the United States; and all right, title, and interest in any property so confiscated shall vest, when, as, and upon the terms directed by the President, in such agency or person as the President may designate from time to time, and upon such terms and conditions as the President may prescribe, such interest or property shall be held, used, administered, liquidated, sold, or otherwise dealt with in the interest of and for the benefit of the United States.

In 2003, Congress again legislated in the area of frozen assets of terrorist-supporting states when it passed section 201 of TRIA. Section 201 states that:

> [N]otwithstanding any other provision of law, and except as provided in subsection (b), in every case in which a person has obtained a judgment against a terrorist party on a claim based upon an act of terrorism, . . . the blocked assets of that terrorist party (including the blocked assets of any agency or instrumentality of that terrorist party) shall be subject to execution or attachment in aid of execution in order to satisfy such judgment to the extent of any compensatory damages for which such terrorist party has been adjudged liable . . . (Judge Katzmann's *Smith* opinion).

The court concluded that "there is no dispute that the Iraqi assets at issue were 'blocked funds' within the meaning of TRIA [section] 201(a) at the time the President issued the confiscation Order."

Table 5.2. *International Emergency Economic Powers Act* before the Federal Courts

	Court upheld executive action	*Court struck down executive action*
Congressional authorization	*Regan v. Wald*, 1984 *U.S. v. Alamdoudi*, 2006 *U.S. v. Arch Trading Co.*, 1993 *U.S. v. Al M. Harb*, 1997 *U.S. v. Rafil Dhafir*, 2006 *U.S. v. Romero-Fernandez*, 1993 *767 Third Avenue v. U.S.*, 1995 *Milena Ship... v. R. Newcomb*, 1993 *Islamic... Relief v. Gonzales*, 2007 *Holy Land... v. Ashcroft*, 2003 *Global Relief... v. O'Neill*, 2002 *Smith v. Federal Bank NY*, 2003	
Congressional inaction	*Dames & Moore v. Regan*, 1981 *Consarc Corporation v. U.S.*, 1995	
No Congressional authorization/contrary to the wishes of Congress		

Table 5.2 shows that when the issue in front of the federal courts concerns the Executive's ability to control foreign assets in American territory, the courts are highly unlikely to challenge the government's authority during times of armed hostilities. Furthermore, while only two challenges to the IEEPA have been granted *certiorari* in front of the Supreme Court, the Court both times has held that the IEEPA does not restrict the Executive when the Congress has allowed the Executive to act in the past. The courts are reluctant to limit executive authority when it comes to controlling foreign assets and have made their decisions based on statutory claims, leaving out arguments in support of rights-based discourse. That Congress has provided the Executive with a number of avenues to control foreign assets makes it difficult for the federal courts to decide cases any differently than they have, unless they are prepared to rule that the federal government as a whole lacks the power to control foreign assets in its effort to protect the national security of the nation.

CONCLUSION

This chapter has looked at two pieces of emergency economic legislation: the *Trading with the Enemy Act* and the *International Emergency Economic Powers Act* where the Executive limits property rights during armed hostilities. This analysis shows that despite the Executive using legislation as its authority to act, the courts were not shy in claiming the office of the Executive went too far in its interpretation of the acts when it was thought that all recourse to due process had been taken away. When applying Jackson's framework at times when the Executive relies on legislation that is specifically for the regulation of the economy in times of emergencies, the president has found himself in the second and third prong of Jackson's framework. This was the case a number of times when the *Trading with the Enemy Act* was in question. Most of these prong-III cases concern property of individuals or corporations that did no wrongdoing, were unconnected with the enemy and sought a return of property erroneously taken from them, which was also a right provided for in the TWEA by Congress.

The IEEPA's adjudication in front of the federal courts presents a different outcome. No federal court has yet to find an officer of the Executive has gone too far in its interpretation of executive authority during times of armed hostilities under the Act. Instead, the courts have found that since Congress passed the IEEPA in an attempt to limit presidential authority, if it failed to limit practices of the Executive that were ongoing, then Congress was in fact consenting, if not authorizing by statute, said actions, leaving the Executive in Jackson's second prong of the separation of powers framework presented in *Youngstown.*

Finally, it should be noted that unlike military detention cases where the courts were reluctant to pass judgment on the decisions of the army and unlike warrantless electronic surveillance cases where the courts decide cases that are either in the domestic sphere or where Congress has legislated on the issue, in the area of emergency economic legislation and property rights, the courts are clearly given jurisdiction to hear cases as parts of the due process afforded individuals who have their property taken away from them during armed hostilities. The courts do not shy away from this jurisdiction.

ENDNOTES

1. Not all scholars agree with the argument that property was so highly regarded at the start of the Republic. William Michael Treanor argues that it was a significant republican notion to "abridge the property right in order to promote common interests" (Treanor, 1985; 700). Evidence to back this claim includes Jefferson's rejection of the Lockean formulation of "life, liberty, and property" in the Declaration of Independence in favor of "life, liberty and the pursuit of happiness" (Treanor, 700). Jefferson's choice of wording is used to suggest the anti-federalists and proponents of republicanism did not consider private property to be an inalienable right.

2. In fact, Nedelsky points out that in a letter to Dewitt Clinton, Gouveneur Morris wrote that "Relying on long experience...I hesitate not to asset, that plenty, power, numbers, wealth, and felicity will ever be in proportion to the security of property and thence is deduced the corollary, that a legislator, who omits securing property neglects his duty" (Nedelsky, 1990; 150).

3. In *United States v. Central Eureka Mining Co.*, 357 U.S. 155; 1958, Justice Burton held that regulation of industry is not the same as taking of property. In October, 1946, the United States government took possession of and operated a major portion of the nation's bituminous coal mines pursuant to Executive Order 9728 due to labor disturbances "interrupting the production of bituminous coal necessary for the operation of the national economy during the transition from war to peace." This action was taken under the authority of both the president being commander-in-chief of the Army and the Navy and by authority conferred upon him by the *War Labor Disputes Act.* In *United States v. United Mine Workers of America*, 330 U.S. 258; 1947, the Court held that other acts of Congress passed which were to regulate employee and employer labor dispute relations could not be used to stop a federal court from filing an injunction on behalf of the Executive to stop a labor strike. The *War Labor Disputes Act* was passed to give the federal government an upper hand in labor disputes and allows "for the seizure of any plant, mine or facility when the President finds that the operation thereof is threatened by strike or other labor disturbance and that an interruption in production will unduly impede the war effort" (Vinson's *Mine Workers* opinion). Also, in *United States v. Pewee Coal Co. Inc.,* 341 U.S. 114; 1951, the owner sued claiming compensation under the Fifth Amendment for operating losses sustained, but the legality of the taking of the property itself was not contested. The Court held that the company was entitled to recover compensation. It must be noted that the loss of property rights in these situations are temporary. Also cases that arise as a result of the Executive nationalizing industry or taking property for war materials are not done through policy created by the Congress. These two arguments make such cases too different from my analysis to include in the case study, though as I said, further study is merited on the situation to see if Jackson's framework is a sufficient guiding post for justices when they adjudicate these issues during times of armed hostilities.

4. Prior to the American entry into World War II, on April 18, 1941, President Roosevelt established the Office of Price Control with Executive Order 8734. Leon Henderson was appointed to be the Administrator. Despite the executive order not being authorized by any specific statute, the administrator was given instructions to

> take all lawful steps necessary or appropriate in order (1) to prevent price spiraling, rising costs of living, profiteering and inflation...; (2) to prevent speculative accumulation, withholding, and hoarding of materials and commodities; (3) to stimulate provision of the necessary supply of materials and commodities required for civilian use, in such manner as not to conflict with requirements for materials, articles and equipment needed for defense; and (4) after the satisfaction of military defense needs, to provide, through the determination of policies and the formulation of plans and programs, for the equitable distribution of the residual supply of such materials and commodities among competing civilian demands (James, 1944; 142).

These duties were initially either fact finding or duties already proscribed to the president, which he could delegate to someone under his authority, such as "the power to call on the Tariff Commission for cost of production studies, and some limited authority to direct the acquisition and disposition of commodities by federal agencies already empowered to deal in them" (James, 1944; 143). The *Emergency Price Control Act* raises questions of due process concerning contractual relations between parties who are engaged in selling and buying commodities. For example, "[w]ould a regulation fixing a maximum price violate any constitutional guarantees of parties to an existing contract calling for the purchase and sale of a commodity or the rendering of a service at a price higher than the maximum established" or, and in the same vein, "[m]ay a manufacturer who is unable to produce profitably at the maximum price fixed for his commodity and is therefore unable to meet his fixed obligations claim that he has been deprived of 'due process' in the event he is forced to close his business (Aidlin, 1942; 649)?"

Laws that call for the confiscation of property contrasts with property-rights cases where infringements are less intrusive and represent an indirect infringement on liberty as ownership of property remain in the hands of the original owner. For this reason, I exclude from my analysis price control legislation. While various price control laws setting up regulatory bodies and administrators to fix prices of commodities for sale during times of armed hostilities limited the right to control economic liberties of the individual, regulating the right to contract is an indirect infringement on personal liberties. I am more concerned with emergency economic legislation policies that explicitly take away property rights of individuals are affected by the Acts of Congress.

While I acknowledge that controlling prices of rent as well as the market price for certain goods does constitute an infringement of rights, it is less striking and severe as the confiscation of property by legislative Act. In an attempt to compare similar cases, the ambiguous nature of how price controls limit property rights versus having assets taken away altogether is too large a difference to consider as likeminded.

5. Military necessity, as defined in Article 14 of the Lieber code, and based on a proclamation from President Lincoln, is "understood by modern civilized nations, consists in the necessity of those measures which are indispensable for securing the ends of the war, and which are lawful according to the modern law and usages of war." The code follows with Article 15 stating that military necessity includes "all destruction of property, and obstruction of the ways and channels of traffic, travel, or communication, and of all withholding of sustenance or means of life from the enemy" (Carnahan, 1998; 215-216). When private property is destroyed during times of armed hostilities, the Court has ruled that citizens risk their property being lost due to the hardships of war. The emergency of war, in fact, creates a justification for army officials to destroy property even if they have the "opportunity to make a calculated choice about the matter" (McCormack, 2005; 78).

If the government destroys property for strategic purposes, done to avoid being destroyed or taken by enemy forces, then the Court sees it as a matter of risk and hardship the citizen burdens due to the war. The federal government is said to have a police power in times of perceived national emergency (Tresolini, 1954; 576) that includes the right to protect the nation at all costs which is based on the law of nations.

6. Other cases include *United States v. Grimaud*, 220 U.S. 506; 1910, *Carter v. Carter Coal Co.*, 298 U.S. 238; 1936.

7. Monaghan notes that the line between applying law and creating it is somewhat blurry at times. Explaining the boundary, Monaghan states that "its applications necessarily will depend upon evolving historical understandings and upon various institutions that cannot be quantified or captured more precisely in any legal formula. Particularly, during periods of national emergency, the distinction will seem problematic" (Monaghan, 1993; 41).

8. In defining emergency, the Congressional Research Service looks to the Webster's *New Collegiate Dictionary* and defines the term as "an unforeseen combination of circumstances or the resulting state that calls for immediate action" (Relyea, 2005; 4). Relyea further denotes four aspects for an emergency to exist. First, an emergency must be temporal in nature. An emergency is unforeseen and its duration is unknown. Second, an emergency is grave in that it may cause danger to the lives and well being of individuals whom are affected. Third, an emergency requires a governmental response. And finally, the governmental response must be immediate (Relyea, 2005; 4-5).

9. The text of the IEEPA is available online at http://www.law.cornell.edu/uscode/. Last accessed, October 11, 2007.

10. Before the matter came to Congress in the North, a statute of the Confederacy of May 21, 1861 forbade citizens from paying debts owed to the Northern States, taking the payments instead for the Confederate Treasury (Randall, 1912; 79). Moreover, an August 30, 1861 Act sequestered all alien property, which meant property belonging to residents of the Union. Proponents of confiscation in the North suggested to Congress that they were forced into such a position due to the acts of the South (Randall, 80).

11. What was considered property of the enemy was vast. In paraphrasing the Act, Samuel Anatole Lourie explains that an enemy and an ally to the enemy by section 2 of the TWEA included:

1. The Government of any nation with which the United States is at war or of any nation which is an ally of such nation, or any political or municipal subdivision thereof, or any officer or official agency thereof.
2. An individual, partnership, or other body of individuals of any nationality, resident within enemy or ally of enemy territories (including territory occupied by their military and naval forces).
3. Any individual resident outside the United States and doing business within enemy or all of enemy territory (or territory occupied by their forces).
4. Corporations incorporated within enemy territory or all of enemy territory or incorporated within any other country than the United States and doing business within such territory.
5. Such other individuals, or body or class of individuals, as may be natives, citizens, or subjects of any nation or an ally of any nation with which the

United States is at war, other than citizens of the United States wherever resident or wherever doing business, as the President may proclaim (Lourie, 1943; 395).

12. *Garvan v. $20000 Bonds* and three other cases, 265 F. 477; 1920.

13. Furthermore, the Court maintains a role in adjudicating such claims because Congress has specifically delegated it one. Holmes continues that "[i]f the Custodian was entitled to demand the delivery of the property in question it does not seem to need argument to show that the demand could be enforced by the District Courts under § 17 of the act, giving to the [federal courts] jurisdiction to make all such orders and decrees as may be necessary and proper to enforce the provisions of the act" (Holmes' *Central Union* opinion).

14. Likewise, in *American Exchange National Bank v. Garvan*, 273 Fed. 43; 1921, money in the sum of upwards to $350,000 was deposited into a bank by an American citizen though the money belonged to a foreign national. The American, John Simon, suggested that the money was owed to him. The Alien Property Custodian demanded the money. The Court held that the sole recourse for the petitioner could be found in section 9 of the Act. Otherwise, the custodian had authority to vest the property.

15. In Vinson's dissent, he believes the Court had been too liberal in its construing of congressional intent and suggested a more literal reading of the Act required that all enemies, regardless of nationality or loyalty who owned property could have it subjected to the Alien Property Custodian's vesting powers.

16. *Uebersee Finanz-Korporation v. Markham*, 158 F. 2d 313; 1946.

17. *Singer v. Yokohama Bank*, 85 N.E. 2d 894; 1949, *McGrath v. Chase National Bank*, 182 F.2d 349; 1950, and *Orvis v. McGrath*, 198 F.2d 708; 1952 respectively.

18. Using *Zittman* as precedent, when the Custodian issued his own vesting orders to vest in himself the proceeds of liquidation that remains after creditors get paid, the New York Supreme Court ruled in favor of the Custodian. The Supreme Court reversed, issued a one word opinion citing the *Zittman* decision. In a strongly worded dissent, Jackson, who wrote the majority opinion in *Zittman* pointed out that "[i]n *Zittman* the Custodian demanded a transfer of a credit from a debtor which had no interest in the credit except that of a stakeholder. Here the Custodian would size a fund from an officer of the State of New York who is administering it pursuant to his statutory duty and under the supervision of the Supreme Court of that State." Furthermore, this case dealt with funds left over after claims had been paid whereas *Zittman* concerned vested debts owed (*Brownell v. Singer*, 347 U.S. 403; 1954).

19. Section 17 of the Act "prescribes fines, sentences and forfeitures as special sanctions to punish willful violations of vesting orders or turnover directives as follows" (Justice Burton's *Manufacturers Trust Co.* opinion):

> That whoever shall willfully violate any of the provisions of this Act or of any license, rule, or regulation issued thereunder, and whoever shall willfully violate, neglect, or refuse to comply with any order of the President issued in compliance with the provisions of this Act shall, upon conviction, be fined not more than $10,000, or, if a natural person, imprisoned for not more than ten years, or both; and the officer, director, or agent of any corporation who knowingly participates in such violation shall be punished by a like fine,

imprisonment, or both, and any property, funds, securities, papers, or other articles or documents,... concerned in such violation shall be forfeited to the United States.

20. That said, however, the *USA PATRIOT Act* did amend the IEEPA to authorize the Executive to confiscate property and to take the title of property of a foreign person, organization or country that is subject to American jurisdiction that has been determined by the president to have been used in planning or perpetrating terrorist attacks (P.L. 107-56, Title I, s 106, October 26, 2001). The TWEA and IEEPA were further amended by Congress with the passage of the *Terrorism Risk Insurance Act* of 2002, ensuring that "the assets of foreign terrorist states that have been frozen in the U.S. pursuant to either statute may be used to satisfy civil judgments against them" (Ackerman and Grimmett, 2003; 29-30).

21. In 1977, there were three presidential national emergency declarations still in effect as a result of the TWEA. There was a banking emergency from 1933, President Truman's declaration of a national emergency as a result of the Korean Conflict in 1950 and finally President Nixon's 1971 balance of payments national emergency (*Harvard Law Review,* Note, 1983; 1104).

22. "This statute instructs the president to use such means, short of war, as he deems necessary to secure the release of citizens imprisoned by foreign governments." The Act was designed to protect European Immigrants who after becoming American citizens returned to their homelands got arrested, because their new status recognized (Cohen et al. 1983; 848).

23. Furthermore, the Court thus "avoided the broader question whether the president could have concluded the Agreement under his plenary constitutional powers: in doing so the Court acted consistently with a venerable principle of constitutional adjudication. The Court also did not consider whether the Agreement should have been concluded through the formal treaty-making process.... This is also consistent with the traditional judicial policy against deciding separation of powers questions" (Cohen et al., 1981; 842).

24. The Supreme Court held that Congress is unable to void the exercise of the Executive's power by use of a concurrent resolution. Congress could only act in this regard by going through the bicameral process of passing legislation and presenting the law to the president for either his signature or veto.

25. http://www.whitehouse.gov/news/releases/2001/09/20010924-1.html (October 11, 2007).

Chapter 6

Free Speech

The First Amendment states that "Congress shall make no law . . . abridging the freedom of speech, or of the press." The Amendment is more than "an order to Congress not to cross the boundary which marks the extreme limits of lawful expression. . . . It is a declaration of national policy in favor of the public discussion of all public questions" (Chafee, 1919; 932). Two societal interests are at play, the individual's right to express themselves freely and a social interest in the attainment of truth for the adoption of the best policies (Pound, 1915; 445). Until the end of the Second World War, the societal importance of free speech was largely left out of federal court decisions, with the justices focusing more squarely on free speech as an individual interest easily dismissed in an attempt to further advance the State's national security (Chafee, 1919; 959). That said, in defense of congressional legislation that limits free speech, Justice Holmes once stated "that neither Hamilton nor Madison, nor any other competent person then or later, ever supposed that to make criminal the counseling of a murder within the jurisdiction of Congress would be an unconstitutional interference with free speech" (Holmes' *Frohwerk* opinion). The message is clear: the right to free speech is not absolute.

State governments place limits on speech in a variety of ways. Obscenity is restricted, as is false advertising, libel and slander. Content neutral regulations of time, place, or manner of speech are not infringements of our First Amendment rights. However, it is only in times of war that the federal government has passed legislation to punish opposition to national policies. So while "dissent that questions the conduct and morality of a war is, on the view, the very essence of responsible and courageous citizenship," it is also the case that dissent is often considered disloyal as it is seen as giving aid and comfort to the enemy (Stone, 2004; 4). When the life of the nation itself is perceived to be at risk, the Executive has limited access to the writ of habeas corpus, wiretapped communications without a warrant, and restricted the assets of the enemy. Can the government also limit the freedom of speech? After all, Justice William O. Douglas pointed out that government's "eternal temptation . . . has been to arrest the speaker rather than to correct conditions about which he complains" (Douglas' *Younger v. Harris,* 401 U.S. 37; 1971, dissent).

In contrast to how the federal courts deal with presidential power, I find that the federal courts decide free speech cases by asking the question whether or not Congress could limit the right to free speech. The constitutional questions are raised and in these cases answered in a way the courts go to great lengths to avoid in my other chapters. When constitutional questions are addressed and answered, the role for Justice Jackson's separation of framework in his *Youngstown* concurrence is no longer applicable as he looks for cooperation amongst the elected branches of government to be key in judicial decisions.

This chapter proceeds in the following fashion. I give a brief account of the major events in criminalizing dissenting opinion of government wartime policies before cases reached the Supreme Court. Second, I examine the World War I, World War II, and Vietnam War cases, and put to the test whether Jackson's framework is applicable. Third, I look at the federal courts today in regard to the public mood during the Bush Administration's war on terrorism and the limitation of free speech, examining whether the federal courts expect the Executive and Congress to work together in a similar fashion as in the past. Throughout the chapter, I emphasize the fact that the courts often decide these First Amendment cases by answering the constitutional questions in contrast to my earlier case studies, where a separation of powers framework is prominent, and I look at the implications of such emphasis on the Bill of Rights for the rights being infringed.

HISTORICAL BACKGROUND

It is suggested that the First Amendment's history is one of "intolerance of political dissent, a story of dark shadows and orthodoxy illuminated periodically by brilliant rays of enlightenment" (Koffler & Gershman, 1984; 858), but there was no common understanding of the meaning of the First Amendment amongst its drafters. Benjamin Franklin stated that no one had any "distinct Ideas of its Nature and Extent." As such, Stone argues that its framers embraced a "broad and largely undefined constitutional principle, not a concrete, well-settled legal principle" (Stone, 2007; 11). Stone's argument comes from an analysis of the English experience. In England, seditious libel was used as a way for the King to have sweeping control over oral and written communication. Anything considered to be "hatred or contempt or to excite disaffection against the king and government and the Constitution of the United Kingdom . . . or to excite British subjects to attempt by otherwise than by lawful means the alteration of any matter in Church or State" was a serious offense (Whipple, 1927; 19). The justification for the English doctrine limiting free speech was that the King was superior to the people and therefore immune to their criticism. The notion of the government being above the people seems contrary to the goals of the American Revolution where the government consists of the people of the United States themselves (Whipple, 19).

Although the issue of limiting free speech during times of war did not make its way through the federal courts until World War I[1], the tradition of repressive laws restricting dissent of government wartime policies goes back to the start of the Republic. The *Alien and Sedition Acts* included four laws passed by Congress in 1798 when Federalist President John Adams was in power. The laws were supposedly to protect the United States from citizens of enemy powers living in the country. The *Alien Enemies Act* allowed the government to detain and deport any citizen of an enemy power living in the United States. This Act is still on the books today. The *Sedition Act* allowed the government to arrest those who published what was considered to be false, scandalous, or malicious content against the president or either Chamber of Congress, but was in reality designed to quiet Republican skeptics of government policies.

Federalists worried about Republicans suggesting the threat from France was exaggerated. In fact, the *Sedition Act* was passed on June 25, two weeks before Congress officially authorized attacks on French ships on July 9, 1798. Congressman John Allen defended the Act "on the ground that a treasonable conspiracy of Republican congressman and editors was attempting to 'ruin the Government by publishing the most shameless falsehoods' and by inciting the people to 'insurrection'" (Stone, 2004; 37).[2] As noted, no cases reached the Supreme Court in regard to the *Sedition Act,* but circuit court cases existed in the form of trials for those tried under the Federalist law.

Under the auspicious of the *Sedition Act,* the Federalists were able to arrest approximately 25 highly regarded Republicans, with ten cases leading to prosecution and conviction (Stone 2004; 63). The Act expired on March 3, 1801, which happened to be Adams last day in office. When Jefferson won the presidency in 1800, he pardoned all those who had been tried under the *Sedition Act,* as he had always maintained its unconstitutionality as a restriction on the First Amendment.

The reason for these acts was the Quasi War with France. Due to waning relations between the two countries, Congress "suspended commercial intercourse with France, denounced treaties with France, established a Department of the Navy and a Marine Corps, augmented the navy, and provided for raising an army in case of need" (Wormuth & Firmage, 1989; 61). While the Federalists, including Adams, preferred good relations with Britain, the Republicans favored the French and saw the French Revolution "as an extension of the American promise of liberty, republicanism, and democracy" (Stone, 2004; 25). Secretary of War, James McHenry recognized the hostility that would come with asking Congress for a declaration of war against France and McHenry suggested Adams seek an undeclared war with France (Sofaer, 1976; 19).

Adams took his case to Congress a number of times between January and July, 1798, suggesting that continued peace with France was unlikely. Adams "called for defensive preparations and unilaterally suspended the order he had issued restricting the arming of merchant vessels" (Sofaer, 1976; 20). Soon thereafter, the details of the XYZ Papers were revealed to Congress. Adams received evidence that his ministers in France, sent to ameliorate diplomatic relations, were not being received. [3] In fact, the ministers were expected to pay a bribe to the French to be recognized. Sentiments toward France cooled considerably and Congress authorized Adams to fight his war, without officially declaring it.

The next time speech criticizing the policies of the government was made punishable by law was when Lincoln suspended the writ of habeas corpus during the Civil War. However, the Republican Party's commitment to freedom of speech should be duly noted. Just as the Federalists had done when the government was at the beginning stages of a conflict with France in 1798, there were some Republicans calling for the federal government to pass legislation making it a crime to question government policies. When states such as North Carolina and Virginia passed laws criminalizing advocating the abolition of slavery, the Republicans maintained these laws were contrary to the First Amendment (Stone, 2004; 95). The federal government would not be held to a lower standard and no law was passed by Congress specifically suppressing free speech.

Despite no law being passed at a federal level to place restrictions on the First Amendment, infringements occurred nonetheless. In *ex parte Vallandigham,* 68 U.S. 243; 1864, Clement Vallandigham, a member of Congress, a former Ohio state Congressman, and the leader of the Copperheads, a group of Northern Democrats opposed to the Lincoln Administration, was arrested for publicly condemning President Lincoln, the war, and the draft. Specifically, Vallandigham gave a speech describing the Civil War as "cruel" and "wicked" and accused Lincoln of being to blame for the start of the conflict. He was arrested on the order of General Burnside, the commanding officer present in Ohio, who had, without direct order from the Executive, declared martial law. Burnside accused Vallandigham of making treasonable utterances. Tried by military commission two days after his arrest, Vallandigham was sentenced to remain in jail for the duration of the war.

Historical accounts suggest that Lincoln was embarrassed about what happened to Vallandigham. Lincoln's secretaries are on the record as saying that had the president been consulted first, he would not have allowed the proceedings against Vallandigham to take place (Nicolay & Hay, 1914; 338). The president stated that "all the Cabinet regretted the arrest, doubting its necessity" (Whipple, 1927; 139). Nonetheless, Lincoln backed General Burnside's arrest and trial of Vallandigham, but ordered the prisoner to be banished to the Confederacy rather than serve out his sentence in jail.[4] These examples of Congress and the Executive limiting the right to free speech were not judged by the federal courts—at least not on the merits of whether or not the policies in question conformed to the Constitution. The lack of First Amendment jurisprudence regarding speech would change during World War I.

The battle for free speech between the Civil and First World War was fought by "libertarian radicals, often on the intellectual and social fringes of American society," looking to secure free speech for those advocating for such issues as radical abolitionism, labor reform and women's rights (Rabban, 1997; 23). Groups were founded to defend freedom of speech when the Congress passed the *Comstock Act* in 1873 that prohibited the interstate mailing of obscene material. The National Defense Association and the Free Speech League were created in 1878 and 1902 respectively to help those prosecuted for their speech. According to Rabban, these early libertarian groups were particularly concerned with the suppression of dissenting opinion during the Spanish-American War as well as laws and prosecution of those advocated anarchist views after President McKinley was assassinated in 1901 (Rabban, 25).

Cases concerning free speech reached the state courts and, at least for Rabban, is satisfying enough evidence to suggest litigation over the constitutional meaning of free speech had already begun when cases reached the Supreme Court (Rabban, 131). However, that is precisely where my analysis begins, as it is the first time we have war time decisions dealing with the First Amendment's guaranteed right to free speech.

THE WORLD WARS

The British liner *Lusitania,* traveling from New York to Liverpool, was sunk by the Germans in 1915, killing 128 Americans that were onboard (Rehnquist, 1998; 171–72). It was feared that the sinking of the *Lusitania* would bring the United States into war, but it was two years later when Germany, in an attempt to limit supplies shipped to the allies, sank three American vessels prompting President Woodrow Wilson to ask Congress for a Declaration of War. Wilson had won reelection on a platform of having kept America out of the war, and his move to now enter the conflict was met with sharp criticism. Republican Senator George Norris argued that the United States was about to commit "a sin against humanity and against our countrymen" (Stone, 2004; 137).[5] Facing criticism from both Republicans and Democrats, Wilson warned that if his decision to go to war was met with "disloyalty, it [would] be dealt with a firm hand of stern repression."[6]

Wilson believed those he considered disloyal "had sacrificed their right to civil liberties" (Murphy, 1979; 53) and Attorney General Thomas Gregory asked Congress to pass the *Espionage Act* of 1917. An amalgamation of 18 bills, the original 1917 *Act* was the first law to make dissent of government policy a crime since the *Sedition Act* of 1798. The Act included the protection of ships in harbors, the protection against spying activities and unlawful military expeditions. It also included Title I, section 3 that created three new offenses, making false statements or reports interfering with military operations or promoting the success of the enemy, causing or attempting to cause insubordination or disloyalty in the armed services, and obstructing enlistments and recruitments in the army (Chafee, 1919; 935).

A year later, the Act was amended by Congress, adding nine more offenses to the books, in what was called the *Sedition Act* of 1918, which included saying or doing anything with the intent to obstruct the sale of American bonds, as well as speech said with the intention of causing contempt to the Constitution, the American flag, or the uniform of the Army or Navy. The encouragement of restricting the production of wartime materials was also made an offense. These crimes came with a possible fine of up to $10 000 as well as a maximum sentence of 20 years in prison or both. By the war's end, over two thousand people were prosecuted for speaking out against the war in a variety of fashions (Cole, 2005; 114).[7] It was only at the war's end that the Supreme Court weighed in on the curtailment of free speech, upholding the *Sedition Act* of 1918 in a small number of cases.

Between 1919 and 1927, the Supreme Court would make a number of rulings on speech that was limited during war and in each case would affirm the lower court ruling that upheld the conviction in question. Neither the Supreme Court, nor the lower courts, were willing to limit the authority of the president, as delegated by Congress with the passage of the *Espionage Act.* While the Supreme Court based its decisions on the limitations of the First Amendment itself, the lower court rulings by and large dealt with errors in respect to admission and exclusion of evidence.

In *Schenck v. United States,* 249 U.S. 47; 1919, the Supreme Court was presented with its first significant First Amendment decision (Stone, 2004; 192).[8] The Court looked at the case challenging the validity of the law through the lens of whether Congress could pass the Act, not whether the Executive had any authority to restrict free speech, and therefore decided the question on the constitutional issue.

The petitioners were members of the Socialist Party. Schenck was the general secretary and was in charge of the headquarters from where 15 000 leaflets were mailed to men drafted into the United States military. The leaflet argued that the draft was unconstitutional and urged readers to protest the *Conscription Act.* Justice Holmes, writing for a unanimous Court, conceded that if the comments were made in peaceful circumstances, the First Amendment probably would protect such speech. However, when the country is at war speech otherwise protected can be regulated by Congress and is not protected by the First Amendment. Holmes argues that the leaflets would not have been sent out if they did not have some intended effect on the readers and that the effect had to be to stop the drafted men from carrying out their duty under the conscription law.

Holmes' continued that "the most stringent protection of free speech would not protect a man in falsely shouting fire in a theatre and causing a panic. It does not even protect a man from an injunction against uttering words that may have all the effect of force" (Holmes' *Schenck* opinion). Holmes thus creates the clear and present danger test and starts to outline where Congress has a duty to protect the nation from certain "substantive evils" and where First Amendment protection exists. With the first important ruling on the First Amendment, Justice Holmes put to rest any notion that the First Amendment means what it says, that "Congress shall make no law abridging the freedom of speech or of the press." The limits on speech presented in the *Schenck* decision would be the benchmark of First Amendment restrictions on speech, slowly to be chipped away at, for decades to come in times of war and in peace.

The Court would follow its ruling in *Schenck* a week later in *Debs v. United States,* 249 U.S. 211; 1919. Eugene V. Debs ran for president for the Socialist Party on a number of occasions, garnering nearly one million votes in 1912. He delivered a speech condemning the war. Debs argued that "wars throughout history have been waged for conquest and plunder . . . The master class has always declared the wars; the subject class has always fought the battles. The master class has had all gain and nothing to lose, while the subject class has had nothing to gain and all to lose—especially their lives" (Schlesinger, 1948; 425). Writing for a unanimous Court, Justice Holmes held that the speech was delivered with the probable effect of preventing recruiting into the armed services and was punishable under the *Espionage Act* and the Act itself was not an infringement of the First Amendment.

On the same day the *Debs* decision was handed down, *Frohwerk v. United States,* 249 U.S. 204; 1919 was also decided. In this case, the Court in upholding a 10-year conviction, reminds Frohwerk that the First Amendment "was not intended to give immunity to every possible use of language." Jacob Frowherk was a copy editor for a German language newspaper that published anti-war material, stating for example that sending American soldiers to fight in France was murder. Again, Holmes writing for a unanimous Court held that the *Missouri Staats Zeitung* in publishing twelve articles between July 6 to December 7, 1917, attempted "to cause disloyalty, mutiny and refusal of duty in the military and naval forces of the United States." Frohwerk, and his employer Carl Gleeser, were held responsible and were punished under the *Espionage Act.* For Holmes, "no significant difference existed, it seemed, between standards that required proof of a clear and present danger (*Schenk*), proof that in the circumstances a little breath would kindle a flame (*Frohwerk*), or proof that the punished expression would generate bad tendencies (*Debs*) (Feldman, 2008; 263).

Only nine months later, another conviction would be upheld under *Schenck,* but Justice Holmes would start to carve out limits to the powers of Congress and the Executive's interpretation of congressional laws when it came to curtailing First Amendment rights. In 1919, law professor Zechariah Chafee wrote an article about free speech during war for the *Harvard Law Review* in which he claimed that Holmes had missed the main point of his own opinion in *Schenck*'s example of the false cry of fire. The clear and present danger test was a legal principle that made it necessary to punish speech only when the words in question would result in unlawful acts—intent alone was not enough (Chafee, 1919; 960). Holmes would come around to this position in his powerful dissent in *Abrams v. United States,* 250 U.S. 616; 1919.[9]

A group of Russian-Jewish emigrants moved to the United States to escape the anti-Semitic policies of the Russian regime and were self-described socialists who backed the Bolshevick overthrow of the Czar (Stone, 2004; 205). The five defendants were convicted under the *Espionage Act* for throwing leaflets out of a window of the building where one of the defendants worked in New York City. The leaflets were printed in English on one side and Yiddish on the other. The English leaflet called the president a coward and a hypocrite because he sent Marines into Russia to defend what was left of the Czarist regime. The leaflet states that "German militarism combined with allied capitalism to crush the Russian Revolution" maintained a common enemy, the working class enlightenment. The Yiddish leaflet tells the workers of the world to unite and workers in factories to stop making bullets and weapons that support the war. The convictions were upheld on the precedent of *Schenck.*

Justice Tom Clark, writing for the Court, held that the leaflets were "not an attempt to bring about a change of administration by candid discussion . . . the manifest purpose of such a publication was to create an attempt to defeat the war plans of the government of the United States, by bringing upon the country the paralysis of a general strike." Clark states that the defendants must be held accountable for the consequences of the intent of their actions. The primary purpose of the leaflets was to help the Russian Revolution, but the message of the leaflets was to bring defeat to the American war program by advocating to the American public not to "work in ammunition factories, where their work would produce 'bullets, bayonets, cannon' and other munitions of war, the use of which would cause the 'murder' of Germans and Russians" (Clark's *Abrams* opinion).

In his dissent, Holmes suggests that the messages of the leaflets are not subject to the limits of free speech put in place by the *Espionage Act.* The legality of the *Espionage Act* here is not questioned by the dissent. Like in the previous case studies where Executive officials overreach in interpreting the will of Congress, here too the arrests are considered by Holmes to be based on too broad a construction of the Act because the message presented in the leaflets "in no way attack the form of government of the United States." The protection of free speech that Holmes offers is actually one that is based on an interpretation of the Act of Congress and is therefore a separation of powers argument, rather than protecting rights using rights-based language.

Holmes further outlines what constitutes a clear and present danger. Rejecting the Court opinion, Holmes does not question the decisions made in the *Schenck, Debs* or *Frohwerk* cases. He reiterates that the Congress "may punish speech that produces or is intended to produce a clear and imminent danger that will bring about forthwith certain substantive evils that the United States constitutionally may seek to prevent," further admitting this power is greater in times of war than would be in times of peace "because war opens dangers that do not exist at other times." However, Holmes outlines when these substantive evils may emerge, arguing that "it is only the present danger of immediate evil or an intent to bring it about that warrants Congress in setting a limit to the expression of opinion" where individual rights are concerned. For Holmes, "nobody can suppose that the surreptitious publishing of a silly leaflet by an unknown man, without more, would present any immediate danger that its opinions would hinder the success of the government arms or have any appreciable tendency to do so" (Holmes' *Abrams* dissent).

Despite Holmes' claims that the clear and present danger test requiring words to actually incite some sort of action, the Supreme Court would continue to uphold convictions under the *Espionage Act* on the basis of *Schenck,* post *Abrams.* In *Schaefer v. United States,* 251 U.S. 466; 1920, the convictions were upheld for employees of another German language newspaper who translated articles from English newspapers to have a German bias. In *Pierce v. United States,* 252 U.S. 239; 1920, four socialists were convicted for passing out leaflets condemning President Wilson and the war stating that the war was started and fought over commercial routes. The petitioners were charged under the publishing false statements provision of the *Espionage Act.* The Act also denied newspapers and other publications being mailed if the publication in question violated provisions of the Act. The Court held that it was within the power of Congress to restrict what is mailed. Likewise, in *United States ex rel. Milwaukee Social Democratic Publishing Company v. Burleson, Postmaster General of the United States,* 255 U.S. 407; 1921, the Court held that denying second class mail privilege to the *Milwaukee Leader* was Constitutional because it "printed articles conveying false reports and false statements with intent to promote the success of the enemies of the United States and constituting a willful attempt to cause disloyalty and refusal of duty in the military and naval forces and to obstruct the recruiting and enlistment service" (Clarke's *Milwaukee* opinion). Clark held that it was within the power delegated to the Postmaster General from Congress to revoke mailing privileges under the nonmailable provision of the *Espionage Act.*[10] The Supreme Court affirmed the lower court opinion that, unlike the other lower court cases, decided the case based on whether or not First Amendment rights were violated. The court held that the First Amendment only goes so far and that to deny that the *Espionage Act* is constitutional would be to deny the United States government that ability of self-preservation (*United States ex rel. Milwaukee Social Democratic Publishing Company v. Burleson,* 258 F. 282; 1919).

State laws were also passed similar in nature to the *Espionage Act.* In *Gilbert v. State of Minnesota,* 254 U.S. 325; 1920, the Court held that it was not only Congress that could pass laws to protect the nation. This ruling came despite it being the federal government that is allocated the war powers, with an additional prohibition on the states to "engage in war, unless actually invaded, or in such imminent danger as will not admit delay." State governments, however, have at their disposal what the federal courts call police powers, the ability of the local government to regulate the welfare, morality and safety of their residents. Justice Joseph McKenna held that it was within these police powers for a state law to declare "it a misdemeanor for any person to teach or advocate by any written or printed matter or by oral speech that citizens of the State would not aid or assist the United States in prosecuting or carrying on war with the public enemies of the United States" (McKenna's Gilbert opinion).

In a striking dissent, Justice Louis Brandeis held while the statute used to convict was enacted during the war, the law itself was unrelated to the war in question. The law was "in fact an act to prevent teaching that the abolition of war is possible." Brandeis goes on to distinguish the federal *Espionage Act* with the local law by pointing out that unlike the *Espionage Act,* the Minnesota law applied equally in times of war and in times of peace. This important note is something that on the one hand makes a big difference in the previously discussed cases where limits to free speech are allowed. The Court notes that Congress is allowed to protect the nation against substantive evils. However, the limits to the First Amendment allowed in times of war remain in times of peace because the cases decided the constitutional questions. Justice Holmes notes on more than one occasion that Congress is given greater leeway during war than in times of peace to restrict freedom of speech.

Despite such claims, starting with falsely crying fire in a crowded theatre, to present day restrictions on obscenity, free speech is limited. Despite the warning presented by Brandeis, the Court would again uphold the state right to limit free speech in the name of national security five years later. In *Gitlow v. People of New York,* 268 U.S. 652; 1925, Justice Edward Sanford held that since a state has the authority to punish "utterances inimical to the public welfare" . . . a part of this police power necessarily includes "punishing utterances advocating the overthrow of organized government by force, violence and unlawful means." Like the Minnesota law, the New York law concerns teaching ideas that the government found objectionable. But in *Gitlow,* the Court refused to apply the clear and present danger rule. The Court held that the state legislature had found a certain form of speech unlawful and the law had to be judged by the Court as whether or not it was reasonable. Since it was reasonable for a state legislature to pass laws to protect itself, the clear and present danger test did not apply. The state court, in *People of New York v. Benjamin Gitlow,* 234 NY 132; 1922, decided similarly as the Court. Like the *Milwaukee Social Democratic Publishing Company* case, the court places a limit to the freedom of speech stating that if the public peace is disturbed by certain messages, the state legislature is able to pass legislation to protect against it.

The *Gitlow* decision made the significant distinction between advocating that the government be changed by lawful means versus the advocacy of overthrowing the government by means that were considered unlawful. Therefore, it was not the speech itself that was problematic but the means to achieve the message.

In *Gitlow,* again Brandeis dissents, this time signing on to an opinion written by Justice Holmes. Offering further clarification on the clear and present danger test, Holmes states that if a written manifesto "was more than a theory, that it was an incitement. Every idea is an incitement . . . If in the long run the beliefs expressed in proletarian dictatorship are destined to be accepted by the dominant forces of the community, the only meaning of free speech is that they should be given their chance and have their way" (Holmes' *Gitlow* dissent). The overarching point of the Brandeis and Holmes dissent, one that would soon make its way into majority opinions, was that speech was protected by the First Amendment if the defendant could show that there was no danger that the substantive evil Congress sought to protect against could actually be brought about.

Gitlow aside, the Court did uphold free speech in a number of cases between 1927 and the start of the Second World War at the state level. The dissenting opinions of Holmes and Brandeis started to become the rationale of court majorities in cases that did not pertain to the war efforts of the nation as diverse as invalidating a tax on newspapers to invalidating a statute that prohibited picketing.[11]

The First World War resulted in Congress passing legislation making it a crime to be critical of the war. This resulted in the creation and growth of the civil liberties movement gaining steam. After WWI, the desire to protect civil liberties also became a new priority for the government, media, and academia (Stone, 2004; 236). The question was whether the federal courts would continue to decide cases the way they had in early years dealing with the suppression of speech.

Dissent during the Second World War was marginal in comparison to the Quasi War with France, The Civil War or World War I. It was believed that one of the reasons France fell to Germany was the existence of Nazi and Communist sympathizers in France. This was alarming to members of Congress who started to restrict First Amendment freedoms by limiting association through its ban on federal employee's membership in any organization that advocated the overthrow of the government (Goldstein, 1978; 248). With dissent being marginal, there was also more toleration for unpopular speech that was considered to be dissention. For example, the president of Yale, Charles Seymour, wrote an editorial in the *New York Times* after the attack on Pearl Harbor reminding Americans that free speech is most essential during times of national emergency and should only be restricted when the security of the nation was endangered by it. Seymour considered the Supreme Court decisions restricting free speech during the First World War as incorrectly decided, noting that these decisions provided a "warning for the future (Seymour, 1942; 13).

During the war, the Supreme Court denied cert, resulting in William Dudley Pelley, a journalist and Hollywood screenwriter, to remain behind bars for 10 years as a result of a number of statements made in the *Galilean* between

December 1941 and February 1942. Among the statements made were accusations that the attack on Pearl Harbor was preventable and that President Roosevelt surrounded himself with Zionists and entered the war as a result of their advice. Pelley further suggested that the United States was bankrupt (*United States v. Pelley,* 132 F2d; 1942). Pelley was convicted under the false statements portion of the *Espionage Act.* However, Stone points out that if this case arose during WWI, Pelley would have no doubt been tried under section 3 of the Act with an attempt to cause insubordination, disloyalty, mutiny or refusal of duty in the military forces.

Pelley's conviction of making false statements only is a show of restraint on the part of the prosecution and the Court of Appeals. This suggests that the *Schenck, Frohwerk, Debs and Abrams* decisions were not in line with constitutional interpretation of the day. That constitutional interpretation is what is relied upon for these First Amendment cases shows why the courts are more consistent when deciding statutory claims over constitutional questions in the other issue areas. Constitutional interpretation can constrain the justices for years by placing limits on individual liberties that become more permanent than a case by case interpretation of the facts applied against a statute.

Another Court of Appeals case that did not reach the Supreme Court was *Dunn et. al. v. United States,* 138 F. 2d 137; 1943, where the court reaffirmed that "the Nation may protect the integrity of its armed forces and may prevent the overthrow of the Government by force and that it may, as a means to those ends, punish utterances which have a tendency to and are intended to produce the forbidden results is not open to question" (Stone's Dunn opinion). Eighteen people were found guilty under the Espionage Act and appealed their decision based on the validity of the Act itself which had been upheld time and time again. The court here does not change its position. The appellants also questioned the indictment itself, arguing that the Espionage Act was not applicable because the supposed crime in question of conspiracy to overthrow the government occurred before the Second World War and the Act was meant to be applicable in times of war alone. The court rejects this claim, stating that the construction of the Act by the members of the Socialist Party was wrong because the Act is just as applicable in times of peace as in times of war. It could be the court was not willing to interpret the Act of Congress any other way because they were in the midst of WWII. However, it goes to show, as noted in the introduction, that I am not making the claim that rights are always protected when the courts use a statutory interpretation to decide war powers cases.

There was only one case that reached the Supreme Court concerning Congress limiting free speech during the war itself. The prosecution of the *Espionage Act* of 1917 was at issue in the 1944 case *Hartzel v. United States,* 322

U.S. 680. Just prior to America's entry into the war, Hartzel wrote several pamphlets attacking the president as well as the English and Jewish people. These writings advocated German victory in Europe that would bring about "increased stability and safety for the West." In 1942, Hartzel wrote three pamphlets expressing similar ideas, which were the basis of the conviction. These new articles were mailed to 600 people, including prominent individuals such as the commanding general of the United States Army Air Forces, the United States Infantry Association, the Airline Pilots Association, and the American Legion, among others. Hartzel argued that his pamphlets were protected speech as they were political in nature. The Court of Appeals in *United States v. Hatzel,* 138 F. 2d 169; 1943, affirmed the convictions based on its interpretation that the *Espionage Act* was in fact applicable because Hartzel willfully and knowingly tried to obstruct enlistment into the services of the United States military, clearly a violation under the Act.

Having already decided that the *Espionage Act* allowed for constitutional limitations on freedom of speech, the Supreme Court looked past the constitutional questions for statutory ones, determining whether or not the articles mailed out by Hartzel fell within the provisions of the congressional act. In reversing the judgment of the court of appeals, the Court held that "there is nothing on the face of the three pamphlets in question to indicate that petitioner intended specifically to cause insubordination, disloyalty, mutiny or refusal of duty in the military forces" (Murphy's *Hartzel* opinion). While the Court acknowledges that the State was participating in World War II at the time, a total war for national survival, "crude appeals to overthrow the government or to discard our arms in open mutiny are seldom made. . . . But the mere fact that such ideas are enunciated by a citizen is not enough by itself to warrant a finding of criminal intent to violate section 3 of the *Espionage Act*" (Murphy's *Hartzel* opinion). In previous cases, pamphlets in question were considered to be more specific in their call for citizens to be disloyal. Because there was no explicit call to action, the Court found that the *Espionage Act* was inapplicable and the speech was therefore protected by the First Amendment. The *Hartzel* decision stands in stark contrast to earlier decisions during the First World War.

Justice Stanley Reed, joined by justices Felix Frankfurter, William Douglas and Robert Jackson, dissented, arguing that "papers or speeches may contain incitements for the military to be insubordinate or to mutiny with scurrilous articles, attacking an ally . . . without words of solicitation." It was possible for the pamphlet to be persuasive because a large segment of the population in 1942 was more interested in focusing the war effort on Japan, not Germany or Italy. The dissent further adopted the argument made by Holmes in *Schenck.* Reed notes that "the documents would not have been sent unless they had been intended to have some effect" and further this intent could be nothing else but to "influence [people in the armed services] to obstruct the carrying on of the war against Germany."

After the war, the Supreme Court would reverse two judgments of the court of appeals, handed down during the war itself, continuing to uphold the right to dissent. The appeals decisions were based on statutory construction, not limiting any constitutionally protected rights. In *Schneiderman v. United States,* 320 U.S. 118; 1948, the case concerned the denaturalization of an individual for disloyal conduct. During the war, the Government had issued 146 decrees of cancellation, mostly former Germans who were sympathetic to Nazi doctrines (Stone, 2004; 280). In 1909, Schneiderman arrived in the United States from Russia. He was three years old. In 1927, he became an American citizen. In 1939, the government started proceedings of denaturalization against him because he was a member of the Communist Party for five years before becoming an American. The government argued that he did not have sincere attachment to the American Constitution due to his membership in a political organization that called for the violent overthrow of the United States government.

Justice Frank Murphy, writing for the Court, held that being a member of the Communist Party itself did not render Schneiderman incapable of sincerely holding dear the principles of the Constitution. This decision reversed *Schneiderman v. United States,* 119 F.2d 500; 1941. Likewise, in *Baumgartner v. United States,* 322 U.S. 665; 1944 when a German-born individual embraced Hitler's philosophy, his naturalization had been canceled. The Supreme Court held, based on the precedent established in *Schneiderman,* citizenship could not be stripped due to holding unpopular views and for speaking "foolishly and without moderation (Frankfurter's *Baumgartner* opinion)," and as a result congressional legislation allowing for the denaturalization of Americans was declared void, reversing *Baumgartner v. United States,* 138 F.2d 29; 1943.

Table 6.1 shows that during World War I, the Supreme Court continuously upheld convictions under the *Espionage Act.* The law was upheld, but the federal courts decided that it was not because Congress authorized the actions of the Executive that allowed for the restrictions on free speech but rather that such speech was not protected under the First Amendment. During World War II, the Court was more willing to strike down executive actions as having authorization from Congress delegated by acts that were unconstitutional violations of free speech, but did so only on statutory grounds. When cases that arose under the *Espionage Act* were held to violate the First Amendment in relation to WWII, the Court held that executive officials had misapplied the intent of the statute, therefore maintaining the legality of the statute itself, as was seen with many cases dealing with the *Trading with the Enemy Act.*

Table 6.1. Restriction to Free Speech During the World Wars

	Court upheld executive action	Court struck down executive action
Congressional authorization	*Pierce v. U.S.,* 1917 *U.S. v. Schaefer,* 1918 *State v. Joseph Gilbert,* 1918 *Schenck v. U.S.,* 1919 *Debs v. U.S.,* 1919 *Frohwerk v. U.S.,* 1919 *Milwaukee... v. Burleson,* 1919 *Abrams v. U.S.,* 1919 *Schaefer v. U.S.,* 1920 *Pierce v. U.S.,* 1920 *Milwaukee v. Burleson,* 1921 *Gilbert v. Minnesota,* 1920 *New York v. Gitlow,* 1922 *Gitlow v. New York,* 1925 *U.S. v. Schneiderman,*1941 *Baumgartner v. U.S.,* 1943 *U.S. v. Hartzel,* 1943 *U.S. v. Pelley,* 1942	
No Congressional authorization/ contrary to the wishes of Congress		*Masse... Co. v. Patten,* 1917 *Hartzel v. U.S.,* 1944 *Baumgartner v. U.S.,* 1944 *Schneiderman v. U.S.,* 1948

THE COLD WAR

After World War II, the start of the Cold War resulted in suspected communists being sought and exposed. Contrary to the World Wars where people were targeted directly for their words, people became targets for their associations and affiliations or even for having sympathies with the Communist Party. While association was now the new target of Congress and the Executive, people were not free to criticize the policies of the government without repercussions. Associations and sympathizes were proven by the speech of the accused (Cole, 2005; 111, 116).

After WWII, two more cases would come before the Supreme Court to act as precedent and shape the circumstances under which limits to free speech could be placed by Congress, all stemming from the original wartime decision in *Schenck.* While the second case would not be decided until 1969, the first was *Dennis v. United States,* 341 U.S. 494; 1951. The *Alien Registration Act,* known as the *Smith Act* required all aliens living in the United States to register with the INS (Immigration and Naturalization Services). The Act also made it a crime to knowingly and willfully advocate the overthrow or the destruction of the government or to organize a group with the mission of overthrowing or destroying the American government. The defendants, twelve members of the national board of the Communist Party, were charged with willfully conspiring to organize the Communist Party of the United States, which had the mission to teach and advocate the overthrow and destruction of the Government of the United States by force and violence (Vinson's *Dennis* opinion).

The Supreme Court affirmed *United States v. Dennis et. al.,* 183 F.2d 201; 1950. The lower court stated that a clear and present danger existed due to the worldly circumstances of the day. As a result, the actions of the appellants were subject to the tenants of the *Smith Act* and were without the protections of the First Amendment. Chief Justice Fred Vinson, writing for the Court plurality of four justices, noted that while the Court never overruled its decisions from World War I, "there is little doubt that subsequent opinions have inclined toward the Holmes-Brandeis rationale" (Vinson's *Dennis* opinion) found in earlier dissents. Vinson explains that the purpose of the *Smith Act* was to protect the government from "change by violence, revolution and terrorism." Because the overthrow of the government by force, including armed rebellion, was considered to be a substantial interest, it was within the power of Congress to limit speech that advocated it.

Vinson adds his own interpretation of what constituted a clear and present danger, arguing that state officials did not have to "wait until the putsch is about to be executed, the plans have been laid and the signal is awaited." If there is evidence that a group is aiming to overthrow the government, that the group "is attempting to indoctrinate its members and to commit them to a course whereby they will strike when the leaders feel the circumstances permit, action by the Government is required." It was up to the Court to decide if "the gravity of the evil, discounted by its improbability, justifies such invasion of free speech as is necessary to avoid danger" (Vinson's *Dennis* opinion). It did not matter for the Court that between 1945 and 1948, the activities of those charged as members in the Communist Party did not result in even a single attempt to overthrow the government. What was relevant was that "there was a group that was ready to make the attempt" (Vinson's *Dennis* opinion).

Vinson argued the convictions were justified because the defendants put in place "a highly organized conspiracy, with rigidly disciplined members subject to call when the leaders . . . felt that the time had come for action" in addition to the "inflammable nature of world conditions, [with] similar uprisings in other countries."

In his dissent, Justice Hugo Black points out that the petitioners were not charged with an attempt to overthrow the government or even with publishing material advocating such an overthrow, but rather were charged with agreeing to meet to talk about their ideas and to publish about those same ideas at a later date. Black argued the prosecution amounted to prior censorship and was concerned with the Court's notion that the "First Amendment permits us to sustain laws suppressing freedom of speech and press on the basis of Congress' or our own notions of mere 'reasonableness.' Such a doctrine waters down the First Amendment so that it amounts to little more than an admonition to Congress." For Black, Vinson's new clear and present danger test amounted to nothing more than the courts approving "suppression of free speech at will."

Black makes a strong argument that gets to the heart of what the previous chapters show. When the Court is faced with constitutional questions limiting rights, they look for statutory answers to the cases because when they allow for limits on rights based on the Bill of Rights, such limits are in place even when the war ends. Black notes that "[p]ublic opinion being what it now is, few will protest the conviction of these [Communists]. There is hope, however, that in calmer times, when present pressures, passions and fears subside, this or some later Court will restore the First Amendment liberties to the . . . place where they belong in a free society" (Black's *Dennis* dissent). It will have to be the Court that restores the liberties it limited by upholding the convictions under *Smith Act.* In the cases concerning military detentions, warrantless electronic surveillance and economic emergency legislation, a dialogue takes place between Congress, the courts and the Executive that shape liberties during times of war due to dependence on statutory rather than constitutional questions that does not occur for the First Amendment cases.

By November 1950, more than 200 organizations were considered to be subversive groups. Any sort of affiliation with these groups targeted by the Attorney General could result in either job loss or testifying before the House Un-American Activities Committee (Bontecou, 1953; 171). Between 1947 to 1953, roughly 350 federal employees lost their jobs due to their loyalty being questioned and another 2,200 federal employees resigned voluntarily to stop the investigation into their suspected disloyalty (Brown, 1958; 487–91). Because losing a job was not a punishment for a crime, these investigations were a way for Congress to punish suspected communist sympathizers without offering those accused of such affiliations the proper criminal protections, namely the right to be presumed innocent as well as the right to confront the evidence of the prosecution.

Congressional committees investigating the loyalty of Americans did not receive a carte blanche from the federal courts. Both the lower and Supreme Court protected an individual's right to keep information private from congressional scrutiny. In *United States v. Rumely,* 197 F.2d 166; 1952, the respondent was the secretary of a group called the Committee for Constitutional Government which sold books that at the time were considered politically unpopular in the United States. When asked by the Congressional House Select Committee on Lobbying Activities to give the names of those who made bulk purchases of books, Rumely refused. The lower court held that the intent of the *Lobbying Act,* which was used to set up the congressional committee, was misapplied. Agreeing with the lower court, the Supreme Court held that the House Committee was without the authority to exact such information. The Resolution setting up the Committee gave Congress jurisdiction to "conduct a study and investigation of (1) all lobbying activities intended to influence, encourage, promote, or retard legislation; and (2) all activities of agencies of the Federal Government intended to influence, encourage, promote, or retard legislation."[12] The Court held that the power of the Committee must be found in that section of the House Resolution, and it was not.

The *Rumely* case was decided along a separation of powers guideline. Justice Frankfurter actually notes the Court's duty to avoid the constitutional issues if at all possible, saying this duty applies not only to legislation but also to congressional resolutions, citing *Federal Trade Comm'n v. American Tobacco Co.,* 264 U.S. 298; 1927, as his source of authority. Because the language of the congressional resolution did not support the idea that it was in fact authorizing a committee to look into the influences that form public opinion, the Court was unwilling to extend the scope of the committee. Frankfurter concludes that "grave constitutional questions are matters properly to be decided by this Court but only when they inescapably come before us for adjudication. Until then it is our duty to abstain from marking the boundaries of congressional power or delimiting the protection guaranteed by the First Amendment." In acknowledging the First Amendment decisions of the past, "only by such self-restraint will [the Court] avoid the mischief which has followed occasional departures from the principles which we profess" (Frankfurter's *Rumely* opinion).

The *Rumely* case would become precedent for other cases that dealt with overzealous investigative congressional committees infringing the First Amendment rights of Americans. In *Watkins v. United States,* 354 U.S. 178; 1957, the petitioner was convicted under 2 U.S.C. section 192 which makes it a crime to refuse answering questions before a committee of Congress if the question pertains to the issue being investigated. When in front of the House Committee on Un-American Activities, Watkins openly answered questions about himself and his own activities but refused to answer questions that concerned other individuals and their potential involvement with the Communist Party. Watkins stated that the questions he refused to answer were outside the scope of the Committee's investigation. The lower court had affirmed the conviction, answering the constitutional question as to whether or not the committee violated the First Amendment. The court held that "[i]f Congress has power to inquire into the subjects of Communism and the Communist Party, it has power to identify the individuals who believe in Communism and those who belong to the party," and that this inquiry was not a violation of the First Amendment.

The Supreme Court, in reversing the lower court decision, held that, as decided in *Rumely,* "when First Amendment rights are threatened, the delegation of power to a congressional committee must be clearly revealed in its charter." Continuing, the Court argued that "it cannot simply be assumed that every congressional investigation is justified by a public need that overbalances any private rights affected." Unlike the lower court, which was willing to limit the scope of the First Amendment, the Supreme Court does not decide the constitutional question, but instead states that if the Court is to seriously consider whether a committee of Congress can delve into the private affairs of citizens restricting the right to free speech then Congress must "spell out the committee's jurisdiction and purpose."

Despite Justice Clark's claim in his dissent that congressional committees have traditionally been given "power in exceedingly broad terms," such as the Committees of the Armed Services having jurisdiction over "common defense generally," Chief Justice Earl Warren's Court opinion makes it clear that "protected freedoms should not be placed in danger in absence of a clear determination by the House or Senate that a particular inquiry is justified by specific legislative need." This suggests that had Congress limited First Amendment rights more specifically in the language of the resolution, that the conviction would have been upheld, thus falling in line with the other case studies in previous chapters as well as Justice Jackson's separation of powers framework presented in *Youngstown Sheet & Tube v. Sawyer.*

The clarity required by Congress to investigate in areas that are generally protected by the Bill of Rights was provided in the case of *Barenblatt v. United States,* 252 F.2d 129; 1958. The lower court distinguished *Barenblatt* from *Watkins,* noting it was the vagueness of the resolution that convinced the Court to reverse the *Watkins* conviction. The petitioner in this case was a graduate assistant and teaching fellow at the University of Michigan. When called upon to testify in front of a subcommittee of the House Committee on Un-American Activities investigating the possible Communist infiltration of the educational fields, Lloyd Barenblatt refused to answer questions regarding his potential membership in the Communist Party.

The Supreme Court agreed in *Barenblatt v. United States,* 360 U.S. 109; 1959 holding that the legislative purpose is valid and "to suggest that because the Communist Party may also sponsor peaceable political reforms the constitutional issues before us should now be judged as if that Party were just an ordinary political party from the standpoint of national security, is to ask this Court to blind itself to world affairs which have determined the whole course of our national policy since the close of World War II" (Justice John Harlan's *Barenblatt* opinion).

Black dissents, disagreeing with the Court's "notion that the First Amendment freedoms must be abridged in order to 'preserve' our country. That notion rests on the unarticulated premise that this Nation's security hangs upon its power to punish people because of what they think, speak, or write about, or because of those with whom they associate for political purposes" (Black's *Barenblatt* dissent).

The *Smith Act* was also given a limited interpretation by the Court. When 14 leaders of the Communist Party in California were charged under section 3 of the *Smith Act* for conspiring to teach about the necessity to overthrow the American Government using force and violence as well as to organize a group that would as their sole goal advocate this duty, petitioners were convicted. However the Supreme Court, in *Yates et. al. v. United States,* 354 U.S. 298; 1957, ordered the convictions to be reversed. The lower court based its decision on an argument that the First Amendment not being violated by the *Smith Act* (*Yates et. al. v. United States,* 225 F.2d 146; 1955). The Supreme Court, not relying on those claims, held that the Communist Party had been organized in 1945 and the indictments were not returned until 1951, therefore the three-year statute of limitations ran its course on the organizational charges. The Court held that the three years applied in this case because organization refers to setting up the Communist Party, not carrying out its activities, as the government contended.

Only six years after *Dennis,* the Court distinguished *Yates* from it, by holding that "the *Smith Act* does not prohibit advocacy and teaching of forcible overthrow of the Government as an abstract principle, divorced from any effort to instigate action to that end." Justice Harlan explains that "the instructions to the jury were fatally defective in that the trial court refused to charge that, in order to convict, the jury must find that the advocacy which the defendants conspired to promote was of a kind calculated to 'incite' persons to action for the forcible overthrow of the Government" (Harlan's *Yates* opinion). *Yates* ensured that the advocacy of overthrowing the government as an abstract doctrine was protected under the First Amendment. The *Smith Act* was now applicable only to teachings that were likely to produce action. Because the instructions to the jury found no distinction between teaching the advocacy of overthrowing the government using violence with an incitement to action and teaching as an abstract theory, the instructions to the jury were beyond the intent of the Act. This case mirrors the *Gitlow* case at the state level, but differs from *Dennis* as the jury was instructed that it was specifically not the teaching about overthrowing the government by use of force or violence but rather the "teaching and advocacy *of action* for the accomplishment of that end" (Harlan quoting *Dennis*).

In *Scales v. United States,* 367 U.S. 203; 1961, prosecutions for merely being a member of the Communist Party under the *Smith Act* came to an end. At the lower court level, in *Scales v. United States,* 260 F.2d 21; 1958, the court would base its decision on its belief that the Communist Party represented a clear and present danger of substantive evils beyond the protection of the First Amendment that Congress could protect against in passing legislation such as the *Smith Act.* The conviction of Scales was upheld at the Supreme Court level. Justice Harlan, however, held that the Court would not attribute to Congress as having the intent to "punish nominal membership, even though accompanied by 'knowledge' and 'intent,' not merely because of the close constitutional questions that such a purpose would raise . . . but also . . . it is not to be lightly inferred that Congress intended to visit upon mere passive members the heavy penalties imposed by the Smith Act."

Between WWII and the Vietnam War, the Court upheld First Amendment rights at the state level as well. For example, *Sweezy v. New Hampshire,* 354 U.S. 234; 1957, dealt with anti-subversion investigations of the Cold War that required a professor in the state of New Hampshire to give detailed accounts of his lectures and political associations. He refused. Chief Justice Warren held that "[r]esponsibility for the proper conduct of investigations rests . . . upon the legislature itself. If that assembly chooses to authorize inquiries on its behalf by a legislatively created committee, that basic responsibility . . . include[s] the duty of adequate supervision of the actions of the committee. This safeguard can be nullified when a committee is invested with a broad and ill-defined jurisdiction." In this case, the Committee had gone too far and infringed upon Sweezy's freedom of speech without having authority from the New Hampshire legislature. The Supreme Court had reversed the state Supreme Court of New Hampshire which argued that any infringements of the First Amendment were reasonable given the committee's scope to protect the government the violent overthrow of the government by Communists.

Justice Frankfurter's concurring opinion stated that examining the content of the professor's lectures was in fact a violation of the First Amendment. Frankfurter argues that "when weighed against the grave harm [to academic freedom] resulting from governmental intrusion into the intellectual life of a university, [ordinary justifications] for compelling a witness to discuss the contents of his lecture [appear] grossly inadequate" (Frankfurter's *Sweezy* concurrence). *Sweezy* shows that when rights are infringed upon, the due process clause of the Fourteenth Amendment requires that the "'subordinating interest of the State must be compelling' in order to overcome the individual constitutional rights at stake."

Before Lyndon B. Johnson committed ground troops to Vietnam in 1964, the Supreme Court had already declared certain nonverbal actions were protected "speech" under the First Amendment. In *Stomberg v. California,* 283 U.S. 359; 1931, the Court allowed for a red flag to be displayed as a symbol against organized government, and in *State Board of Education v. Barnette,* 319 U.S. 624; 1943, the Court struck down a law forcing students to recite the pledge of allegiance. During the Vietnam War, the Court was faced with the question as to whether an action was protected as speech if it violated a law, but the purpose of the action was to show protest to the law in question.

The Court allowed for convictions to stand where defendants burnt their Selective Services registration certificate. The *Universal Military Training and Service Act* made it a crime for anyone who "forges, alters, knowingly destroys, knowingly mutilates, or in any manner changes any such certificate." David Paul O'Brien, along with three other individuals who had been drafted, burned their draft cards on the front steps of the South Boston courthouse. During his trial, O'Brien testified that he burned the card with the intention of inspiring others to "reevaluate their positions" about registering with the army after being drafted. The lower court opinion upheld the convictions on the basis that the defendants were without their draft cards which was also a crime, but stated that burning the card was protected under the First Amendment, so the federal government as a whole lacked authority in this regard (*O'Brien v. United States,* 376 F.2d 538; 1967). In a rare instance where the court used the First Amendment to strike down congressional legislation, the federal government found itself within the first prong of Jackson's framework and still the court did not allow the conviction to stand.

However, in a blow to First Amendment liberties, in *United States v. O'Brien,* 391 U.S. 367, 1968, the Supreme Court reinstated the district court convictions, holding that the amendment to the *Universal Training and Military Service Act* did not infringe upon the First Amendment's protection of free speech on its face. Congress has the authority to pass legislation concerning the Selective Service registration card within its authority to raise and support armies. Warren argued that "a law prohibiting destruction of Selective Service certificates no more abridges free speech on its face than . . . a tax law prohibiting the destruction of books and records." The First Amendment did not protect O'Brien and his friends because the government regulation furthers a substantial societal interest—the ability of Congress to conscript manpower for military service. It should be noted that Justice Douglas dissents on the basis that there was no Declaration of War; therefore, the power of Congress to raise and support armies should not be construed as broadly as the Court allowed for.

Though the destruction of Selective Service certificates was not protected by the First Amendment, the Court did protect free speech when Daniel Jay Schacht was convicted of wearing a military uniform without permission in *Schacht v. United States,* 398 U.S. 58; 1970. Schacht and his colleagues performed a skit in front of the Armed Forces induction center, showing an American soldier accidentally killing a pregnant woman in Vietnam. The petitioner was charged under a law that allowed for the uniform to be worn when depicting a soldier in a play or a movie so long as the production did not "discredit" the Armed Services. Justice Black, reversing the lower court decision that held Congress was within its right to restrict the use of the military uniform when used in a disparaging manner, decided that such a restriction on the use of the uniform was a violation of the First Amendment. Black reasoned that "an actor, like everyone else in our country, enjoys a constitutional right to freedom of speech, including the right to openly criticize the Government during a dramatic performance" (Black's *Schacht* opinion). The federal courts at the appeals and Supreme Court levels decided the case by answering the constitutional issues.

During the Vietnam War, no law was passed by Congress suppressing the speech of those critical of government policy. At the start of the war, the constitutionality of § 305 (a) of the *Postal Service and Federal Employees Salary Act* of 1962 was challenged in *Lamont, DBA Basic Pamphlets v. Postmaster General,* 381 U.S. 301; 1965. The section required the Postmaster General to detain foreign mailings considered communist propaganda and to send an addressee a card to have checked, asking for the mail to be delivered. While there was no list being kept as to who was requesting their mailings to be sent, the Court held that it was nonetheless a violation of the First Amendment. The Court decides the case on "the narrow ground that the addressee in order to receive his mail must request in writing that it be delivered" (Douglas' *Lamont* opinion). Because § 3 of the Act placed on the addressee an affirmative obligation to ask for the mail to be sent, a deterrent effect results where some "might think they would invite disaster if they read what the Federal Government says contains the seeds of treason" such as those in sensitive positions like teachers and government employees. The Court continues, even those who are not in sensitive positions are still "likely to feel some inhibition in sending for literature which federal officials have condemned as 'communist political propaganda.'"

The issue area of First Amendment rights being curtailed in the name of national security sees the courts deciding such cases often by addressing the constitutional question, rather than determining the constitutional of the government's actions based on cooperation of the elected branches of government. During the Cold War, when the lower courts decide these cases, they often continued to limit the First Amendment's applicability, while the Supreme Court would reverse, offering a limited construction of whatever Act of Congress was being used to suppress the First Amendment.

Following the same patterns as my previously discussed issue areas, when laws of Congress are considered constitutional, the Supreme Court looked to see if the Executive's actions fall within the scope of the law in question rather than a discussion of whether the First Amendment restricts the president. In *Schneider v. Smith, Commandant, United States Coast Guard,* 390 U.S. 17, 1968, the Court upheld the rights of a merchant mariner to become a second assistant engineer after he refused to answer questions about past organizations of which he was once a member. Schneider was a member of the Communist Party but quit because he disagreed with their method of achieving their ends. President Truman decided that the Commandant of the Coast Guard had the authority to withhold validation if "the character and habits of life of such person are such as to authorize the belief that the presence of the individual on board would not be inimical to the security of the United States" (Justice Douglas' *Schneider* opinion). Though the president is authorized by the *Magnuson Act,* 64 Stat. 427, 50 U.S.C. s 191 (b), to issue rules and regulations "to safeguard against the destruction, loss, or injury from sabotage or other subversive acts" all "vessels in territories or waters subject to the jurisdiction of the United States," determining one's character was an overstretch of the intentions of Congress in passing the Act. The Act spoke of actions, not beliefs and ideas which are protected under the First Amendment. The Supreme Court reversed the lower court decision that held the Act was applicable to the situation at hand because the president had a vested interest in protecting the military vessels (*Schneider v. Roland,* 263 F. Supp 496; 1967). As such, First Amendment freedoms were appropriately guarded.

Similarly, *Watts v. United States,* 394 U.S. 705; 1969, the Court reversed the conviction of a man who stated at a public rally that if given a rifle by the military the first person he would aim towards would be President Johnson. The lower court held that uttering threats against the president was beyond the protections offered by the First Amendment (*Watts v. United States,* 402 F.2d 676; 1968). The 18 year old was convicted under the 1917 *Threats Against the President Act* that made it a crime to make a threat to either kill or cause bodily harm to the president. The Court reversed the conviction on the basis that the statements made were nothing more than a "crude offensive method of stating a political opposition to the president." The Court held that Congress did not intend to limit this sort of speech, as "debate on public issues should be uninhibited, robust, and wide-open, and that it may well include vehement, caustic, and sometimes unpleasantly sharp attacks on government and public officials" (per Curiam *Watts* opinion).

The freedom of the press was also protected during the Vietnam War when the government tried to stop the *New York Times* from publishing a classified study entitled "History of U.S. Decision-Making Process on Viet Nam Policy," otherwise known as the *Pentagon Papers*. In *New York Times Co. v. United States,* 403 U.S. 713; 1971, the *Pentagon Papers* were given to the newspaper by Daniel Ellsberg, a former employee of the Department of Defense who was a consultant under Secretary of Defense Robert MacNamara. Ellsberg, having read the entire Pentagon Papers, decided that withdrawal from Vietnam was the best course of action and gave the *Times* a redacted copy of the document, taking out anything thought to be a detriment to the national security of the nation.

Justice Black's concurring opinion notes that the press has the freedom, under the First Amendment, to "publish news, whatever the source, without censorship, injunctions, or prior restraints, and that the guarding of military and diplomatic secrets at the expense of informed representative government was not justified." Black concludes that "every moment's continuance of the injunctions against these newspapers amounts to a flagrant, indefensible, and continuing violation of the First Amendment."

Justice Harlan's dissent points to the Government's power resting on the construction and validity of the *Espionage Act* which prohibits the publication of information that will help the enemy. Harlan notes that what is and is not a threat to national security are political decisions, not judicial ones, and the elected representatives, Congress and the president, should be making these calls since they alone are directly responsible to the people. The lower court's per curiam opinion sent the case back to the district court for in camera proceedings to determine if the information to be published would be harmful to the national security of the United States.

In the first case concerning the distribution of pamphlets since the First World War, the Supreme Court upheld the right of John Thomas Flower to distribute pamphlets on a San Antonio military base in *Flower v. United States,* 407 U.S. 197; 1972. Flower was the Peace Education Secretary of the American Friends Service Committee. Because the military allows civilians on the particular road in question, the Court held that "the military has abandoned any claim that it has special interests in who walks, talks, or distributes leaflets on the avenue." As a result, "the base commandant can no more order petitioner off this public street because he was distributing leaflets than could the city police order any leafleteer off any public street (per curiam *Flower* opinion). Again, the lower court held that restricting the ability of Flower to pass out pamphlets on the base was a reasonable restriction on free speech in order to maintain morale and order on the base.

While the freedom of press was safeguarded, speech of members of the Armed Services was limited. The lower court attempted to protect the First Amendment, basing its ruling on an interpretation of Article 134 of the *Uniform Code of Military Justice.* If a soldier was convicted under Article 134, it was for attempting to "publish a statement disloyal to the United States to members of the Armed Forces 'with design to promote disloyalty and disaffection among the troops." The court held that the Article was unconstitutionally vague (*Avrech v. Secretary of the Navy,* 477 F. 2d 1237; 1973). However, in *Secretary of the Navy v. Avrech,* 418 U.S. 676; 1974, the Supreme Court reversed, upholding the Air Force regulations that required members to obtain the approval of commanding officers before they circulate petitions meant to be sent to Congress did not violate the First Amendment. The Court held that such regulations "protect a substantial Government interest unrelated to the suppression of free expression—the interest in maintaining the respect for duty and discipline so vital to military effectiveness" (Powell's *Glines* opinion). Again, we have an example of one decision being based on the applicability of the First Amendment itself, with the right being limited, and another court basing its ruling on an interpretation of a congressional statute, protecting the First Amendment.

Furthermore, we also have the Supreme Court limiting First Amendment rights based on acts of Congress as not all cases are decided squarely by an interpretation of what is and is not protected speech. In *Brown, Secretary of Defense, et. al. v. Glines,* 444 U.S. 348; 1980, and *Secretary of the Navy et al. v. Huff et. al.,* 444 U.S. 453; 1980, the Court held that military regulations prohibiting letters being sent to Congress do not violate the Act of Congress (10 U.S.C. s 1034) allowing for service members to have an unrestricted right to communicate with members of Congress because members of the Armed Services retain the ability to write to his or her individual member of Congress. The lower courts disagreed, believing the military regulations ignored the chosen policy of Congress, placing the actions of the Executive in the third prong of the Youngstown framework in Jackson's concurring opinion (*Glines v. Wade,* 586 F.2d 675; 1978 and *Huff et. al. v. Secretary of the Navy,* 575 F.2d 907; 1978).

JUDICIAL INCONSISTENCIES

During World War I, it was typically the case that the federal courts limited the protection of free speech under the First Amendment by holding that speech that is detrimental to the national security of the nation is beyond the scope of the Amendment. During World War II, the Supreme Court would reverse lower court decisions that would take away the citizenship of naturalized Americans accused of not being loyal to the United States for being members of the Communist Party. During the Communist scare of the Cold War and the Vietnam War, free speech cases show no consistent pattern of judicial decision making. At times, we have the lower courts upholding individual liberties based on statutory interpretation just to be reversed by the Supreme Court. Other times, we have the Supreme Court upholding First Amendment rights based on statute and likewise based squarely on our constitutional rights. The following section shows this lack of consistency.

In *Kleindienst, Attorney General, et. al. v. Mandel et. al.,* 408 U.S. 753, 1972, the Court allowed for Congress to deny a Marxist Belgian journalist entry into the country. Having been invited to speak at a variety of academic conferences and events around the country, including at Stanford, Columbia and Princeton universities, Mandel brought the case to the federal courts arguing that a visa could not be denied because the First Amendment rights of those at the universities that had invited Mandel to speak included the right to speak, hear and debate ideas in person. The Court held that Congress had plenary authority as to who could gain entry into the country and that it was the choice of Congress to delegate a conditional exercise of that authority to the Executive. The Court here reversed the lower court opinion *Mandel et. al. v. Mitchell,* 325 F. Supp. 620; 1971. Though the Supreme Court was willing to allow government to deny entry into the country based on political opinion, the lower court held it was a violation of the First Amendment because Congress was not protecting the nation from any threat and instead was only protecting the state from "disfavored political doctrine."

The right to free speech was also an issue at the state level during the war. In contrast with *Mandel,* the lower court is willing to limit free speech whereas it is the Supreme Court that will uphold it. In *Bond et al v. Floyd et. al.,* 385 U.S. 116; 1966, Bond, newly elected to the Georgia House of Representatives was a member of a civil rights organization that issued an anti-war statement. While Bond was not a signatory to the statement, he did say he agreed with the message. Bond endorsed it, "first, because [he likes] to think of [himself] as a pacifist and one who opposes that war and any other war . . . Secondly . . . [he thought] it [was] . . . hypocritical for us to maintain that we are fighting for liberty in other places and we are not guaranteeing liberty to citizens inside the continental United States" (quoted in Warren's *Bond* opinion). The result was that the Georgia House of Representatives refused to seat Bond as a member. House members said the statement aided the enemies of the United States because it gave them comfort and that such statements violated the Selected Services laws. The Court held that disqualifying Bond was a violation of his First Amendment rights because opposition to national foreign policy, including the war in Vietnam, is protected political speech. The lower court would have allowed the state legislature to choose qualifications that would disqualify someone from holding office as a matter of federalism (*Bond et. al. v. Floyd* et. al, 251 F. Supp 333; 1966).

Also at the state level, the Court struck down a California law that made it illegal to "maliciously and willfully disturb the peace or quiet of any neighborhood or person . . . by . . . offensive conduct." When Paul Cohen wore a jacket in a courtroom that had the words "Fuck the Draft" on the back he was charged with offensive conduct that could have provoked others to act violently in turn resulting in further disturbances of the peace. The Court reversed the lower court decision that would have upheld the California law based on the state's right to prohibit what is considered obscene (*People of California v. Cohen,* 1 Cal. App. 3d. 94; 1969).

The Supreme Court upheld an individual's right to protest the draft by noting that Cohen's behavior rested solely on speech and did not necessarily have any attached message that incited action. In *Cohen v. California,* 403 U.S. 15; 1971, Justice Harlan stated that "the ability of the government, consonant with the Constitution, to shut off discourse solely to protect others from hearing it is, in other words, dependent upon a showing that substantial privacy interests are being invaded in an essentially intolerable manner" (Harlan's *Cohen* opinion).

The Court continued that if it interpreted the power of Congress any broader, it would result in the government having the authority to censure minority views. Similarly, while the lower court did not think a law restricting the use of the American flag was a limit to expression protected under the First Amendment (*State of Washington v. Spence,* 81 WN.2d 788; 1973), the Supreme Court upheld the right of an individual to place the American flag in his apartment window upside down with a peace sign taped to it as political speech in *Spence v. Washington,* 418 U.S. 405; 1974.[13]

Not all cases resulted in favorable outcomes for First Amendment defenders. A variety of civil disorders prompted the government to ask the Army to develop a data-gathering system. Petitioners would argue that what amounted to electronic surveillance would create a prior restraint on speech as individuals, upon becoming aware of the surveillance, would be less inclined to speak freely. This claim is often cast aside as the federal courts rule that having rights "chilled," or being afraid to freely exercise one's rights, is not the same thing as proving a right has been violated (*United States v. Ahmad,* 347 F. Supp. 912; 1972). The Department of the Army created a program for the surveillance of domestic groups which was challenged in court. In *Tatum v. Laird,* 444 F.2d 947; 1971, the lower court dismissed the complaint due to lack of evidence, or at least available information, for the court to decide the issue, but the Supreme Court in *Laird v. Tatum,* 408 U.S. 1; 1972, reversed, holding that the Department of the Army created a program for the surveillance of domestic groups but that "to pass judgment on whether the army should have such a program" would see the federal courts monitor the "wisdom" and the "soundness" of the Executive's actions. The Court held that it was for Congress to act in this oversight role "absent actual present or immediate threatened injury resulting from unlawful government action."[14]

In *Socialist Workers Party v. Attorney General,* 419 U.S. 1314; 1974, a chilling effect of having the FBI attend the Socialist Workers Party Youth National Convention was sufficient enough to warrant the federal courts having jurisdiction to decide the case, but a stay on the part of the Court was considered "improper, since the FBI . . . represented that it plan[ned] no disruptive activity at the convention and [would] not transmit information to nongovernmental entities." Despite the Court's concern for abuses of government power, such a concern, it was held, "cannot be permitted to lead to an indiscriminate willingness to enjoin undercover investigation of any nature, whenever a countervailing First Amendment claim is raised" (Marshall's *Socialist Workers Party* decision).

The last and to this day controlling opinion on when the Congress can limit free speech is from 1969 and concerns a leader of the Klu Klux Klan in Ohio, not the ongoing Vietnam War. In *Brandenburg v. Ohio,* 395 U.S. 444; 1969, in question was an Ohio Criminal Syndicalism statute for "'advocat[ing] . . . the duty, necessity, or propriety of crime, sabotage, violence, or unlawful methods of terrorism as a means of accomplishing industrial or political reform' and for voluntarily assembl[ing] with any society, group or assemblage of persons formed to teach or advocate the doctrines of criminal syndicalism (per curiam *Brandenburg* opinion)" was challenged as unconstitutional.

A man telephoned a television station and invited a reporter to a Ku Klux Klan rally. The KKK rally was taped by the reporter and put on the news. The video showed 12 hooded individuals, some with guns. A cross was burned and an address was delivered. At the end of the speech the speaker noted that "we are marching on Congress July the Fourth, four hundred thousand strong." The per curiam decision of the Court finally placed rigid restrictions on what used to be the clear and present danger test that the only recourse for Congress to limit the First Amendment rights was "where such advocacy is directed to inciting or producing imminent lawless action and is likely to incite or produce such action." The key change here from the decision in *Dennis* in 1951 was the emphasis on action likely to occur, as the Court continued that "the mere abstract teaching . . . of the moral propriety or even moral necessity for a resort to force and violence, is not the same as preparing a group for violent action and steeling it to such action" (per curiam *Brandenburg* decision). What started with the *Schenck* decision during World War I where the Court answered the constitutional question head on was finally resolved 50 years later in 1969.

Table 6.2. Restriction to Free Speech During the Cold War

	Court upheld executive action	*Court struck down executive action*
Congressional authorization/no First Amendment protection	*U.S. v. Dennis*, 1950 *Dennis v. U.S.*, 1951 *Yates v. U.S.*, 1957 *Watkins v. U.S.*, 1956 *Wyman v. Sweezy*, 1956 *Barenblatt v. U.S.*, 1958 *Scales v. U.S.*, 1958 *Barenblatt v. U.S.*, 1959 *Scales v. U.S.*, 1961 *Bond v. Floyd*, 1966 *Schneider v. Roland*, 1967 *U.S. v. O'Brien*, 1968 *Watts v. U.S.*, 1968 *Schacht v. U.S.*, 1969 *California v. Cohen*, 1969 *U.S. v. Flower*, 1971 *Laird v. Tatum*, 1972 *U.S. v. Ahmad*, 1972 *Kleindienst v. Mandel*, 1972 *Fifth Ave... v. Gray*, 1973 *Navy v. Avrech*, 1974 *Washington v. Spence*, 1974 *Zweibon v. Mitchell*, 1975 *Brown v. Glines*, 1980 *Navy v. Huff*, 1980 *ACLU v. Barr*, 1991	
No Congressional authorization/ contrary to the wishes of Congress		*Rumely v. U.S.*, 1952 *U.S. v. Rumely*, 1953 *Watkins v. U.S.*, 1957 *Yates v. U.S.*, 1957 *Sweezy v. N. H.*, 1957 *Lamont v. Postmaster*, 1965 *Bond v. Floyd*, 1966 *O'Brien v. U.S.*, 1967 *Schneider v. Smith*, 1968 *Watts v. U.S.*, 1969 *Schacht v. U.S.*, 1970 *Mandel v. Mitchell*, 1971 *Cohen v. California*, 1971 *Flower v. U.S.*, 1972 *Avrech v. Navy*, 1973 *Spence v. Washington*, 1974 *Glines v. Wade*, 1978 *Huff v. Navy*, 1980

Table 6.2 shows the federal courts more inclined to protect First Amendment rights post-World War II, but the cases show little in the way of judicial patterns. As previously stated, at times the Supreme Court reverses lower court decisions which uphold individual rights on the basis on the First Amendment in favor of allowing for rights to be limited through statutory interpretation. The same can be said for the lower courts. That said, however, the courts were still willing to strike down executive actions based on a misinterpretation of congressional statutes as was the case in decisions with a after the year. In *Schacht,* the Court actually strikes down a law as unconstitutional, thus denying the federal government as a whole the ability to dictate under what conditions the uniform of a soldier can be worn in dramatic reenactments. The First Amendment cases between the end of World War II and the end of the Cold War present the most puzzling findings, but what remains constant is when the federal courts decide cases using the language found in the Bill of Rights, and they limit the application of the Amendment, what has occurred is that the right is limited in times of peace as well as times of war.

WAR ON TERRORISM

In the months after the 2001 terrorist attacks in New York and Washington, criticism of the government's policies was described by government officials as seditious (Lapham, 2002; 7), and, in the words of former Attorney General John Ashcroft, as giving "aid to terrorists."[15] Staffers at American newspapers in Texas and Oregon got fired for writing columns that were critical of the Bush Administration after the terrorist attacks (Sarat, 2005; 7). Despite political speech being protected by the First Amendment, evolving from the days of the *Schenck* decision, on September 12, 2001, a journalism professor at the University of Texas, Robert Jensen, wrote a newspaper editorial stating that "[m]y anger on this day is directed not only at individuals who engineered the September 11 tragedy but at those who have held power in the United States and have engineered attacks on civilians every bit as tragic."[16] There was public outcry demanding Jensen be dismissed. Though the professor kept his job and did not face any sort of disciplinary actions, the president of the university, Larry R. Faulkner, wrote a letter stating that he disagreed with the letter and considered the arguments made to be a "fountain of undiluted foolishness on issues of public policy." There were concerns from the faculty, however, that the negative backlash Faulkner created by his response would result in a chilling effect on other members of the University community (Bird and Barker Brandt, 2002; 435).[17]

There has been a small number of federal court cases pertaining to free speech after 9/11. While there is a broader acceptance of dissent during times of war, the results of these particular cases are less than promising. In *Sheehan v. United States,* 896 F.2d 1168, 2006, the District Court for the District of Columbia upheld the conviction of demonstrators protesting without a permit, violating the National Park Service regulations (36 C.F.R., s 7.96 (g)(2). More than 300 people gathered on the sidewalk of the White House to protest the Iraq War. The National Park Service issued a permit to the Iraq Pledge of Resistance group to demonstrate at the Ellipse and Lafayette Parks, but not at the White House, where a permit is required for demonstrations of more than 25 people. The organizers of the demonstration were warned to leave the premises, seek a permit and return. Cindy Sheehan and the other appellants protested their convictions based on a claim that the regulation was an unconstitutional infringement of their freedom of speech and expression as guaranteed under the First Amendment. Sheehan's conviction was upheld by the court of appeals (*United States v. Sheehan,* 512 F. 3d 621; 2008).

Other First Amendment legal battles have arisen in the federal courts since 9/11. As discussed in the chapter on warrantless electronic surveillance, President Bush authorized the National Security Agency to implement the Terrorist Surveillance Program which included the interception of telephone and email communications without a warrant where one party was located outside of the United States. The plaintiffs were lawyers who had overseas clients arguing their clients feared to speak freely because their conversations could be wiretapped. As such, their First Amendment rights were chilled. In reversing a district court decision, on July 6, 2007, the 6th U.S. Circuit Court of Appeals dismissed the case in *ACLU v. NSA,* 438 F. Supp. 2d 754 because plaintiffs had no standing as it was impossible for them to demonstrate they were direct targets of warrantless electronic surveillance. As discussed in chapter 4, Judge Batchelder, relying on the *Laird* precedent, reminds the plaintiffs that they "must establish that he or she is regulated, constrained, or compelled directly by the government's action instead of by his or her own subjective chill." Because the plaintiffs were unable to show that they were personally subject to surveillance, the court was unable to address their potential First Amendment claims. The Supreme Court denied cert in 2008.

CONCLUSIONS

The Constitution gives Congress the power to declare war, raise armies, and support a navy. However, Zechariah Chafee Jr. long ago pointed out that "one provision of the Constitution cannot be used to break down another provision, and consequently freedom of speech cannot be invoked to break down the war power (Chafee, 1919; 955). While the Bill of Rights and the war powers of the federal government must exist side by side in times of war as in times of peace, congressional action was shown to be restricted by the Bill of Rights in *ex parte Milligan,* 4 Wall. U.S.; 1866, during the Civil War. Chafee continues by arguing that "if the First Amendment is to mean anything, it must restrict powers which are expressly granted by the Constitution to Congress, since Congress has no other powers. It must apply to those activities of government which are most liable to interfere with free discussion, namely, the postal service and the conduct of war" (1919; 956). Evidence shows that the dissent in *Milligan,* which suggests had Congress authorized the military commissions then the conviction may have been upheld, has become the majority rationale in war powers cases when individual rights are limited.

Would First Amendment jurisprudence have been any different had the Court decided *Schenck* based primarily on statutory claims not constitutional ones? David Cole notes that the history of the First Amendment during times of war shows the government repeating history while refusing to acknowledge it as such and in fact insisting that it has learned from its past individual rights infringements. Restrictions on speech progressed to restrictions on association. Today, the government does not make it a crime to association with groups that are considered terrorist organizations but it has "made guilt by association the linchpin of the war's strategy, penalizing people under criminal and immigration laws for providing 'material support'" for such groups even if the support was intended to further an activity that was not terrorist in nature (Cole, 2005; 112).

ENDNOTES

1. I will discuss *ex parte Vallandigham* in this historical background section, but label it as a case about the writ of habeas corpus and not the First Amendment, despite the reasons for Clement Vallandigham's arrest in the first place.

2. James Madison opposed the *Alien and Sedition Acts.* In fact, Madison wrote the Virginia Resolutions in 1798, officially stating Virginia's opposition to the federal government's initiative. In his *Report of 1800,* Madison declared that the *Alien Act,* being in force during times of peace, exercises a power that is nowhere delegated to the federal government as a whole (noting that in times of war the power of reprisal does allow Congress to make laws concerning the declaration of who is an enemy to the State). Furthermore, Madison argued that the *Sedition Act* was contrary to the First Amendment and rejected the argument in favor of the *Sedition Act* that freedom of the press meant whatever the government says it meant (*Madison Papers,* Vol. 17; 326). In a letter to Thomas Jefferson, Madison reported that the Virginia Resolutions passed 60 votes in favor and 40 against after a five-day debate (*Madison Papers,* Vol. 17; 336).

3. France was at war with Great Britain and depended on American ships to bring goods back and forth from France to the United States. However, the Jay Treaty, signed on November 19, 1796, brought peace between Great Britain and the United States, with President Washington insisting on American neutrality in regard to European wars (Stinchcombe, 1977; 590). This displeased the French. Three French officials, at the time known as X, Y, and Z (the identities of the French diplomats were X = Jean Conrad Hollinguer, Y = Pierre Bellamy and Z = Lucien Hauteval), demanded bribes from the American envoy to be received in response to American neutrality. The Americans refused to pay. Two of the convoy members, John Marshall and Charles Pinckney, were sent home, while Elbridge Gerry stayed in France.

4. At the Supreme Court, Justice Swayne, writing for a unanimous Court, stated that "whatever may be the force of Vallandigham's protest that he was not triable by a court of military constitution, it is certain that his petition cannot be brought within the 14th section of the Judiciary Act of 1789" (Swayne's *Vallandigham* opinion).

5. 65th Cong, 1st Sess, in 55 Cong Rec S 214 (April 4 1917).

6. 65th Cong, Spec Sess, in 55 Cong Rec S 214 (April 4, 1917).

7. The Wilson Administration asked for what Stone calls a "press censorship" to be included in the Act that would, if agreed to, make it illegal for any information to be published in a time of war that the president decided was useful to the enemy. The provision was voted down in the House by a vote of 184 to 144 (Stone, 2004; 147-149). Two other clauses were amended in significant ways that showed the concern Congress had for First Amendment rights. The "disaffection provision" made it a crime to "'make or convey false reports or false statements with intent to interfere with the operation or success' of the military forces of the United States or to 'promote the success of its enemies,' or (b) willfully to 'cause or attempt to cause disaffection in the'" armed forces of the United States. Congress thought disaffection was too broad and added that the goal of the speech had to be to "cause or attempt to cause insubordination, disloyalty, mutiny, or refusal of duty." The nonmailability provision allowed the Postmaster General to exclude mail that violated any provision of the *Espionage Act* or was considered to be treasonable or anarchistic. The phrase "treasonable and anarchistic" posed problems for Congress and was amended to narrow the delegation of authority, allowing the Postmaster General to disallow mail that expressed advocacy of action that urged "treason, insurrection or forcible resistance to any law of the United States."

8. In one attempt to get at the meaning of the First Amendment's freedom of speech and press prior to the First World War, Justice Holmes did suggest the First Amendment was intended to prevent prior restraint on publication by the government, but once something was published, the author would be held accountable if the printed comments were contrary to the public welfare. In *Patterson v. Colorado*, 205 U.S. 454; 1907, Holmes' emphasized that free speech and free press were relative terms and were subject to the limitations society dictated.

9. Stone suggests that Holmes' change of position on the protection of free speech, while officially remaining a "delicious mystery," probably has to do with

his 1919 summer correspondence with Judge Learned Hand, Zechariah Chafee, and political scientist Harold Laski, all three of whom championed the rights of those convicted under the *Espionage Act* of 1917 (Stone, 2007; 61).

10. At the district court level, in *Masse Publishing Co. v. Patten*, 244 Fed. 535 (S.D.N.Y.); 1917, the court was asked to decide whether the postmaster of the state was allowed to exclude mailing *The Masses,* a journal containing articles and poems that carried an anti-war message. Under the *Espionage Act,* the postmaster could refrain from mailing any publication that was in violation of the law. In constructing what he thought to be the proper intent of Congress, Judge Hand argued that the Act was meant to prohibit mail that would interfere with the conduct of military affairs and was not meant to suppress opinion that was critical of the government's war policies. This point of view would not reach majority opinions in the cases that arose out of World War I.

11. In *Grosjean v. American Press Co.*, 297 U.S. 233; 1936, the Court invalidated a law taxing newspapers. *Thornhill v. Alabama*, 310 U.S. 88; 1940 put an end to a law prohibiting picketing, with the Court stating that the Supreme Court protects protests about the facts of a labor dispute. Other examples of speech protection between the two world wars include *Near v. Minnesota,* 283 U.S. 697; 1931, where the Court held that freedom of the press included freedom from prior restraint in publishing and *Cantwell v. Connecticut*, 310 U.S. 296; 1940 the conviction of a Jehovah's Witness for breaching the peace through an attack on the Catholic Church was reversed.

12. H. Res. 298, 81 Cong., 1st Sess.

13. More than a decade after troops were pulled out of Vietnam, at the national level, in *United States v. Eichman,* et. al., 496 U.S. 310; 1990, an act of Congress (*Flag Protection Act*, 1989), that made it illegal to burn the American flag for other purposes than to dispose of one, was an unconstitutional violation of the First Amendment as held in *Texas v. Johnson,* 491 U.S. 397; 1989. The Court in *Johnson* held that the interest of the State in preserving the flag as a symbol of national unity was an interest related to the suppression of expression within the meaning of *O'Brien* because the state's concern was with protecting the flag from being destroyed when that destruction conveyed some sort of political message. The demonstrator's First Amendment rights outweighed the government's interest under the "most exacting scrutiny." Note the terminology. A level of heightened scrutiny is used in evaluating this First Amendment case that occurs during a time of perceived peace.

14. Similar results at circuit court level were held in *Fifth Avenue Peace Parade Committee v. Gray*, 480 F. 2d 326; 1973, *Zweibon et. al. v. Mitchell*, 516 F.2d 594; 1975, and *ACLU v. Barr*, 952 F.2d 457; 1991.

15. Dan Eggan, "Ashcroft defends Anti-Terrorism steps: Civil Liberties Groups' Attacks 'Only aid Terrorists' Senate Panel Told" *Washington Post*, December 7, 2001.

16. Robert Jensen, September 26, 2001. Full text of editorial is available online. http://www.chron.com/cs/CDA/story.hts/editorial/1047072 (April 2, 2007).

17. In another widely publicized account, University of South Florida professor Sami Al-Arian founded an organization called the World Islamic Studies Enterprise. A guest on *The O'Reilly Factor* on September 26, 2001, Bill O'Reilly asked about comments Al-Arian made in 1988 when he stated that "Jihad is our path. Victory to Islam. Death to Israel." Though the Professor stated such comments were taken out of context, the university received phone calls and email messages in protest (Bird and Barker Brandt, 2002; 455). Al-Arian was fired and subsequently charged by the FBI with providing financial assistance to terrorists.

Conclusion

Protecting Individual Rights: Guidance for both Congress and the Executive

When our individual rights, guaranteed by the Constitution, are limited by executive action, we expect judicial challenges to be adjudicated using a rights-based discourse. Executive actions should stand or fall depending on whether the president's orders are contrary to the Bill of Rights. This is not predominantly the case, as my examination of military detentions, warrantless electronic surveillance, and emergency economic legislation shows. When the Executive claims to be limiting rights in the name of national security, the federal courts will often look for the presence of congressional approval, or disapproval, of the actions in question. I have called this a separation of powers framework for judicial decision making. In other words, the federal courts often decide war-powers questions where individual liberties are limited by the Executive on statutory grounds, not by looking at the constitutional questions involved.

Free speech cases show an entire issue-area that is an exception to my analysis. In these cases, during WWI, the Judiciary decided the constitutional claims but did not protect the liberty in question, allowing for the infringement of the First Amendment. In later cases, the courts would revert to deciding free speech claims using a separation of powers framework by interpreting the intent of congressionally enacted statutes. This would occur only after the initial damage of limiting the scope of the First Amendment had already occurred.

The federal courts' emphasis on the separation of powers is a way to protect both the Judiciary and the Constitution itself from overzealous justices who in a time of great panic might grant too much authority to the Executive, thus potentially damaging rights enumerated in the Constitution beyond repair after the end of hostilities. Alternatively, the separation of powers framework also protects against the courts limiting the Executive to the peril of national security, leaving our elected political actors either powerless or willing to ignore the ruling of the courts, either way weakening not only the institution of the Judiciary but also the Constitution.

This analysis is not the first to suggest the federal courts decide war powers cases within a separation of powers framework. As noted in the introduction, Issacharoff and Pildes point out that the scholarly debate concerning the curtailment of individual rights during war is centered on rights-based discourse while the cases themselves are decided using the language of institutional roles and rules (Issacharoff and Pildes, 2003; 7). Silverstein notes, "[f]rom the beginning, the Court has maintained that one of its primary obligations in foreign and domestic policy disputes is to police the separation of powers" (Silverstein, 1997; 22). The preceding chapters show there is consistency in the reasoning used by the federal courts in deciding cases where the Executive has implemented a policy which limits individual liberties during times of war. Justice Jackson's *Youngstown* concurrence is used as a framework to show how the separation of powers rationale of deciding war powers cases works. Jackson's vision of the interconnectedness between the elected branches of government mirrors the vision shared by some of the framers of the Constitution, most notably James Madison. Showing the historical accuracy in the Jackson framework also shows an extra layer of protection for individual rights that would not exist if the courts deferred to the Executive alone.

This institutionalist approach to deciding war-powers cases concerning limitations on individual liberties necessarily brings into question claims to the contrary which might suggest that a more behavioralist approach is key to such analysis. Showing that the courts look for cooperation amongst the elected branches of government during times of armed hostilities stands in contrast to the behavioralist arguments that a) justices vote based on their policy preferences and b) justices vote in accordance with the ruling elite, which is considered to be the Executive. This is because the courts actually defer to Congress by seeking its approval for executive policies. In contrast, since proponents of a rational choice analysis of judicial decision making suggest that good legal policy is a legitimate preference for justices (Baum, 2006; 14), the institutionalist argument emerging in consideration of limiting rights during war is a mix between strategic and historical institutionalist approaches to judicial decision making. The strategic component consists of the federal courts' efforts at maintaining the institutional integrity of the Judiciary and the Constitution itself. The historical institutionalist component is found in the courts' consistency of rationales for how decisions are made during war over time. This is significant because while the adjudication of the war powers have been an often discussed topic for analysis by scholars, the language of judicial decision making itself is not often a part of the analysis. In other words, while the outcomes of the cases themselves are often analyzed, less emphasis on providing a theory for how the courts decide the cases the way they do in the first place has emerged.

Deference to Congress and not to the Executive is in fact a significant finding because we tend to argue that the president has flat-out usurped the war powers of Congress. It is true that presidents have been very creative in their abilities to link wartime actions with statutes. It is also true that the courts have not willingly held the Executive to strict interpretations of statutory authority that it requires, as is illustrated in more recent times with the federal judiciary's lofty interpretations of the AUMF (chapter 3). Yet, just like choosing the appropriate level of scrutiny to apply to a case, whether or not the Executive has congressional approval is a question that remains up to the Judiciary itself to decide. Furthermore, as chapter 1 indicated, some of the major contributors to war powers analysis, such as Louis Fisher, Louis Henkin, and John Hart Ely, suggest that the president has consistently aggrandized the war powers for the Executive since Truman held the office, with the courts doing nothing to stop the power grab. However, this analysis differs from those of the past because the focus is on the curtailment of individual liberties and not the initiation of hostilities. As in the case with the initiation of hostilities, it is true that Congress allows the president to aggrandize the powers of his office through years of acquiescence and the passage of statutes delegating authority to the Executive. Unlike the initiation of hostilities, the federal courts have not declined to get involved in the institutional battle over the war powers and have continuously decided cases before it concerning the limitation of individual rights.

There is another theme running through the previous chapters and that is the apparent deference to the military, as an extension of the Executive, when it is military policies in question. We saw the Supreme Court uphold freedom of speech in *Flower,* striking down military regulations that prohibited passing out pamphlets near military bases. Such cases, however, are far and few between. As far back as the Civil War, in *ex parte Milligan,* Justice Davis notes the Judiciary was not the proper branch of government to judge military initiatives as "the tempter of the times did not allow that calmness in deliberation and discussion so necessary to a correct conclusion of a purely judicial question." Close to a century later, similar sentiments were expressed. In *In re Yamashita,* 327 U.S. 1, 1946 Justice Stone held that "the extent to which the power to prosecute violations of the law of war shall be exercised before peace is declared rests, not with the courts, but with the political branch of the Government, and may itself be governed by the terms of an armistice or the treaty of peace." Justices Murphy and Douglas echo these sentiments in *Hirabayashi v. United States,* 320 U.S. 81; 1943. Justice Douglas stated that "we cannot sit in judgment on the military requirements of that hour," with Murphy adding that when the president and the Congress act together they "may generally employ such measures as are necessary and appropriate to provide for the common defense and to wage war 'with all force necessary to make it effective.'"

More recently, in *Rasul v. Bush,* 542 U.S. 466; 2004, Kennedy's concurrence, while agreeing with the decision to allow foreign nationals access to the federal courts system, acknowledges that there is indeed an area of power "where judicial power may not enter" that engages the "joint role of the president and the Congress, in the conduct of military affairs (Kennedy's *Rasul* concurrence). The Court rationale is clear; if Congress has endorsed the role the military is playing, then it is for the elected branches of government to deal with such issues.

However, when we look at issues concerning warrantless electronic surveillance, restrictions on private property, and free speech, the federal courts sing a different tune. It is not the military, Congress and the Executive whose decisions are being judged, but rather Congress and the Executive alone. The courts remain weary of limiting the power of the federal government as a whole during armed hostilities, but as an institution, the courts are more likely to adjudicate cases dealing with warrantless electronic surveillance, property rights, and free speech because these issues include matters of domestic policy that are regulated by acts of Congress and provide to the federal courts jurisdiction to make important decisions. In fact, Justice Powell notes that there is no reason to believe that the courts would be "insensitive to or uncomprehending of the issues involved in *domestic* security cases (Powell's *United States District Court* opinion).

The warrantless electronic surveillance cases showcase Powell's point. When Congress has created rules in a particular area and when domestic policy is in play, the federal courts are willing to get involved. When, however, the issue of foreign intelligence gathering emerged in front of the courts, like military policy cases, the courts place themselves outside the area of expertise, and therefore outside the ability to limit executive authority until, that is, Congress passed the *Foreign Intelligence Surveillance Act* of 1978. Judge Ainsworth noted that before the passage of FISA, "further judicial inquiry would be improper and should not occur. It would be intolerable that courts, without the relevant information, should review and perhaps nullify actions of the Executive taken on information properly held secret" (Ainsworth's *Clay* opinion, citing *Chicago & Southern Airlines v. Waterman SS Corp.,* 333 U.S. 103; 1948).

When jurisdiction is unclear and Congress has remained silent on the issue, the courts will defer to the Executive, unless the issue is considered one with a domestic component, despite claims of national security. When Congress has passed legislation on the issue, the courts abide by the requirements Congress has placed on executive actions. When Congress passes laws which specifically state it is not limiting any powers of the Executive that it might possess on its own, this policy position, too, is respected by the courts. This back and forth between Congress, the federal courts and the Executive creates a constitutional dialogue (Hogg and Bushell, 1997; 75) where the branches of government work together within their proper institutional spheres of authority to create war powers policies.

Similarly, in regard to property rights, the courts look for the proper role of the court noting that emergency economic laws have clauses giving jurisdiction to the federal courts to hear cases where due process to determine if property was erroneously confiscated is questioned. Because the *Trading with the Enemy Act* calls for it, the courts maintain an active role in interpreting the Act, which has resulted in the courts finding that executive officials have gone too far in interpreting the intent of Congress.[1] While the courts have not always held that Congress explicitly delegated authority to the president, they used the Act of Congress to show it did not explicitly forbid actions of the Executive either. That the federal courts place emphasis in its decisions on its own jurisdictional role as mandated by Congress is telling.

Policy implications

Given the reliance on the separation of powers where rights-based claims are rejected by the federal courts when Congress has consented to the actions of the Executive, it should come as no surprise that the courts reject, simply by not addressing, claims made by the president that the Executive possesses some sort of inherent authority to unilaterally act in using the war powers. That the federal courts have not accepted such arguments and instead base their decisions on statutory grounds rather than answering the constitutional questions at hand, should be noted by those involved in the decision-making process.

The position of the federal courts is one that has remained relatively constant. Because historically it is the case that the courts seek some sort of congressional approval for executive actions when the president spearheads efforts to curtail individual liberties, this brings into question the actions of presidents starting with Truman's efforts during the Korean War up to and including George W. Bush's establishment of military commissions to try suspects detained on the battlefield in Afghanistan without congressional authorization. All modern presidents made a claim of possessing inherent authority as Executive and commander-in-chief of the Armed Forces. The courts, however, will not allow the president to act unilaterally in limiting individual rights, even when the argument is made that it is necessary for the protection of national security.

The best position for the Executive to be in is one where the Congress is on board by authorizing, paying for, sanctioning after the fact, or explicitly not limiting (though not conferring power either) whatever action the Executive takes in its attempt to secure the public's safety. The worst position for the president is the Executive acting alone. Of course, it should also be mentioned that even the presence of congressional legislation does not guarantee that the Executive's actions will not end up in the second or third prong of Jackson's framework. As the emergency economic legislation case study details, the government's claims of having legislative backing does not mean the courts will accept suggestions that the law in question does in fact grant the authorization claimed. An example is the *Trading with the Enemy Act* where the courts found that the Executive's officials misinterpreted or misapplied legislation thus resulted in grants of power to the Executive that Congress had not intended with the passage of the Act. As a result, the actions of the Executive were left in the third prong of Jackson's framework.

On the surface, unless Congress has forbidden such actions, it would appear that the Executive would find itself in Jackson's second prong of the framework where the president and "Congress may have concurrent authority, or in which its distribution is uncertain. Therefore, congressional inertia, indifference or quiescence may sometimes, at least as a practical matter, enable, if not invite, measures on independent presidential responsibility" (Jackson's *Youngstown* concurrence). But Jackson continues by pointing out that "[i]n this area, any actual test of power is likely to depend on the imperatives of events and contemporary imponderables rather than on abstract theories of law." While the courts often do not address the constitutional questions regarding rights violations or claims of inherent power made by the Executive, by deciding questions on statutory grounds the president is left, if acting alone, in the third prong of Jackson's framework. This is because the federal courts have reinterpreted the war powers to add a component that requires congressional authorization. Without authorization, the president's "power is at its lowest ebb, for then he can rely only upon his own constitutional powers minus any constitutional powers of Congress over the matter. Courts can sustain exclusive presidential control in such a case only by disabling the Congress from acting upon the subject" (Jackson's *Youngstown* concurrence).

This analysis of presidential war powers decision making is shared in Jack Goldsmith's book, *The Terror Presidency* (2007). As head of the Justice

Department's Office of Legal Counsel from October 2003 to July 2004, Goldsmith's firsthand experience in making war powers policy makes his observation more startling. Goldsmith clearly supports the claim of shared powers arguing that "[g]etting Congress on board would thus place whatever emerged from the process-an admitted risk-on a solid legal foundation appropriate for this new type of war, and would diminish many complaints about legitimacy" (Goldsmith, 2007; 123).

Goldsmith does not speak against the Bush Administration's actions because he disagrees with the objectives of the government in its fight against global terrorism. Goldsmith in fact sees the future threat to American national security coming from non-state actors, such as terrorist organizations. It is because Goldsmith shares the security vision posited by those who fear future terrorist attacks that he lodges his criticism of President Bush. The hope in Goldsmith's work is for future presidents to learn from the mistakes of the Bush Administration (Goldsmith, 140). It is essential, according to Goldsmith, for the Executive to reach out to Congress and get approval of its foreign policy agenda, especially when that agenda involves the curtailment of individual liberties. The patterns of judicial decision making that has emerged shows that Goldsmith's advice is sound, finding its logic in historical practice of rights-based cases adjudicated by the federal courts during war.

Goldsmith actually advocated going to Congress to ask for legislation signing off on the Administration's military detention program. As chapter 3 presents, the policy in question saw American citizens Yasser Hamdi and Jose Padilla held as enemy combatants and denied basic rights afforded to American citizens when tried by jury in the civilian courts. Goldsmith's efforts at securing explicit congressional authorization failed.[2] The Supreme Court's ultimate rebuke of presidential unilateral authority came in 2006 with the *Hamdan* decision. While Congress would pass a law legalizing the military commissions the Court said were illegal due to a lack of congressional legislation establishing such tribunals, Goldsmith's concludes that the president "could have achieved all that he wanted to achieve, and put it on firmer foundation, if he had been willing to reach out to other institutions of government" (Rosen, 2007; 9). Due to an insistence on working alone, Goldsmith points out that the Supreme Court "forced" the Executive to ask Congress for help (Goldsmith, 2007; 139). The federal courts do not actively rebuke the notion that the president possesses inherent authority in times of armed hostilities.[3] Instead, the courts show they are unwilling to decide war powers cases on constitutional grounds if they do not have to and that during times of armed hostilities courts decide cases based on "the ever-shifting balance of power among branches of government" (Greenhouse, 2006; A1).[4]

The second policy implication of the courts seeking congressional authorization of executive war powers actions is that Congress must act to limit the power of the Executive. The federal courts have not taken to arguments by the Executive that it has the inherent power to act alone. However, the federal courts look for Congress to act in passing legislation before limiting executive authority. The federal courts defer to Congress and by passing legislation that continues to aggrandize the powers of the Executive, Congress should be held accountable. Since the courts place emphasis first and foremost on whether or not Congress has given its approval to the Executive's efforts, it is up to Congress to stop the Executive if it decides that the powers of the Executive have been exercised too far.

The utility of the separation of powers framework

The framers viewed the separation of powers as a safeguard of liberty. That does not mean to suggest that every time the Court invalidates some action by the president it has advanced the cause of liberty. Admittedly, the president will often claim that its actions are designed to further liberty, regardless of the Court's ruling. This begs the question, are our rights destined to remain in a zone of twilight not unlike Justice Jackson's second prong in his concurrence to *Youngstown?* In a way, the answer is yes because our rights dependent on the will of Congress to protect individual liberties in the face of powerful Executives that may limit individual rights, making arguments these rights need to be infringed for national security purposes. Political pressure will often ensure no action on the part of Congress to stop the president and more often than not, action on the part of Congress to in fact sanction the actions of the Executive. With these possible limitations to the separation of powers framework, should the federal courts continue to behave this way? Alternatively, should the courts decide war powers, rights-based cases using rights-based discourse? After all, there is only one Constitution and there is no suspension clause for emergency situations, an exception being the strict criteria imposed for suspending the writ of habeas corpus. If we understand the Constitution's distribution of the war powers among the branches of government as shared among Congress and the Executive, as interdependent and connected, then an argument can be made to justify the courts deciding war-powers cases based on a separation of powers framework rather than using rights-based language. Ultimately, as noted in chapter 2, the federal courts tread lightly in foreign affairs because the Constitution itself is at stake. As Silverstein notes, "if the justices choose to base their justification on a broad reading of the Constitution, they take the risk that this reading will return to haunt them later . . . broad readings in foreign policy cases can become precedents for equally broad readings in domestic policy cases drawing on the same constitutional phrases" (Silverstein, 1997; 23).

In their attempt to avoid making mistakes that will weaken the Constitution and the Judiciary, it is reasonable for the federal courts to look to statutory questions over constitutional ones in deciding war powers issues. Agreement amongst the elected branches of government brings legitimacy to otherwise controversial decisions to limit individual liberties. Jackson's *Korematsu* dissent highlights this argument. Jackson maintains the military initiatives that limit individual liberties and that are sanctioned by Congress have a shelf life as long as the conflict at hand. Deciding cases based on statutory questions thus leaves the rights protected in the Constitution intact so far as peacetime is concerned. The alternative sees the federal courts deferring straight to the Executive handing the office the blank check in foreign affairs that the president is often accused of already possessing, because the courts seem unlikely to answer war-powers questions where the Executive curtails individual liberties by answering the constitutional questions. Jackson is a realist. He knows that with the passions of the people high during war there will be pressure on the courts to defer to the Executive. By not simply deferring to the Executive, the courts do allow for some protection of individual liberties. In other words, by using a separation of powers framework, the courts require some deliberation, or at least acknowledgment, by both branches of government before individual liberties are limited, thus expecting that any curtailments upheld by the federal courts would be, at the very least and under the circumstances at hand, reasonable.

Jackson, in *Johnson v. Eisentrager,* 339 U.S. 763, sums up why it is impractical for the federal courts to use rights-based language in times of armed hostilities. Enemies of the United States could be protected under the laws of the United States. At the same time, enemies of the State could receive protections not extended to American soldiers under the jurisdiction of martial regulations. If the enemy is going to demand a right to bear arms as stipulated in the Second Amendment, how can the integrity of the Bill of Rights be upheld in times when national security is at stake? Jackson argued that while no statutes existed which extended the Bill of Rights to alien enemies, he also added more practical reasons to limit its applicability to the enemies of the United States. "To grant the writ [of habeas corpus] to these prisoners might mean that our army must transport them across the seas for hearing," which would also potentially entail the transportation of witnesses the prisoners in question wished to call in their defense. Furthermore, and important to note, since the writ "is held to be a matter of right, would be equally available to enemies during active hostilities as in the present twilight between war and peace. Such trials would hamper the war effort and bring aid and comfort to the enemy" (Jackson's *Eisentrager* opinion). Such legalities would also be contrary to the law of nations which allows governments to hold prisoners until the end of hostilities so they are not released at which point they would be likely to return to the battlefield to continue their fight against American forces. And, "it would be difficult to devise more effective fettering of a field commander than to allow the very enemies he is ordered to reduce to submission to call him to account in his own civil courts and divert his efforts and attention from the military offensive abroad to the legal defensive at home" (Jackson's *Eisentrager* opinion).

FUTURE DIRECTIVES

The separation of powers argument presented here shows a vision of the war powers held by James Madison, among other framers of the Constitution, where the branches of government worked together to solve national-security issues. It merits further examination to see if the emphasis on the separation of powers between the Executive and Congress as the focus of the federal courts decision making can be more generally applied to other areas of decision-making where congressional action cannot be looked to for legitimization of executive policy during armed hostilities. Where there may be a limited role for Congress to play, the federal courts are not necessarily helpless in determining the limits of presidential power. Congress can be substituted for another body that functions as conferring authority on the president to act in limiting individual liberties. Likewise, the absence of this conferring power, or substitute to Congress, can also be used to limit the ability of the Executive to curtail individual liberties. Take for consideration the example of prize cases. When prize cases came before the federal courts, they looked to Congress when statutes were in place authorizing or limiting, as the case may be, specific actions of the Executive. Otherwise, the federal courts looked to international law to act as the second governing body with which the Executive is required to cooperate to have validity in limiting rights. When the Executive was said to be acting in accordance with international law, the limits were upheld by the federal courts, thus creating a situation that is analogous to the executive-congressional relationship. This analogous relationship thus maintains the separation of powers emphasis the federal courts place on war-powers adjudication that has been drawn. When prize cases concerning the Executive establishing policy curtailing individual liberties reached the Supreme Court, both international law and the laws of the land were looked to for guidance in determining the constitutionality of executive actions. This was reasonable because prize controversies have traditionally been considered in the realm of international law.[5] According to Louis Henkin, "early United States courts and legislators regarded customary international law and treaty obligations as part of the domestic legal system. International law *was* domestic law" (emphasis in original; Henkin, 1987; 868). Furthermore, the framers never intended for prize cases to be decided based on domestic law alone, "anticipating that international disputes would regularly come before the United States courts, and that the decisions in those cases could rest on principles of international law, without any necessary reference to the common law or to constitutional doctrines" (White, 1989; 83). Eventually, parts of the law of nations were domesticated into general common law in the United States. By the mid-to late nineteenth century, dualism began to take shape, with the belief that international and domestic law "constitute rigidly separate systems" taking hold of the American legal system (Koh, 1991; 2353). Courts began to decide cases of maritime law using international customs but subjecting them to congressional modification (Koh, 2353). The relevant prize cases during the Civil War are used to illustrate the point.

During the Civil War, the Supreme Court held the blockade that the Executive placed on the states of the Confederacy was legal. In what would be known as the *Prize Cases,* in the *Amy Warwick,* 67 U.S. 635; 1862, Justice Grier argued that for a ship to capture a neutral vessel, "a war must exist de facto, and the neutral must have knowledge or notice of the intention of one of the parties belligerent to use this mode of coercion against a port, city, or territory, in possession of the other." A civil war exists when "the party in rebellion occupy and hold in a hostile manner a certain portion of territory; have declared their independence . . . have organized armies; have commenced hostilities against their former sovereign, the world acknowledges them as belligerents, and the contest a war" (Grier's *Prize Cases* opinion). The reasoning of the Court was that because this situation was recognized under international law as war, war in fact did exist in the United States. International law dictated that war existed, so the blockade of the Executive was deemed essential in fighting the enemy. Justice Grier explains that "[i]f a war be made by invasion of a foreign nation, the president is not only authorized but bound to resist force by force. He does not initiate the war, but is bound to accept the challenge without waiting for any special legislative authority." International law was used in the place of congressional authority to legitimize the president's actions.

Cases concerning the application of the blockade also went before the Court where it was decided in a number of cases that it was lawful for neutral ships to trade goods to neutral territories or to enemy territory if such trade was not in violation of the blockade.[6] In *The Bermuda,* 70 U.S. 514; 1866, the Court holds, based on international law, "neutral trade is entitled to protection in all courts" (Chase's *Bermuda* opinion). However, once the federal courts determine the vessel not to be neutral, it is subjected to the laws in place governing the hostilities in question, in this case, the Executive's blockade. Here we have an example of international law placing a layer of protection on individual liberties that the Executive, according to the Court, must respect in regard to who is subject to executive-imposed blockades. However, in *The Venice,* 69 U.S. 258; 1865, a property owner's rights were protected under international law when no congressional statutes directing the Executive on how to treat neutrals existed. International custom did allow "a pretended destination to a neutral port, coupled with the intent to break blockade or carry articles ultimately destined for the enemy and obviously for warlike or contraband use, even if innocent and commercial in themselves" to serve as protection (Hoyt, 1903; 310). The Executive had authority to issue orders for the seizure of such vessels. This was the case in *The Hart,* 70 U.S. 559; 1866. Justice Chase held that

> neutrals who place their vessels under belligerent control, and engage them in belligerent trade; or permit them to be sent with contraband cargoes, under cover of false destination, to neutral ports, while the real destination is to belligerent ports; impress upon them the character of the belligerent in whose service they are employed . . . and the vessels may be seized and condemned as enemy property.

Under these enumerated circumstances, vessels from neutral territory could in fact be seized and condemned as enemy property.

In *The Peterhoff,* 72 U.S. 28; 1867, the ship was captured in the West Indies by the United States vessel *Vanderbilt,* in 1863, on suspicion of being destined for the rebel states. Claims to the contrary were made by the British owner, stating he was going to conduct trade in Mexico. The government held that trade with Matamoras was unlawful under the blockage on the mouth of the Rio Grande. Justice Chase notes that "it must be premised that no paper or constructive blockage is allowed under international law." The Rio Grande was within Mexican territory and was as much Mexican as it was American. As a result, there had be a clear expressed declaration by the Executive that the blockade included the Rio Grande and that the blockade could not be extended by construction.

The Executive's actions here are upheld or struck down based on international law that the Court accepts as applicable to these wartime situations in contrast to cases during the Quasi War with France and the War of 1812 where the actions of the Executive either stood or fell based on congressional statutes. The Civil War also saw a plethora of cases where Acts of Congress were used to justify a variety of presidential proclamations, orders and instructions concerning the conduct of American vessels with regard to maritime issues of property confiscation through capture.

One such example of presidential authority delegated to the Executive from Congress was the Executive's power to decide who can trade with whom and under what conditions in times of war. Congress passed an Act July 13th, 1861 which gave the president the authority to, by proclamation, declare that those inhabiting the states where the insurrection is taking place are thus "in a state of insurrection against the United States, and thereupon all commercial intercourse by and between the same and the citizens thereof and the citizens of the rest of the United States, shall cease and be unlawful so long as such condition of hospitality shall continue" (Swayne's *Ouachita* Cotton opinion). Furthermore, the Act provided that the president could, at his discretion, allow for commercial intercourse with any inhabitant of the insurrection states as he so chooses and deems required for the public interest. Several cases concerning the blockade of New Orleans reached the Court after the city had been taken by Union forces (*The Ouachita Cotton,* 73 U.S. 521; 1868).

That Congress had delegated authority to the president to allow for exceptions to trading in rebel territory was first affirmed in *The Reform,* 70 U.S. 617; 1865 and *The Sea Lion,* 72 U.S. 630; 1866. In *The Circassian,* 69 U.S. 135; 1865, the Court decided whether if the capture of New Orleans by Union troops made the blockage on the city's ports thus void. The Court pointed out that only the city was occupied, not the port and not the entire state. The rebel army was still in the area and hostile to union forces. Chief Justice Chase added that "the moment the capture [of New Orleans] was established, the municipal laws of that government took the place of the international law upon which the blockade rested" (Chase's *Circassian* opinion). The Court also upheld the capture of *The Baigorry,* 69 U.S. 474; 1865, as being in violation of the blockade based on a presidential proclamation as authorized by Congress. Each of these cases saw the Court authorize presidential actions based on congressional delegation of power. This preliminary analysis, though much more must be conducted, shows that international laws guided the American courts when cases pertaining to the regulation of trade and commerce on international waters were brought to the fore.

The Supreme Court relied on international law if Congress had not created America-specific policy. The rationale maintains constant as to why the presence of approval or disapproval in international law would aid the courts in their prize-cases judicial decision making. Instead of allowing the Executive to create policy where it at best shares power with the law of nations, the Court maintains the legitimacy of the Judiciary and the Constitution by again not deciding such cases based on the constitutional questions, but, in the absence of statutory questions, based its decision on the realm of the law of nations.

Table 7.1. Prize Cases in Front of the Supreme Court

	Court upheld executive action	*Court struck down executive action*
Congressional authorization	*Talbot v. Seaman,* 1801 *Bas v. Tingy,* 1801 *The Circassian,* 1865 *The Baigorry,* 1865	
No Congressional authorization/ contrary to the wishes of Congress		*Barreme v. Little,* 1804 *The Ouachita Cotton,* 1868 *The Reform,* 1866 *The Sea Lion,* 1867
International law	*The Hart,* 1866 *The Prize Cases,* 1862	*The Bermuda,* 1866 *The Springbok,* 1866 *The Peterhoff,* 1867 *The Venice,* 1865

Table 7.1 shows a mix of international law with domestic law that is relied upon for deciding prize cases where the Executive limits property rights. There are a number of cases where the actions of executive agents are struck down as contrary to international laws or congressional statutes, placing the actions of the Executive in Jackson's third prong of the *Youngstown* framework. The executive authority to issue executive orders concerning ships condemned as prize was an issue to be handled within a separation of powers framework because in the Constitution, rules for ships captured rests with Congress, not the Executive. This was the case despite the president issuing orders on the matter. However, many situations arose outside ships being captured that required the Court's attention, resulting in the liberties of the people being in jeopardy of infringement. The Court needed to find a way to make not only its decisions legitimate but the actions of the Executive legitimate too. When issues were decided based on international law, it was in regard to whether or not the Executive had authority in relation to the law of nations. If the Court held that authority existed, power to do so would fall within the Executive's power as commander-in-chief. The cases do not fall within one of the three prongs of Jackson's framework, because the framework looks specifically at Congressional-Executive relations. I suggest, however, when the Court looks for the Executive to be working within the framework of international law, it is not necessarily contrary to Jackson's vision. International law can be understood as a parallel, or at least as applicable as, a domestic law in the absence of congressional legislation, therefore creating a Jackson-like framework where international law works as the legitimizing force that

Congress usually plays. This framework shows the federal courts looking for some authority of executive actions in the absence of congressional action from international law.

CONCLUSIONS

In crafting its foreign policies, especially those that will involve the curtailment of individual liberties, the Executive cannot, in the words of Goldsmith, "go-it-alone" (Goldsmith, 2007; 205). In my suggesting that the Executive must find institutional legitimacy from a source outside its own authority granted in the text of the Constitution, I echo the likes of Richard Neustadt who several decades ago argued the power of the president is found in the Executive's ability to persuade (Neustadt, 1960; 122). Neustadt's suggestion proved to stand the test of time and in 1999 was restated by Arthur Schlesinger Jr. who suggested that "the power to manage the vast, whirring machinery of government derives from individual skills as persuader, bargainer, and leader" (Schlesinger, 1999; 284). Goldsmith also invokes the messages of Neustadt and Schlesinger, pointing out that the go-it-alone approach to government escapes the political process that has developed in the United States which encompasses "the need to explain, to justify, to convince, to get people on board, to compromise" (Goldsmith, 2007; 205).

Despite the warnings, the go-it-alone approach is not new. Schlesinger's term for such action is imperial. Schlesinger called the Nixon presidency imperial and argued that the Executive had gained control over areas that the framers had never intended to be solely in the hands of the presidency, namely the war powers. The imperial presidency "created wars abroad" producing "an unprecedented concentration of power in the White House and an unprecedented attempt to transform the presidency of the Constitution into a plebiscitary presidency" (Schlesinger, 1973; 377). The result was that the "traditional constitutional assumptions based on shared powers and collective judgment [gave] way as the political and structural conditions on which they were based were altered" (Boylan, 1999; 232). In other words, the president was able to achieve a more powerful office at the expense of the other branches of government. Andrew Rudavilege argues that "when George W. Bush took the oath of office for the second time in January 2005, he presided over a presidency much stronger in absolute and relative terms than the framers has conceived it" (2006; 16). Just like Schlesinger maintained in 1973, the powers Bush enjoyed unilaterally were those in the domain of the war powers. Though the federal courts will be looked to as the last line of defense for the protection of individual liberties, it is the Congress that should be looked to, as the growth of executive authority has not ended with the election of the Obama administration.

Using the three prongs of Jackson's framework to classify how justices decide war-powers cases when the Executive has limited individual liberties shows that the courts look to see if Congress has authorized the actions of the Executive or not. If they have not and the Executive finds itself in Jackson's third prong, the courts will not allow the Executive's actions. This being the case, it is clear that it is up to Congress to again reassert itself in reclaiming power away from the Executive. When Congress limits executive authority by reasserting itself, putting forth its own war powers policies, the courts will follow suit by reaffirming the need for the Executive to seek, and achieve, some sort of congressional approval of its war-powers policies. That we now know the courts defer to the Congress and not the Executive places the onus on the Congress to take decisive action.

ENDNOTES

1. However, during armed hostilities, the courts have yet to reject the actions of the Executive as misinterpreting the intent of Congress in regard to the *International Emergency Economic Powers Act*.

2. Goldsmith himself had admitted that his legal analysis was not one that incorporated concerns for civil liberties. Instead, Goldsmith reasoned that "the Supreme Court would be less likely to strike down a detention program in wartime if Congress had explicitly supported it" (Goldsmith, 2007; 122).

3. There are exceptions, of course. During the Civil War, in protecting the writ of habeas corpus in *ex parte Milligan* the Court denied the president possessed the authority to suspend the writ. Justice Black's court opinion in *Youngstown* is not even a rebuke of inherent authority in times of armed hostilities. Though Black is firmly making an argument that the president has no inherent power to take possession of an industry without appropriate congressional legislation to back up such decisions, he argues that the president's policy was domestic in nature, whereas the other opinions in the case address the international crisis at hand.

4. Linda Greenhouse, "Justices, 5-3, Broadly Reject Bush Plan to Try Detainees," *New York Times,* June 30, 2006. http://www.nytimes.com/2006/06/30/washington/30hamdan.html (July 2, 2008).

5. In no way do I mean to suggest that Congress had been unable or unwilling to regulate prize cases. To the contrary, Congress passed laws that created policy which would regulate how the courts decided many prize cases. However, it is also the case that at times Congress remains silent on the issue, but international laws were in place which regulate the circumstances under consideration. Instead of looking to Jackson's second prong when Congress is silent, the courts turn to international law to see if there was some authority upon which the Executive's actions

could be based. While I want to show that the courts also look to international law for validation of executive action, the courts have at times depended on congressional legislation. A number of examples can be used to illuminate this claim. I offer a couple examples from the early republic before the notion of dualism set in. As early as 1801, the Court held that the Executive overstepped its boundaries when it gave instructions to commanders of vessels that contradicted laws passed by Congress. During the Quasi War with France, Congress passed legislation that would allow for the president to

> give instructions to the commanders of the public armed ships of the United States, to stop and examine any ship or vessel of the United States on the high sea, where there may be reason to suspect to be engaged in traffic or commerce contrary to the true tenor hereof; and if, upon examination, it shall appear that such a ship or vessel is bound or sailing to any port or place within the territory of the French republic, or her dependencies, contrary to the intent of this act, it shall be the duty of the commander of such public vessel, to seize every such ship or vessel engaged in such illicit commerce, and to send to the nearest port in the United States (Marshall's *Barreme* opinion).

In *Little v. Barreme*, 6 U.S. 170; 1804, a ship coming from a port of France was seized upon the orders of the Executive. The ship owner sued for his property citing the law of Congress quoted above as having been violated, because the Executive was authorized to issue orders to seize ships sailing *to,* not *from* French ports. The Court held that:

> A commander of a ship of war of the United States, in obeying his instructions from the President of the United States, acts at his peril. If those instructions are not strictly warranted by law he is answerable in damages to any person injured by their execution. The Act of the 9th of February, 1799, did not authorize the seizure upon the high seas of any vessel sailing from a French port; and the orders of the President of the United States could not justify such a seizure (Marshall's *Barreme* opinion).

It was for Congress to make laws concerning punishment on the high seas and not the president. In this case, Congress decided to "indemnify the naval officer, because his unlawful actions had aided the nation during wartime" (Lobel, 1989; 1394). Once the laws were written, they had to be followed by the Executive's orders to the commanders of his warships. In this case, the Executive Order was in violation of a congressional statute, placing Adams' orders in the third prong of Jackson's framework. The president would have to be judged on his own authority as stated in the Constitution, and the Court found that the Constitution confers no such authority on the Executive.

The Court would also find Congress authorized the Executive to issue orders in regard to prize cases. In *Bas v. Tingy*, 4 U.S.; 37; 1800, the Court held that since Congress recognized a state of war between France and the United States, its legislation must be interpreted to allow for the president to send warships abroad to capture French vessels and the property within such vessels as prize (Moore's *Tingy* opinion). Likewise, in *Talbot v. Seeman*, 5 U.S. 1; 1801, the Court recognized a state of hostilities between the two nations as a result of a number of congressional statutes. Marshall concluded that

> if by the laws of Congress on this subject, that body shall appear to have legislated upon a perfect conviction that the state of war in which this country was placed, was such as to authorize re-captures generally from the enemy; if one part of the system shall be manifestly founded on this construction of the other part, it would have considerable weight in rendering certain what might before have been doubtful (Marshall's *Talbot* opinion).

The same issues arose during the War of 1812, where the president gave instructions for capturing vessels which the Court held to have either been authorized by Congress or to which pieces of legislation which appear to limit the executive's authority in issuing instructions need not apply to the president's orders.

6. This was the case in not only *The Venice* and *The Bermuda* and *The Peterhoff*, 5 Wall, 28; 1867, but also in *The Springbok*, 5 Wall. 1; 1866.

Cases

Note: Cases included are all those mentioned both in substance and those merely referenced in the body of the text.

767 Third Avenue Associates et. al. v. United States, 48 F.3d 1575; 1995
ACLU v. Barr, 952 F.2d 457; 1991
ACLU v. NSA, 438 F. Supp. 2d 754; 2006
Ahrens et al v. Clark, 335 U.S. 188, 1948
Alderman et al. v. United States, 394 U.S. 165; 1969
American Exchange National Bank v. Garvan, 273 Fed. 43; 1921
Amos v. United States, 255 U.S. 313
Amy Warwick, 67 U.S. 635; 1862 (The Prize Cases)
The Baigorry, 69 U.S. 474; 1865
Bas v. Tingy, 4 U.S.; 37; 1800
Behn, Meyer & Company, Limited v. Miller, 266 U.S. 457; 1925
Berger v. New York, 388 U.S. 41; 1967
The Bermuda, 70 U.S. 514; 1866
Buena Ventura v. the United States, 175 U.S. 384; 1899
Bevans v. United States, 16 U.S. 336 1818
Billeci v. United States, 87 U.S. App. D.C. 274; 1950
Boumediene v. Bush, 476 F.3d 981 (D.C. Cir. 2007)
Bowles v. Seminole Rock & Sand Co., 325 U.S. 410; 65; 1945
Bowles v. Willingham et. al., 321 U.S. 503; 1944
Boyd v. United States, 116 U.S. 616, 1886
Brandenburg v. Ohio, 395 U.S. 444; 1969
Brown v. United States, 8 Cranch 110; 1814
Brownell v. Singer, 347 U.S. 403; 1954

Carter v. Carter Coal Co 298 U.S. 238; 1936
Central Union Trust Co. v. Garvan, 254 U.S. 554; 1921
The Circassian, 69 U.S. 135; 1865
Cities Services Co. et. al. v. McGrath, 342 U.S. 330; 1952
Chicago & Southern Airlines v. Waterman SS Corp., 333 U.S. 103; 1948
Chimel v. California, 395 U.S. 752; 1969
Clark v. Allen et al, 331 U.S. 503; 1947
Clark v. Uebersee Finanz-Korporation, A.G., 332 U.S. 480; 1947
Commercial Pacific Cable Company v. Burleson et al; 250 U.S. 360; 1919
Consarc Corp. v. United States Treasury Department, 315 U.S. App. D.C. 201; 1995
Cox v. Wood, 247 U.S. 3, 1918
Cudahy Packing Co. v. Holland, 315 U.S. 357; 1942
Currin v. Wallace 306 U.S. 1; 1939
Curtiss-Wright Export Corp. v. United States, 299 U.S. 304; 1936
Dames & Moore v. Regan, 453 U.S. 654; 1981
Dennis v. United States, 341 U.S. 494; 1951
Duncan v. Kahanamoku, 327 U.S. 304; 1946
Eisentrager v. Johnson, 339 U.S. 763, 1950
El-Masri v. Tenet, 437 F. Supp. 2d 530; 2006
Ex parte Benedict, 3 Fed. Cas. 159 (D. N.Y. 1862)
Ex parte Bollman, 8 U.S. 75, 1807
Ex parte Field, 9 Fed. Cas. 1, 3 (C.C. Vt. 1862)
Ex parte McCardle, 74 U.S. 506, 1869
Ex parte Merryman, 17 F. Cas. 144; 1861
Ex parte Milligan, 71 U.S. (4 Wall.) 2 1866
Ex parte Mitsuye Endo, 323 U.S. 283; 1944
Ex parte Quirin, 317 U.S. 1, 1942
Ex parte Vallandigham, 68 U.S. 243; 1864
Ex parte Yerger, 75 U.S. 85, 1868
Field v. United States, 143 U.S. 649; 1892
Fifth Avenue Peace Parade Committee v. Gray, 480 F. 2d 326; 1973
Flanders v. United States, 222 F.2d 163; 1955
Fleming v. Mohawk Wrecking & Lumber Co., 331 U.S. 111; 1947
Givens v. Zerbst, 255 U.S. 11, 1921
Goldman v. United States, 316 U.S. 129; 1942
Goldstein v. United States, 316 U.S. 114; 1941
Gouled v. United States, 255 U.S. 298, 1921
Grant v. United States, 1 Ct. Cl. 41, 1863
Griswold v. Connecticut, 381 U.S. 479
Guessefeldt v. McGrath, 342 U.S. 308; 1952

The Guido, 175 U.S. 382; 1899
Halkin et al. v. Helms,194 F.2d 598, 1979
Halperin v. Kissinger et al, 606 F.2d 1192; D.C.Cir.1979
Hamdan v. Rumsfeld, 548 U.S. ___, 2006
Hamdan v. Rumsfeld, 464 F. Supp. 2d 9 (D.D.C. 2006)
Hamdi v. Rumsfeld, 542 U.S. 507, 2004
Hampton & Co. v. United States, 276 U.S. 394; 1928
The Hart, 70 U.S. 559; 1866
Hepting v. AT&T Corporation, 2006, No. C-06-672
Hirabayashi v. United States, 320 U.S. 81; 1943
Hirota v. MacArthur, 338 U.S. 197, 1948
Hoffa v. United States, 385 U.S. 293; 1966
Holy Land Foundation for Relief . . . v. Ashcroft, 357 U.S. App. D. C. 35; 2003
Honda et al. v. Clark, 386 U.S. 484; 1967
Humphrey, Warden v. Smith, 336 U.S. 695, 1949
Illinois v. McArthur, 531 U.S. 326; 2001
In re Grand Jury Proceedings, 856 F.2d 685; 4th Cir. 1988
In re Dunn, 8 Fed. Cas. 93 (N.Y. 1863)
In re Egan, 8 Fed. Cas. (N.Y. 1866)
In re Fagan, 8 Fed. Cas. 947 (D. Mass. 1863)
In re All Matters Submitted to the FISC, 218 F. Supp. 2d. 611; 2002
In re Sealed Case, Case No. 02-001; 2002
In re Winder 30 Fed. Cas. 288 (1862)
In re Yamashita, 327 U.S. 1, 1946
In the Matter of Kevork, F.2d 566; 9th Cir.1986
INS v. Chadha, 462 U.S. 919; 1983
Islamic American Relief Agency v. Gonzales, 375 U.S. App. D.C. 93; 2007
Jabara v. Kelley et al, 476 F. Supp. 561; 1979
Juraga Iron Co. v. United States, 212 U.S. 297; 1909
Johnson v. United States, 333 U.S. 10; 1948
Jones v. Perkins, 245 U.S. 390, 1918
Kahn v. Anderson, 255 U.S. 1, 1921
Katz v. United States, 389 U.S. 347; 1967
Kaufman et al. v. Societe Internationale pour participations industrielle et commerciales et. al., 343 U.S. 156; 1952
Kimball Laundry Co. v. United States, 338 U.S. 1; 1949
Korematsu v. United States, 323 U.S. 214, 1944
L.P. Steuart & Bro. Inc. v. Bowles, 322 U.S. 398; 1944
Laird v. Tatum, 408 U.S. 1; 1972
Little v. Barreme, 6 U.S. 170; 1804

Lopez v. United States, 373 U.S. 427; 1963
Lyon v. Singer, 339 U.S. 841; 1950
Marion & Rye Valley Railway Company v. United States, 270 U.S. 280; 1926
Markham v. Allen, 326 U.S. 490; 1946
Markham v. Cabell, 326 U.S. 404; 1945
The Mary, 13 U.S. 126; 1815
The Mayor v. Cooper, 73 U.S. 247, 1868
McConnell v. Hampton, 12 Johns, 234 (N.Y. 1815)
McCulloch v. Maryland, 17 U.S. 316; 1819
McGrath v. Manufacturers Trust Co., 338 U.S. 241; 1949
McVeigh v. United States, 11 Wallace 259; 1871
McDonald et al. v. United States, 355 U.S. 451; 1948
Milena Ship Management Company v. R. Richard Newcomb, 995 F. 2d 620; 1993
Miller v. United States, 11 Wall. 268; 1870
Miller v. United States, 317 U.S. 369; 1943
Miranda v. Arizona, 384 U.S. 436; 1966
Missouri Pacific R.R. Co. v. Ault, 256 U.S. 554; 1921
Mitchell v. Harmony, 54 U.S. 115; 1851
Monongahela Navigation Co v. United States, 143 U.S. 312; 1893
Mostyn v. Fabrigas, 1 Cowp. 180; 1774
Mulford v. Smith 307 U.S. 38; 1939
Nardone v. United States, 302 U.S. 379; 1937
Nardone v. United States, 308 U.S. 338; 1939
National Board of Young Men's Christian Assns. Et al. v. United States, 395 U.S. 85; 1969
National Broadcasting Co. v. United States, 319 U.S. 190; 1943
Northern Pacific Ry. Co. v. North Dakota, 250 U.S. 135; 1919
Olmstead v. United States, 277 U.S. 438; 1928
Olson v. United States, 292 U.S. 246; 1934
Opp Cotton Mills v. Administrator, 312 U.S. 126; 1941
Orvis et al. v. Brownell, 345 U.S. 183; 1953
The Ouachita Cotton, 73 U.S. 521; 1868
The Panama, 176 U.S. 535; 1899
Panama Refining Co. v. Ryan, 293 U.S. 388; 1935
Paracha v. Bush, D.C. Cir. No. 05-5194, 2007
The Pedro, 175 U.S. 354; 1899
The Peterhoff, 72 U.S. 28; 1867
Porter v. Warner Holding Co., 328 U.S. 395; 1946
Portsmouth Harbor Land & Hotel v. United States, 260 U.S. 327; 1922.

Poultry Corp. v United States, 295 U.S. 495; 1935
Propper v Clark, 337 U.S. 472; 1949
Rasul et al. v. Bush, 542 U.S. 466, 2004
Rathburn v. United States, 355U.S. 107; 1957
Regan v. Wald, 468 U.S. 222; 1984
The Reform, 70 U.S. 617; 1865
Rumely v. McCarthy, 250 U.S, 283; 1919
Rumsfeld v. Padilla, 542 U.S. 426, 2004
Russian Volunteer Fleet v. United States, 282 U.S. 481; 1931
St. Louis, Kennett & Southeastern R.R. Co. v. United States, 267 U.S. 346; 1925
Schenck v. United States, 249 U.S. 47; 1919
The Sea Lion, 72 U.S. 630; 1866
Selective Draft Law Cases, 245 U.S. 366, 1918
Silesian-American Corp. et al v. Clark, 332 U.S. 469; 1947
Silverman v. United States, 365 U.S. 505; 1961
Silverthorne Lumber Comp. v. United States, 251 U.S. 385, 1920
Shapiro v. United States, 335 U.S. 1; 1948
Smith v. Federal Reserve Bank of New York, 346 F.3d 264; 2003
Smith v. Shaw, 12 Johns 257 (N.Y. 1815)
The Springbok, 5 Wall. 1; 1866
Stoehr v. Wallace, 255 U.S. 239; 1921
Sunshine Anthracite Coal Co. v. Adkins, 310 U.S. 381; 1940
Talbot v. Seeman, 5 U.S. 1; 1801
Terkel et al. v. AT&T, 441 F. Supp. 2d 899; 2006
Terry v. Ohio, 392 U.S. 1; 1968
The Thomas Gibbons, 12 U.S. 421; 1814
Uebersee Finanz-Korporation, A. G. v. McGrath, 343 U.S. 205; 1952
Union Insurance Company v. United States, 73 U.S. 759; 1867
United States v. Abdurahman M. Alamdoudi, 452 F.3d 310; 2006
United States v. Ahmad, 347 F. Supp. 912; 1972
United States v. Al M. Harb, 111 F.3d 130; 1997
United States v. Arch Trading Company, 987 F. 2d 1087; 1993
United States v. Belfield, 223 App D.C. 417; D.C. Cir. 1982
United States v. Bookie, 229 F.2d 130; 1956
United States v. Brown, 484 F.2d 418; 5th Cir.; 1973
United States v. Buck, 548 F. 2d 871; 9th Cir.; 1977
United States v. Butenko, 494 F. 2d 593; 3rd Cir.; 1974
United States v. Caltex Inc., 344 U.S. 149; 1952
United States v. Causby, 328 U.S. 256; 1946.
United States v. Cavanagh, 807 F.2d 787, 790-92; 9th Cir. 1987

United States v. Chemical Foundation, 272 U.S. 1; 1926
United States v. Clay, 430 F. 2d 165, 171; 5th Cir. 1970
United States v. Commodities Trading Corp., 339 U.S. 121; 1950.
United States v. Coplon,185 F. 2d. 629; 1950
United States v. Enten et al. 388 F. Supp. 97; 1971
United States v. Central Eureka Mining Co., 357 U.S. 155; 1958
United States, ex rel John Murphy v. Porter, Provost Marshal, 2 Hay & Hays 395; 1861
United States v. Falvey, 540 F. Supp. 1306; E.D.N.Y. 1982
United States v. Fox 455 F.2d 131; 5th Cir. 1972
United States v. General Motors Corp, 323 U.S. 373; 1945
United States v. Giordano, 416 U.S. 505; 1974
United States v. Grimaud, 220 U.S. 506; 1910
United States v. Hoffman, 334 F. Supp. 504; D.D.C. 1971
United States v. Humphrey, 456 F. Supp 51 E.D. Va. 1978
United States v. John J. Felin & Co., 334 U.S. 624; 1949
United States v. Johnson, 979 F.2d 396, 400; 6th Cir. 1992
United States v. Lewis, 87 F. Supp. 970; 1950
United States v. Manuel Romero-Fernandez. 983 F. 2d 195; 1993
United States v. Martinez-Fuerte, 428 U.S. 543; 1976
United States v. Megahey, 553 F. Supp. 1180; E.D.N.Y. 1982
United States v. Miller, 425 U.S. 435, 1976
United States v. New River Collieries Company, 262 U.S. 341, 1923
United States v. Nicholson, 955 F. Supp 550; 1997
United States v. Ott 827 F. 2d 473; 9th Cir. 1987
United States v. Pacific Railroad, 120 U.S. 227; 1887
United States v. Petty Motor co., 327 U.S. 372; 1946
United States v. Pewee Coal Co., Inc. 341 U.S. 114; 1951
United States v. Pelton, 835 F.2d 1067; 4th Cir. 1987
United States v. Percheman, 32 U.S. 51; 1833
United States v. Pierce, 124 F. Supp. 264; 1954
United States v. Polakoff, 112 F.2d 888; 2d Cir. 1940
United States v. Rafil Dhafir, 461 F. 3d 211; 2006
United States v. Rock Royal Co-Op 307 U.S. 533; 1939
United States v. Santana, 427 U.S. 38; 1976
United States v. The Schooner Peggy, 5 U.S. 103; 1801
United States v. Sinclair, 321 F. Supp. 1074; 1971
United States v. Smith, 321 F. Supp 424; 1971
United States v. Sullivan, 116 F. Supp. 480; 1953
United States v. Toronto Navigation Co., 338 U.S. 396; 1949
United States v. Truong Dinh Hung, 629 F. 2d 908; 1982

United States v. United Mine Workers of America, 330 U.S. 258; 1947
United States v. United States District Court, 407 U.S. 297; 1972
United States v. Verdugo-Urquidez, 494 U.S. 259; 1990
United States v. Westinghouse Electric & Manufacturing Co., 339 U.S. 261; 1950
United States v. White, 228 F.2d 832; 1956
The Venice, 69 U.S. 258; 1865
Vinson, Director of Economic Stab. v. Washington Gas Light Co. 321 U.S. 489; 1944
Wayman v. Southard, 23 U.S. (10 Wheat.) 1; 1825
Weiss v. United States, 308 U.S. 321; 1939
Weeks v. United States, 232 U.S. 383, 1914
Wiggins v. United States, 3 Ct. Cl. 412, 1867
Wong Sun v. United States, 371 U.S. 471; 1963
Yakus v. United States, 321 U.S. 414; 1944
Youngstown Sheet & Tube v. Sawyer, 343 U.S. 579; 1952
Zittman v. McGrath, 341 U.S. 471; 1951
Zittman v. McGrath 341 U.S. 446; 1951
Zweibon et al. v. Mitchell, 516 F.2d 594; 1975

Bibliography

Ackerman, Bruce. *We the People: Foundations, Volume I.* Cambridge, MA: Harvard University Press, 1993.

Ackerman, David, and Bruce Grimmett. "Declarations of War and Authorizations for the Use of Military Force: Historical Background and Legal Implications." *Congressional Research Service Report,* 2003.

Adams, John. "Thoughts on Government, 1776." In *The Works of John Adams.* Edited by Charles Francis Adams. Boston: Little, Brown, 1851.

Aidlin, Joseph. "The Constitutionality of the 1942 Price Control Act." *California Law Review* 30, no. 6 (September 1942): 648–654.

Alder, David Gray. "The Steel Seizure Case and Inherent Presidential Power" (President Truman's 1952 seizure of U.S. steel mills). *Constitutional Commentary* 19, no. 1 (Spring 2002): 155–214.

Alder, David Gray, and Larry N. George. *The Constitution and the Conduct of Foreign Affairs.* Lawrence: University of Kansas Press, 1996.

Baker, Joseph, and Henry Crocker. *The Laws of Land Warfare Concerning the Rights and Duties of Belligerents as Existing on August 1, 1914.* Wilmington, DE: Scholarly Resources, 1974.

Baker, Nancy. *The Law: The Impact of Antiterrorism Policies on Separation Of Powers: Assessing John Ashcroft's Role.* Washington, DC: Center for the Presidential Studies, 2001.

———. "National Security versus Civil Liberties." *Presidential Studies Quarterly* 33, no. 3 (2003): 547–567.

Bailyn, Bernard. *The Ideological Origins of the American Revolution.* Cambridge, MA: Harvard University Press, 1967.

Banks, William, and Peter Raven-Hansen. *National Security Law and the Power of the Purse.* New York: Oxford University Press, 1994.

Barber, N. W. "Prelude to the Separation of Powers." *The Cambridge Law Journal* 60, No. 1 (March 2001): 59–88.

Baum, Lawrence. *Judges and Their Audiences: A Perspective on Judicial Behavior.* Princeton, NJ: Princeton University Press, 2006.

Bazan, Elizabeth, and Jennifer Elsea. "Presidential Authority to Conduct Warantless Electronic Surveillance to Gather Foreign Intelligence Information." *Congressional Research Service Report*. January, 2006.

Beale, Howard K. *The Diary of Edward Bates, 1859–1866: Vol. IV of the American Historical Association Annual Report.* Washington, DC: Washington Government Printing Office, 1933.

Bellia, Patricia. "Executive Power in Youngstown's Shadow" (President Truman's 1952 seizure of U.S. steel mills). *Constitutional Commentary* 19, no. 1 (Spring 2002): 87–155.

Berdahl, Clarence Arthur. *War Powers of the Executive in the United States.* Urbana: University of Illinois Press, 1921.

Berger, Raoul. *Executive Privilege: A Constitutional Myth.* Cambridge, MA: Harvard University Press, 1974.

Bergh, Albert. *The Writings of Thomas Jefferson.* Washington, DC: Thomas Jefferson Memorial Association, 1903.

Bestor, Arthur. "Separation of Powers in the Domain of Foreign Affairs: The Intent of the Constitution Historically Examined." *Seton Hall Law Review* 5 (Spring 1974): 527–665.

Bickel, Alexander. *The Least Dangerous Branch: The Supreme Court at the Bar of Politics.* Indianapolis: Bobbs-Merrill, 1962.

———. "The Need for a War-Powers Bill." *The New Republic* 17, no. 18 (January 1972).

Bigel, Alan I. *The Supreme Court on Emergency Powers, Foreign Affairs, and the Protection of Civil Liberties: 1935–1975.* New York: University Press of America, 1986.

Bird, Kenton, and Elizabeth Barker Brandt. "Academic Freedom and 9/11: How the War on Terrorism Threatens Free Speech on Campus." *Communication Law and Policy* 7, no. 4 (2002): 431–459.

Blackstone, William. *Commentaries on the Laws of England.* Chicago: University of Chicago Press, 1979.

Bobbitt, Philip. "Youngstown: Pages from the Book of Disquietude" (President Truman's 1952 seizure of U.S. steel mills). *Constitutional Commentary* 19, no. 1 (Spring 2002): 3–36.

Bontecou, Eleanor. *The Federal Loyalty-Security Program.* Ithaca, NY: Cornell University Press, 1953.

Borchard, Edwin. "The Effect of War on Law." *American Journal of International Law* 40, no. 3 (1946): 620–623.

Boylan, Timothy S. "War Powers, Constitutional Balance, and the Imperial Presidency." *Presidential Studies Quarterly* 29, no. 2 (1999): 232–249.

Bradley, Curtis A., and Jack L. Goldsmith. "Congressional Authorization and the War on Terrorism." *Harvard Law Review* 118, no. 7 (2005): 2047–2133.

Brant, Irvine. *James Madison: Secretary of State, 1800–1809* 6, vols. 1941–1969. Indianapolis: Bobbs-Merrill Company, 1953.

———. *James Madison: Father of the Constitution, 1787–1800.* Indianapolis: Bobbs-Merrill Company, 1950.

———. *James Madison.* New York: Bobbs-Merrill, 1950.

Brest, Paul et al. *Processes of Constitutional Decision Making: Cases and Materials Supplement.* 4th ed. New York: Aspen Publishers, 2003.

———. *Processes of Constitutional Decision Making: Cases and Materials.* 4th ed. New York: Aspen Publishers, 2000.

Brace, Paul, and Melinda Hall. "Integrated Models of Judicial Dissent." *Journal of Politics* 55, no. 4 (1993): 914–935.

Breyer, Stephen. "Liberty, Security, and the Courts. Association of the Bar of the City of New York." New York, April 14, 2003. http://www.supremecourtus.gov/publicinfo/speeches/sp_04-15-03.html (April 10 2008).

Brinkley, Alan. "A Familiar Story: Lessons from Past Assaults on Freedoms." In *The War on Our Freedoms. Civils Liberties in an Age of Terrorism,* edited by Richard C. Leone and Greg Anrig Jr., 23–46. New York: Public Affairs, 2003.

Brown, Ralph S. *Loyalty and Security: Employment Tests in the United States.* New Haven, CT: Yale University Press, 1958.

Brownell, Herbert. "The Public Security and Wire Tapping." *Cornell Law Quarterly* 39, no. 195 (1954): 201–203.

Bruff, Harold. "Judicial Review and the President's Statutory Powers." *Virginia Law Review* 68, no. 1 (January 1982): 1–61.

Bussiere, Elizabeth. *(Dis)Entitling the Poor: The Warren Court, Welfare Rights and the American Political Tradition.* University Park: Pennsylvania State University Press, 1997.

Butterfield, Lyman H., et al., eds. *Adams Family Correspondence.* Cambridge, MA: Belknap Press of Harvard University Press, 1963.

Carnahan, Burrus M. "Lincoln., Lieber and the Laws of War: The Origins and Limits of the Principle of Military Necessity." *The American Journal of International Law* 92, no. 2 (Apr., 1998): 213–231.

Casper, Jonathan. "The Supreme Court and National Policy Making." *American Political Science Review* 70 (March 1976): 50–63.

Campbell, Tom. *Separation of Powers in Practice.* Palo Alto, CA: Stanford University Press, 2004

Ceasar, James W. *Presidential Selection: Theory and Development.* Princeton, NJ: Princeton University Press, 1987.

Chafee, Zechariah. "Freedom of Speech in Wartime." *Harvard Law Review* 32, no. 8 (1919): 932–973.

Clayton, Cornell, and Howard Gillman. *Supreme Court Decision Making: New Institutionalist Approaches.* Chicago: Chicago University Press, 1999.

———. *Institutional Approaches to Supreme Court Decision-Making.* Chicago: University of Chicago Press, 1999.

Clayton, Cornell. *Government Layers: The Federal Legal Bureaucracy and Presidential Politics.* Lawrence: University of Kansas Press, 1995.

———. "Separate Branches–Separate Politics: Judicial Enforcement of Congressional Intent." *Political Science Quarterly* 109 (1994): 843–872.

———. *The Politics of Justice: The Attorney General and the Making of Legal Policy.* New York: M.E. Sharpe, 1992.

Cohen, Shlomo, et al. "The Iranian Hostage Agreement under International and United States Law." *Columbia Law Review* 81, no. 4 (1981): 822–901.

Cole, David. "The New McCarthyism: Repeating History in the War on Terrorism." In *Dissent in Dangerous Times,* edited by Austin Sarat. Ann Arbor: University of Michigan Press, 2005.

Cole, David, and Marty Lederman. *The National Security Agency's Domestic Spying Program: Framing the Debate.* 2006. http://www.acslaw.org/files/Microsoft%20Word%20-%2012_NSA_Debate.pdf (May 2, 2007).

Collins, Paul M., Jr. "Friends of the Court: Examining the Influence of Amicus Curiae Participation in U.S. Supreme Court Litigation." *Law and Society Review* 807 (December): 2004.

Coolidge, Francis L. "The War-Making Powers: The Intention of the Framers in the Light of Parliamentary History." *Boston Law Review* 50 (1970): 5–18

Corwin, Edward S. "The Steel Seizure Case: A Judicial Brick without Straw." *Columbia Law Review* 53, no. 1 (1953): 53–66.

Covey, Russell Dean. "Adventures in the Zone of Twilight: Separation of Powers and National Economic Security in the Mexican Bailout." *The Yale Law Journal* 105 no. 5 (1996): 1311–1345.

Cox, Archibald. "Internal Affairs of Labor Unions under the Labor Reform Act of 1959." *Michigan Law Review* 58, no. 6 (April 1960): 819–854.

Cox, Charles, C. "The Enforcement of Public Price Controls." *The Journal of Political Economy* 88, no. 5 (October 1980): 887–916.

Crushman, Barry. *Rethinking the New Deal Court: The Structure of a Constitutional Revolution.* Oxford: Oxford University Press, 1998.

Cunningham, Noble E., Jr. *The Process of Government under Jefferson.* Princeton, NJ: Princeton University Press, 1978.

Cushman, Robert. *Cases in Constitutional Law.* New York: FS Crofts and Co. Inc., 1925.

Dahl, Robert. "Decision Making in a Democracy: The Supreme Court as a National Policy Maker." *Journal of Public Law* 6 (Fall 1957): 279–295.

Darmer, M., Katherine B., et al., eds. *Civil Liberties vs. National Security in a Post-9/11 World.* New York: Prometheus Books, 2004.

Dempsey, James, and David Cole. *Terrorism and the Constitution: Sacrificing Civil Liberties in the Name of National Security.* Washington, DC: First Amendment Foundation, 2002.

Devins, Neal, and Louis Fisher. "The Steel Seizure Case: One of a Kind?" (President Truman's 1952 seizure of U.S. steel mills). *Constitutional Commentary* 19, no. 1 (Spring 2002): 63–87.

Dickinson, Laura. "Using Legal Process to Fight Terrorism: Detentions, Military Commissions, International Tribunals, and the Rule of Law." *Southern California Law Review*, 75 (2002): 1407–1492.

Donnelly, Richard, C. "Comments and Caveats on the Wire Tapping Controversy." *The Yale Law Journal* 63, no. 6 (April 1954): 799–810.

Duker, William. *A Constitutional History of Habeas Corpus*. Westport, CT: Greenwood, 1980.

Dunlop, C. R. Reviewed Works: *Prize Law during the World War: A Study of the Jurisprudence of the Prize Courts, 1914–1924* by J. W. Garner and *A Treatise on the Law of Prize* by C. John Colombos. *Journal of Comparative Legislation and International Law* 10, no. 1 (1928): 151–157.

Dworkin, Ronald. *Taking Rights Seriously*. 2d ed. Cambridge, MA: Harvard University Press, 1991.

Eggert, David S. "Executive Order 12,333: An Assessment of the Validity of Warrantless National Security Searches." *Duke Law Journal* 1983, no. 3 (June 1983): 611–644.

Elkin, Stephen L., and Karol E. Soltan, eds. *A New Constitutionalism: Designing Political Institutions for a Good Society*. Chicago: Chicago University Press, 1993.

Elster, Jon. *Ulysses Unbound: Studies in Rationality, Precommitment, and Constraints*. Cambridge: Cambridge University Press, 2002.

Ely, James Jr. "Property Rights and Liberty: Allies or Enemies?" *Presidential Studies Quarterly* 22, no. 4 (1992): 703–711.

Ely, John Hart. *War and Responsibility*. Princeton, NJ: Princeton University Press, 1993.

———. "Suppose Congress Wanted a War Powers Act that Worked." *Columbia Law Review* 88, no. 7 (November 1988): 1379–1431.

Epstein, Lee, and Jack Knight. *The Choices Justices Make*. Washington, DC: CQ Press, 1998.

Epstein, Lee, and Joseph F. Kobylka. *The Supreme Court and Legal Change: Abortion and the Death Penalty*. Chapel Hill: University of North Carolina Press, 1992.

Epstein, Lee, et al. *The Effect of War on the U.S. Supreme Court*. Presented at the Annual Meeting of the Midwest Political Science Association, Chicago, IL, April 2004.

Fairfield, Roy P., ed. *The Federalist Papers*. Baltimore, MD: Johns Hopkins University Press, 1991.

Farrand, Max, ed. *The Records of the Federal Convention of 1787*. 3 vols. New Haven, CT: Yale University Press, 1911. http://memory.loc.gov/ammem/amlaw/lwfr.html (September 2 2008).

Fehrenbacher, Don E., ed. *Abraham Lincoln: Speeches and Writings 1832–1858 by Abraham Lincoln*. New York: Penguin USA, 1989.

Fein, Bruce. "Presidential Authority to Gather Foreign Intelligence." *Presidential Studies Quarterly* 37, no. 1 (March 2007): 23–36.

Fisch, William B. "Emergency in the Constitutional Law of the United States." *The American Journal of Comparative Law 38, Supplement. U.S. Law in an Era of Democratization*. (1990): 389–420.

Fisher, Louis. "Invoking Inherent Powers: A Primer." *Presidential Studies Quarterly* 37, no. 1 (2007): 1–22.

———. *Constitutional Dialogues: Interpretation as Political Process.* Princeton, NJ: Princeton University Press, 2006.

———. *Military Tribunal and Presidential Power: American Revolution to the War on Terrorism.* Lawrence: University Press of Kansas, 2005.

———. *Nazi Saboteurs on Trial: A Military Tribunal and American Law.* 2d ed. Lawrence: University Press of Kansas, 2005b.

———. *Presidential War Power.* Lawrence: University Press of Kansas, 2005.

———. *Presidential War Power.* Lawrence: University Press of Kansas, 2004.

———. "Military Tribunals: A Sorry History." *Presidential Studies Quarterly* 33, no. 3 (2002): 484–508.

———. "Congressional Abdication: War and Spending Powers." *St. Louis University Law Journal* 43 (Summer 1999): 931–1012.

———. "Delegating Power of the President." *Journal of Public Law* 19 (1970): 251–282.

Freedman, Eric. *Habeas Corpus: Rethinking the Great Writ of Liberty.* New York: New York University Press, 2001.

Freund, Paul A. "The Emergency Price Control Act of 1942: Constitutional Issues." *Law and Contemporary Problems* 9, no. 1 (1942): 77–88.

———. "The Supreme Court, 1951 Term–Foreword: The Year of the Steel Seizure Case." *Harvard Law Review* 66, no. 1 (1952): 89–184.

Funston, Richard. "The Supreme Court and Critical Elections." *American Political Science Review* 69, no. 3 (1975): 795–811.

Gates, John B. *The Supreme Court and Partisan Realignment: A Macro- and Micro-level Perspective.* Boulder, CO: Westview Press, 1992.

———. "Partisan Realignment, Unconstitutional State Policies, and the U.S. Supreme Court: 1837–1964." *American Journal of Political Science* 31, no. 2 (May 1987): 259–80.

George, Alexander. "Case Studies and Theory Development: The Method of Structured, Focused Comparison." In *Diplomacy: New Approaches in History, Theory and Policy,* edited by Paul Lauren. New York: Free Press, 1979.

George, Alexander, and Timothy J. McKeown. "Case Studies and Theories of Organizational Decision Making." *Advances in Information Processing in Organizations* 2 (1985): 21–58.

George, Tracey E., and Lee Epstein. "On the Nature of Supreme Court Decision Making." *American Political Science Review* 86, no. 2 (1990): 323–337.

Gillman, Howard. *The Constitution Beseiged: The Rise and Demise of Lochner Era Police Powers Jurisprudence.* Durham, NC: Duke University Press, 1993.

———. "The Court Is an Idea, Not a Building (or a Game): Interpretive Institutionalism and the Analysis of Supreme Court Decision Making." In *Supreme Court Decision-Making: New Institutionalist Approaches,* ed. Cornell and Gillman, 1999: 65–87.

———. "Placing Judicial Motives in Context." *Law and Courts* (Newsletter of the Law and Courts Section of the American Political Science Association) 7 (Spring 1997): 10–13.

Glennon, Michael J. *Constitutional Diplomacy.* Princeton, NJ: Princeton University Press, 1990.

Goldsmith, Jack. *The Terror Presidency: Law and Judgment Inside the Bush Administration.* New York: W. W. Norton & Company, 2007.

Goldstein, Robert J. *Political Repression in Modern America: From 1870 to the Present.* Boston: G. K. Hall Press, 1978.

Gould, Jon B. "Playing with Fire: The Civil Liberties Implications of September 11th." *Public Administration Review* 62, no. 1 (2002): 74–79.

Graber, Mark. "Constructing Judicial Review." *Annual Review of Political Science* 8 (June 2005): 425–451.

———. "The Non-Majoritarian Difficulty: Legislative Deference to the Judiciary." *Studies in American Political Development,* 7 (1993): 35–73.

Gross, Oren. "Once More unto the Breach: The Systemic Failure of Applying the European Convention on Human Rights to Entrenched Emergencies." *Yale Journal of International Law* 23 (1998): 437–491.

Gusterson, Hugh. "The Weakest Link? Academic Dissent in the War on Terrorism." In *Dissent in Dangerous Times,* edited by Austin Sarat. Ann Arbor: University of Michigan Press, 2005.

Gwyn, William B. *The Meaning of the Separation of Powers: An Analysis of the Doctrine from Its Origin to the Adoption of the US Constitution*, vol. 9. New Orleans, LA: Tulane University Press, 1965.

Hamilton, Alexander. *The Papers of Alexander Hamilton.* 26 vols. Edited by Harold C. Syrrett and Jacob E. Cooke. New York: Columbia University Press, 1961–1979.

Harbaugh, William H. Review: The Steel Seizure Reconsidered: *Truman and the Steel Seizure Case: The Limits of Presidential Power* by Maeva Marcus. *The Yale Law Journal* 87, no. 6 (1978): 1272–1283.

Hardaway, Robert, and Christopher Hardaway. "Military Tribunals and Civil Liberties in Time of National Peril: A Legal and Historical Perspective." *Law in the War on International Terrorism.* Ardsley, NY: Transnational, 2005: 169–208.

Hays, Arthur Garfield. Enemy Property in America. *The Virginia Law Register* 9, no. 1 (1923): 80.

Henkin, Louis. "The Constitution for Its Third Century: Foreign Affairs." *The American Journal of International Law* 83, no. 4 (1989): 713–717.

———. *Constitutionalism, Democracy and Foreign Affairs.* New York: Columbia University Press, 1990.

———. *Foreign Affairs and the United States Constitution.* 2d ed. Oxford: Oxford University Press, 1996.

Hirsch, Ran. *Toward Juristocracy: The Origins and Consequences of the New Constitutionalism.* Cambridge, MA: Harvard University Press, 2004.

Hollis, Martin, and Steve Smith. *Explaining and Understanding International Relations.* Oxford: Clarendon Press, 1990.

Holmes, Oliver Wendall. "The Path of Law." *Harvard Law Review* 10 (1897): 460–461.

Hoyt, Henry. "Recent Development and Tendency of the Law of Prize." *Yale Law Journal* 12, no. 5 (1903): 306–317.

Hurst, William. "Review and the Distribution of National Powers." In *Supreme Court and Supreme Law.* Edited by Edmond Cahn. New York: Greenwood Press, 1954.

Huzar, Elias. "Reorganization for National Security." *The Journal of Politics* 12, no. 1 (1950): 128–152.

Irons, Peter. *War Powers: How the Imperial Presidency Hijacked the Constitution.* London: Metropolitan, 2005.

Issacharoff, Samuel, and Richard Pildes. "Between Civil Libertarianism and Executive Unilateralism: An Institutional Process Approach to Rights During Wartime," pp. 161–97. In *The Constitution in Wartime: Beyond Alarmism and Complacency.* Edited by Mark Tushnet. Durham, NC: Duke University Press, 2005.

Jackson, Robert. "Wartime Security and Liberty Under Law." *Buffalo Law Review* 1, no. 2 (1951): 103–117.

Jackson, Donald, and Dorothy Twohig, eds. *The Diaries of George Washington.* 6 vols. Charlottesville: University of Virginia Press, 1976–1979.

Jefferson, Thomas. *The Writings of Thomas Jefferson.* Edited by P. L. Ford. New York: Putnam, 1895.

Jeffreys-Jones, Rhodi. *Cloak and Dollar: A History of American Secret Intelligence.* New Haven, CT: Yale University Press, 2002.

Jones, Charles. "The Separated Presidency." In *The New American Political System,* 2d ed. Edited by Anthony King. Washington, DC: American Enterprise Institute, 1990.

Kahn, Ronald. *The Supreme Court and Constitutional Theory, 1953–1993.* Lawrence: University Press of Kansas, 1994.

Kang, Jerry. "Watching the Watchers: Enemy Combatants in the Internment's Shadow." *Law and Contemporary Problems* 68 (2005): 255–284.

Keck, Thomas. *The Most Activist Supreme Court in History: The Road to Modern Judicial Conservatism.* Chicago: Chicago University Press, 2004.

Kenny, David. "The Vicarious Exclusionary Rule in California." *Stanford Law Review* 24, no. 5 (1972): 947–964.

Ketcham, Ralph. *Selected Writings of James Madison.* New York: Hackett Publishing Company, 2006.

———. *James Madison, a Biography.* New York: Macmillan, 1971.

Keynes, Edward. *Undeclared War: Twilight Zone of Constitutional Power.* University Park: Pennsylvania State University Press, 1982.

King, William B. "The Constitutional Foundation of War Claims for Property." *The American Law Register (1852–1891)* 29, no. 4 (1881): 226–239.

King, Kimi Lynn, and James Meernik. "The Supreme Court and the Powers of the Executive: The Adjudication of Foreign Policy." *Political Science Quarterly* 52, no. 4 (December 1999): 801–824.

Klarman, Michael. *From Jim Crow to Civil Rights: The Supreme Court and the Struggle for Racial Equality.* New York: Oxford University Press, 2004.

Knight, Jack. *Institutions and Social Conflict.* Cambridge: Cambridge University Press, 1992.

Koffler, Judith, and Bennett Gershman. "The New Seditious Libel." *Cornell Law Review* 69 (1984): 816–882.

Koh, Harold. "Why the President (Almost) Always Wins in Foreign Affairs." *Yale Law Journal* 97, no. 7 (June 1998): 1255–1342.

———. The Constitutional Roles of Congress, the Executive and the Courts in the Conduct of U.S. Foreign Policy, Woodrow Wilson Center monograph, 1991.

———. *The National Security Constitution.* New Haven, CT: Yale University Press, 1990.

Kohn, Richard. "The Constitution and National Security: The Intent of the Framers." *The United States Military under the Constitution of the United States, 1789–1989.* New York: New York University Press, 1991.

Korn, Jessica. *The Power of Separation: American Constitutionalism and the Myth of the Legislative Veto.* Princeton, NJ: Princeton University Press, 1998.

Koelble, Thomas A. "The New Institutionalism in Political Science and Sociology." *Comparative Politics* 27 (1995): 231–243.

Klieman, A. A. "Preparing for the Hour of Need: Emergency Powers in the United States." *The Review of Politics* 41, no. 2 (1979): 235–255.

Knauth, Arnold W. "Prize Law Reconsidered." *Columbia Law Review* 46, no. 1 (1946): 69–93.

Lapham, Lewis H. "American Jihad." *Harper's Magazine.* (January 2002): 7–10.

Leigh, Monroe. American International Group, Inc., et al. v. Islamic Republic of Iran, et al. 493 F.Supp. 522. *The American Journal of International Law* 75, no. 2 (April 1981): 371–373.

Leone, Richard, and Greg Anrig, Jr. *The War on Our Freedoms: Civil Liberties in an Age of Terrorism.* New York: Public Affairs, 2003.

Lewis, Anthony. "Security and Liberty: Preserving the Values of Freedom." In *The War on Our Freedoms. Civil Liberties in an Age of Terrorism,* edited by Richard C. Leone and Greg Anrig, Jr., New York: Public Affairs, 2003.

Llewellyn, Karl. "Some Realism about Realism—Responding to Dean Pound." *Harvard Law Review* 44, 1931: 1237.

Lobel, Jules. "The Commander in Chief and the Courts." *Presidential Studies Quarterly* 37, no. 1 (2007): 49–65.

———. "Emergency Power and the Decline of Liberalism." *Yale Law Journal* 98, no. 7 (May 1989): 1385–1433.

Locke, John. *Second Treatise of Government.* Indianapolis: Hackett Publishing Company, 1980.

Lofgren, Charles. "War-making under the Constitution: The Original Understanding." *Yale Law Journal* 81, no. 4 (March 1972): 672–702.

Lourie, Samuel Anatole. "Enemy under the Trading with the Enemy Act and Some Problems of International Law." *Michigan Law Review* 42, no. 3 (1943): 383–408.

———. "The Trading with the Enemy Act." *Michigan Law Review* 42, no. 2 (1943): 205–234.

Lovell, George. *Legislative Deferrals: Statutory Ambiguity, Judicial Power, and American Democracy*. New York: Cambridge University Press, 2003.

Lund, Nelson. "Second Amendment Decision Breaks New Ground." *Civil Rights Practice Groups Newsletter* 3 (Spring 1999): 10.

Maltzberg, Forrest, and Paul J. Wahlbeck. "Strategic Policy Considerations and Voting Fluidity on the Burger Court." *American Political Science Review* 90, no. 3 (1996): 581–92.

Mansfield, Harvey. "The Law and the President." *The Weekly Standard,* January 16, 2006. http://www.weeklystandard.com/Content/Public/Articles/000/000/006/563mevpm.asp (July 2008).

March, James, and Johan Olsen. *Rediscovering Institutions: The Organizational Basis of Politics*. New York: Free Press, 1989.

Marcus, Maeva. "Will Youngstown Survive?" *Duquesne Law Review* 41 (2003): 725–733.

———. *Truman and the Steel Seizure Case: The Limits of Presidential Power*. New York: Columbia University Press, 1977.

Martinek, Wendy, et al. "Comparing Attitudinal and Strategic Accounts of Dissenting Behavior on the U.S. Courts of Appeals." *American Journal of Political Science* 48, no. 1 (January 2004): 123–137.

McGuire, Kevin, and James Stimson. "The Least Dangerous Branch Revisited: New Evidence on Supreme Court's Responsiveness to Public Preferences." *The Journal of Politics* 66, no. 4 (November 2004): 1018–1035.

McMahon, Kevin. *Reconsidering Roosevelt on Race: How the Presidency Paved the Road to Brown*. Chicago: University of Chicago Press, 2004.

McNulty, George A. "Constitutionality of Alien Property Controls." *Law and Contemporary Problems* 11, no. 1 (1945): 135–148.

Melnick, Shep. "Courts and Agencies." In *Making Policy, Making Law: An Interbranch Perspective*. Edited by Mark C. Miller and Jeb Barnes. Washington, DC: Georgetown University Press, 2004.

Moe, Terry. "The Politics of Bureaucratic Structure." In *Can the Government Govern?* Edited by John E. Chubb and Paul E. Peterson. Washington, DC: Brookings Institution Press, 1989.

Moeckli, Daniel. "The U.S. Supreme Court's 'Enemy Combatant' Decisions: A Major Victory for the Rule of Law." *Journal of Conflict and Security Law* 10, no. 1 (2005): 75–99.

Monaghan, Henry P. "The Protective Power of the President." *Columbia Law Review* 93, no 1 (1993): 1–74.

Montesquieu, Charles de. *The Spirit of the Laws*. Cambridge: Cambridge University Press, 1989.

Moore, J. B. "Maritime Law in the War with Spain." *Political Science Quarterly* 15, no. 3 (1900): 399–425.

Murphy, Paul. *World War I and the Origin of Civil Liberties in the United States.* New York: Norton, 1979.

Murphy, Walter. *Elements of Judicial Strategy.* Chicago: University of Chicago Press, 1964.

Murphy, Walter, et al. *Courts, Judges, and Politics.* Columbus, OH: McGraw-Hill Humanities, 2005.

Nedelsky, Jennifer. *Private Property and the Limits of American Constitutionalism: The Madisonian Framework and its Legacy.* Chicago: The University of Chicago Press, 1990.

Neely, M. *The Fate of Liberty: Abraham Lincoln and Civil Liberties.* New York: Oxford University Press, 1991.

Nelson, Michael. *The Presidency and the Political System.* 4th ed. Washington, DC: CQ Press, 1995.

Neustadt, Richard. *Presidential Power: The Politics of Leadership.* New York: Wiley, 1960.

Nichols, David. "Congressional Dominance and the Emergence of the Modern Presidency: Was Congress Ever the First Branch of Government?" In *Separation of Powers and Good Governance.* Edited by Bradford P. Wilson and Peter W. Schramm. Lanham, MD: Rowman & Littlefield, 1994.

Niskanen, William A. "Legislative Implications of Reasserting Congressional Authority over Regulations." *Cardozo Law Review* 20 (1999): 939.

Oppenheim, L. *International Law.* Vol. I, 8th ed., London: Longmans, Green, 1955.

Ordershook, Peter, and Olga Shvetsova. "Federalism and Constitutional Design." *Journal of Democracy* 8, no. 1 (1997): 27-42.

Orren, Karen, and Stephen Skowronek. *The Search for American Political Development.* Cambridge: Cambridge University Press, 2004.

O'Toole, G. A. J. *The Encyclopedia of American Intelligence and Espionage: From the Revolutionary War to the Present.* New York: Facts on File, 1988.

Peretti, Terry Jennings. *In Defense of a Political Court.* Princeton, NJ: Princeton University Press, 1999.

Pierson, Paul. "When Effect becomes Cause: Policy Feedback and Political Change." *World Politics* 45 (1993): 595-628.

Pious, Richard. "Inherent War and Executive Powers and Prerogative Politics," *Presidential Studies Quarterly* 37, no. 1 (2007): 66–84.

Pohlman, Harry. *Terrorism and the Constitution: Post 9–11 Cases.* Lanham, MD: Rowman & Littlefield, 2007.

Posner, Richard. *Not a Suicide Pact.* New York: Oxford University Press, 2006.

Posner, Eric, and Adrian Vermeule. "Accommodating Emergencies," pp. 55–94. In *The Constitution in Wartime: Beyond Alarmism and Complacency.* Edited by Mark Tushnet. Durham, NC: Duke University Press, 2005.

Pound, Roscoe. "Interests of Personality." *Harvard Law Review* 28, no. 5 (March 1915): 453–556.

Powell, Walter W., and Paul DiMaggio, eds. *The New Institutionalism in Organizational Analysis.* Chicago: University of Chicago Press, 1991.

Powell, Thomas Reed. "The Logic and Rhetoric of Constitutional Law." *Journal of Philosophy* 15 (1918): 645–658.

Prakash, Saikrishna B., and Michael D. Ramsey. "The Executive Power over Foreign Affairs." *Yale Law Journal* 111, no. 2 (November 2001): 231–356.

Prichett, Herman C. *The Roosevelt Court.* New York: MacMillan, 1948.

Quint, Peter. "The Separation of Powers under Nixon: Reflections on Constitutional Liberties and the Rule of Law." *Duke Law Journal* 1981, no. 1 (1981): 1–70.

Rabban, David. "Free Speech in its Forgotten Years." Cambridge: Cambridge University Press, 1997.

Ragin, Charles. *The Comparative Method: Moving Beyond Qualitative and Quantitative Strategies.* Berkeley: University of California Press, 1987.

Rakove, Jack. "Taking the Prerogative out of the Presidency: An Originalist Perspective." *Presidential Studies Quarterly* 37, no. 1 (2007): 85–100.

Randall, James G. "Some Legal Aspects of the Confiscation Acts of the Civil War." *The American Historical Review* 18, no. 1 (1912): 79–96.

Raven-Hansen, Peter. "Detaining Combatants by Law or by Order?: The Rule of Lawmaking in the War on Terrorists." *Louisiana Law Review* 64, no. 4 (2004): 831–850.

Raven-Hansen, Peter, and William C. Banks. "Pulling the Purse Strings of the Commander in Chief." *Virginia Law Review* 80, no. 4 (1994): 833–944.

Rehnquist, William H. "Seizing Power: The Steel Seizure Case Revisited." Stanford University, Recorded 2002.

———. *All the Laws but One: Civil Liberties in Wartime.* New York: Vintage, 2000.

———. *The Supreme Court.* New York: Knopf, 1987.

Reisman, Michael W. "War Powers: The Operational Code of Competence." *The American Journal of International Law* 83, no. 4 (1989): 777–785.

Relyea, Harold. *Terrorist Attacks and National Emergencies Act Declarations.* Congressional Research Service Report. January 2005.

———. *National Emergency Powers.* Congressional Research Service Report. September 2005.

———. *A Brief History of Emergency Powers in the United States.* Washington, DC: Government Printing Office, 1974.

Reveley, W. Taylor, III. *War Powers of the President and Congress: Who Holds the Arrows and Olivebranch?* Charlottesville: University of Virginia Press, 1981.

———. Review: Undeclared War: Twilight Zone of Constitutional Power by Edward Keynes. *Columbia Law Review* 83, no. 8 (December 1983): 2117–2129.

Richardson, Neal, and Spencer Crona. "Detention of Terrorists as Unlawful Combatants and their Trial by American Military Commissions." In Nanda, Ved, P. *Law in the War on International Terrorism.* Adrsley, NY: Transnational Publishers, 2005.

Richardson, Elliot L. "Checks and Balances in Foreign Relations." *The American Journal of International Law* 83, no. 4 (1989): 736–739.

Richardson, J., ed. *Compilation of the Messages and Papers of the Presidents,* vol. 1. New York: Bureau of National Literature, 1897.

Richberg, Donald R. "The Steel Seizure Case." *Virginia Law Review* 38, no. 6 (1952): 713–727.

Rhode, David, and Harold J. Spaeth. *Supreme Court Decision Making.* San Fransisco, CA: W. H. Freeman, 1976.

Roach, J. Ashley. "The Law of Naval Warfare at the Turn of Two Centuries." *The American Journal of International Law* 94, no. 1 (2000): 64–77.

Robertson, James. "Quo Vadis, Habeas Corpus?" *Buffalo Law Review* 55 (January 2008): 1063–1087.

Roche, John P. "Executive Power and Domestic Emergency: The Quest for Prerogative." *The Western Political Quarterly* 5, no. 4 (1952): 592–618.

Rockman, Bert. "The New Institutionalism and the Old Institutions." In *Perspectives on American Politics.* Edited by Lawrence C. Dodd and Calvin Jillson. Washington, DC: Congressional Quarterly Books, 1994.

Rockoff, Hugh. "Price and Wage Controls in Four Wartime Periods." *The Journal of Economic History* 41, no. 2 (1981): 381–401.

Rogers, William. "The Case for Wire Tapping." *Yale Law Journal* 63, no. 6 (April 1954): 792–798.

Rosen, Mark D. "Revisiting Youngstown: Against the View that Jackson's Concurrence Resolves the Relation between Congress and the Commander-in-Chief." *UCLA Law Review* 54, no. 1 (2007): 1–44.

Rosen, Jeffrey. "Conscience of a Conservative." *New York Times.* September 9, 2007.

Rosen, Lawrence. *Law as Culture: An Invitation.* Princeton, NJ: Princeton University Press, 2006.

Rosenberg, Gerald N. *The Hollow Hope: Can Courts Bring about Social Change?* Chicago: University of Chicago Press, 1991.

Rossiter, Clinton. *Constitutional Dictatorship: Crisis Government in the Modern Democracies.* Westport, CT: Greenwood Press, 1948.

———. "Constitutional Dictatorship in the Atomic Age." *Review of Politics* 2, no. 4 (October 1949): 395–418.

Rostow, Eugene. "Great Cases Make Bad Law: The War Powers Act." *Texas Law Review* 50 (1972): 833.

———. "President, Prime Minister or Constitutional Monarch?" *The American Journal of International Law* 83, no. 4 (1989): 740–749.

Rudalevige, Andrew. *The New Imperial Presidency: Renewing Presidential Power after Watergate.* Ann Arbor: University of Michigan Press, 2006.

Rudko, Frances. *Truman's Court: A Study in Judicial Restraint.* Westport, CT: Greenwood Press, 1988.

Rutland, Robert, and William M. E. Rachal. *Papers of James Madison.* Chicago: University of Chicago, 1975.

Sarat, Austin. *Dissent in Dangerous Times.* Ann Arbor: University of Michigan Press, 2005.

Sartori, Giovanni. *Comparative Constitutional Engineering: An Inquiry into Structures, Incentives and Outcomes.* 2d ed. New York: New York University Press, 1997.

Schubert, Glendon. "Behavioral Research in Public Law." *American Political Science Review* 57, no. 2 (June 1963): 433–445.

———. "The Steel Seizure Case: Presidential Responsibility and Judicial Irresponsibility." *George Washington Political Quarterly* 61 (1953): 6.

Scheiber, Harry. "Property Rights versus 'Public Necessity': A Perspective on Emergency Powers and the Supreme Court." *Journal of Supreme Court History* 28, no. 3 (2003): v–386.

Schlesinger Jr. Arthur M., Introduction in *Writings and Speeches of Eugene V. Debs,* Eugene Debs. New York: Hermitage, 1948.

———. *The Cycles of American History.* New York: Houghton Mifflin, 1999.

———. *The Imperial Presidency.* Boston: Houghton Mifflin, 1973.

Scott, Winfried. *Memoirs of Lieut.-General Scott, L.L.D.* Freeport, NY: Books for Libraries Press, 1864.

———. "Statutory Interpretation and the Balance of Institutional Power." *The Review of Politics* 56, no. 3 (1994): 475–501.

Segal, Jeffrey A. "Separation of Powers Games in the Positive Theory of Congress and Courts." *American Political Science Review* 91, no. 1 (March 1997): 28–44.

Segal, Jeffrey A., et al. "Decision Making on the U.S. Court of Appeals." In *Contemplating Courts.* Edited by Lee Epstein. Washington, DC: CQ Press. 1995, 227–243.

Segal, Jeffrey, and Harold Spaeth. *The Supreme Court and the Attitudinal Model Revisited.* Cambridge: Cambridge University Press, 2002.

———. "Decisional Trends on the Warren and Burger Courts: Results from the Supreme Court Data Base Project." *Judicature* 73 (1989): 103.

Seymour, Charles. "How Free Can Speech Be in Time of War." *New York Times Magazine.* April 12, 1942.

Shapiro, Martin. *The Supreme Court and Administrative Agencies.* New York: Free Press, 1968.

Sharman, Jackson R. "Note: Covert Action and Judicial Review." *Harvard Journal of Law and Public Policy* 12, no. 2 (1989): 569–609.

Sheffer, Martin S. *The Judicial Development of Presidential War Powers.* London: Praeger Press, 1999.

Sidak, J. Gregory. "The Price of Experience: The Constitution after September 11, 2001" (President Truman's 1952 seizure of U.S. steel mills). *Constitutional Commentary* 19, no. 1 (Spring 2002): 37–62.

Silverstein, Gordon. *Imbalance of Powers.* Oxford: Oxford University Press, 1997.

Skowronek, Stephen. *Building a New American State: The Expansion of National Administrative Capacities.* Cambridge: Cambridge University Press, 1982.

Smith, Rogers M. "If Politics Matters: Implications for a New Institutionalism." *Studies in American Political Development* 6 (1992): 1–36.

Sofaer, Abraham. "Presidential Power and National Security." *Presidential Studies Quarterly* 37, no. 1 (2007): 101–123.

———. *War, Foreign Affairs, and Constitutional Power.* Cambridge, MA: Ballinger Press, 1976.

Sommerich, Otto C. "A Brief against Confiscation." *Law and Contemporary Problems* 11, no. 1 (1945): 152–165.

Spaight, J.M. *War Rights on Land.* New York: MacMillan Company, 1911.

Spindler, John F. "Constitutional Law: Eminent Domain: Destruction of Private Property to Prevent Enemy Capture." *Michigan Law Review* 51, no. 5 (1953): 739–742.

Stagg, J. C. A., *James Madison and the Spanish Borderlands: Three Episodes in Early American Foreign Policy.* New Haven, CT: Yale University Press. Forthcoming.

———. *The Papers of James Madison: Secretary of State Series,* vol. 2. Edited with Mary A. Hackett and Jeanne K. Cross. Charlottesville: University of Virginia Press, 1993.

———. *The Papers of James Madison: Presidential Series,* vol. 2. Edited with Jeanne K. Cross and Susan H. Perdue. Charlottesville: University of Virginia Press, 1992.

———. *Mr. Madison's War: Politics, Diplomacy, and Warfare in the Early American Republic, 1783–1830.* Princeton, NJ: Princeton University Press, 1983.

Steinmo, Sven, Kathleen Thelen, and Frank Longstreth, eds. *Structuring Politics: Historical Institutionalism in Comparative Analysis.* New York: Cambridge University Press, 1992.

Steyn, Johan. "Guantanamo Bay: The Legal Black Hole." *International and Comparative Law Quarterly* 53, no. 1 (January 2004): 1–15.

Stinchcombe, William. "The Diplomacy of the WXYZ Affair." *The William and Mary Quarterly* 34, no. 4 (1977): 590–617.

Stokes Paulsen, Michael. "Youngstown Goes to War" (President Truman's 1952 seizure of U.S. steel mills). *Constitutional Commentary* 19, no. 1 (Spring 2002): 215–245.

———. "The Most Dangerous Branch: Executive Power to Say What the Law Is." *Georgetown Law Journal* 83 (1994): 217.

Stone, Geoffrey. *War and Liberty: An American Dilemma 1790 to the Present.* New York: Norton, 2007.

———. *Perilous Times: Free Speech in Wartime from the Sedition Act of 1798 to the War on Terrorism.* New York: Norton, 2004.

———. "Civil Liberties in Time of National Emergency." *Journal of the Supreme Court Historical Society* 28 (2003): 215.

Story, Joseph. *Commentaries on the Constitution of the United States.* Boston: Hilliard Gray and Company, 1833.

Storing, Herbert. *The Complete Anti-Federalist.* Chicago: University of Chicago Press, 1981.

Stromseth, Jane E. "Understanding Constitutional War Powers Today: Why Methodology Matters." *Yale Law Journal* 106 (1996): 845, 847.

———. "Collective Force and Constitutional Responsibility: War Powers in the Post-Cold War Era." *University of Miami Law Review* 145 (1995): 168–72.

Sundquist James, L. *Beyond Gridlock? Prospects for Governance in the Clinton Years—And After.* Washington, DC: Brookings Institution Press, 1993.

Sunstein, Case. *One Case at Time: Judicial Minimalism on the Supreme Court.* Cambridge, MA: Harvard University Press, 1999.

Taft, William Howard. *Our Chief Magistrate and His Powers.* 2d ed. New York: Columbia University Press, 1925.

Tannenhaus, Joseph. "The Supreme Court and Presidential Power (in Legislative and Judicial Relations)." *Annals of the American Academy of Political and Social Science* 307 (1956): 106–113.

Taylor, Alan. "The Alien and Sedition Acts." In *The American Congress.* Edited by Julian E. Zelizer. Boston: Houghton Mifflin, 2004.

Theoharis, Athan, and Meyer Theoharis. "The 'National Security' Justification for Electronic Eavesdropping: An Elusive Exception." *Wayne Law Review* 19 (1968): 749.

Tigar, Michael. "Judicial Power, The 'Political Questions Doctrine,' and Foreign Relations." *U.C.L.A. Law Review* 17 (1970): 1135, 1163.

Tobias, Carl. "Detentions, Military Commissions, Terrorism, and Domestic Case Precedent." *Southern California Law Review* 76, no. 6 (2003): 1371–1408.

Treanor, William. "The Origins and Original Significance of the Just Compensation Clause of the Fifth Amendment." *The Yale Law Journal* 94, no. 3 (1985): 694–716.

Trevelyan, G. M. *History of England.* London: Longsman, 1926.

Tresolini, R. J. "Eminent Domain and the Requisition of Property during Emergencies." *The Western Political Quarterly* 7, no. 4 (1954): 570–587.

Turner, Robert. "Legal Responses to International Terrorism: Constitutional Constraints on Presidential Power." *Houston Journal of International Law* 22, no. 1 (Fall 1977): 1999.

———. *The U.S. Constitution and the Power to Go to War.* Westport, CT: Greenwood Press, 1994.

Tushnet, Mark V. "The State of Constitutional Theory in U.S. Law Schools in the 2000s." *The Good Society* 13, no. 2 (2004): 21–24.

———, ed. *The Constitution in Wartime: Beyond Alarmism and Complacency.* Durham, NC: Duke University Press, 2005.

Vile, M. J. C. *Constitutionalism and the Separation of Powers.* Oxford: Clarendon Press, 1967.

Vladeck, Steve. "Congress, the Commander-in-Chief, and the Separation of Powers after Hamdan." *Transnational Law and Contemporary Problems* 16 (2007): 933–964.

Waldron, J. "Judicial Review and the Conditions of Democracy." *Journal of Political Philosophy* 6, no. 4 (2003): 335–355.

Walker, Ronald E. "War-Time Economic Controls." *The Quarterly Journal of Economics* 58, no. 4 (1944): 503–520.

Washington, George. *The Writings of George Washington,* vol. XII. Edited by W. C. Ford. New York: Putnams, 1891.

Weaver, Kent R., and Bert A. Rockman, eds. *Do Institutions Matter? Governing Capabilities in the United States and Abroad.* Washington, DC: Brookings Institution Press, 1993.

Weir, Margarett, Ann S. Orloff, and Theda Skocpol, eds. *The Politics of Social Policy in the United States.* Princeton, NJ: Princeton University Press, 1988.

Westin, Alan F. *The Anatomy of a Constitutional Law Case: Youngstown Sheet and Tube Co. v. Sawyer.* New York: Columbia University Press, 1958.

———. "The Wire-tapping Problem: An Analysis and a Legislative Proposal." *Columbia Law Review* 52, no. 2 (1952): 165–173.

Whipple, Leon. *The Story of Civil Liberties in the United States.* New York: De Capo Press, 1970.

White, Donald. "History and American Internationalism: The Formulation from the Past after World War II." *Pacific Historical Review* 58, no. 2 (1989): 145–172.

Wilson, Woodrow. *Congressional Government.* New York: Houghton Mifflin, 1885.

Wormuth, Francis D. "Nixon Theory of the War Power: A Critique." *California Law Review* 60, no. 3 (May 1972): 623–703.

———. "Presidential Wars: The Convenience of 'Precedent.'" *The Nation* 9 (1972): 301.

Wormuth, Francis D., and Edwin B. Firmage. *To Chain the Dog of War: The War Power of Congress in History and Law.* Dallas, TX: Southern Methodist University Press, 1989.

Wood, Gordon. *The Creation of the American Republic: 1769–1789.* Chapel Hill: University of North Carolina Press, 1968.

Wright, Louis B., and Julia H. MacLeod. *The First Americans in North Africa: William Eaton's Struggle for a Vigorous Policy Against the Barbary Pirates, 1799–1805.* Westport, CT: Greenwood Press, 1969.

———. "William Eaton's Relations with Aaron Burr." *The Mississippi Valley Historical Review* 31, no. 4 (1945): 523–536.

Yosal, Rogat. "Legal Realism." In Paul Edwards, ed., *The Encyclopedia of Philosophy.* New York: MacMillan. 1972

Yoo, John. *The Powers of War and Peace.* Chicago: University of Chicago Press, 2005.

———. *War by Other Means: An Insider's Account of the War on Terror.* New York: Atlantic Monthly Press, 2006.

Zaller, John. *The Nature and Origins of Mass Opinion.* New York: Cambridge University Press, 1992.

Zeisberg, Mariah. "Constitutional Fidelity and Interbranch Conflict." *The Good Society* 13, no 3 (2004): 24–30.

Index

About the Author

Amanda DiPaolo is an assistant professor of Constitutional Law at Middle Tennessee State University. She received a Ph.D. in political science from Syracuse University.